# JEWISH LIFE UNDER ISLAM

# *Jewish Life under Islam*

## JERUSALEM IN THE SIXTEENTH CENTURY

*Amnon Cohen*

HARVARD UNIVERSITY PRESS
Cambridge, Massachusetts
and London, England
1984

Printed in the United States of America
10 9 8 7 6 5 4 3 2 1

This book is printed on acid-free paper,
and its binding materials have been chosen
for strength and durability.

LIBRARY OF CONGRESS CATALOGING IN PUBLICATION DATA

Cohen, Amnon, 1936–
Jewish life under Islam.

Translation of: Yehudim be-shilṭon ha-Islam.
Bibliography: p.
Includes index.
1. Jews—Jerusalem—History—16th century.
2. Jerusalem—History.
3. Jerusalem—Ethnic relations.
I. Title.
DS109.92.C6313 1984 956.94′4004924 83-13025
ISBN 0-674-47436-8

# *Contents*

# *Preface*

THE POLITICAL and administrative importance of Jerusalem has varied dramatically in the course of its long history. During the time of the First and Second Temples the city reached significant heights; during the Middle Ages it declined. In modern times—after the British conquest of 1918 and, above all, since the establishment of the State of Israel—it has come into its own again. Jerusalem's religious significance, however, has never decreased but has increased greatly over the centuries. In biblical days, during the reign of the House of David, the city was established as the ritual and spiritual center for Jewry. Since the day Jesus was crucified there, it has also been central to Christianity. Under Islam, Jerusalem was designated the first *qibla,* the place toward which believers direct their prayers; though later reduced in importance to the third *ḥaram,* after Mecca and Medina, the city has remained one of Islam's holiest places. In the Middle Ages, under Islamic rule—both Mamluk and Ottoman—Jerusalem was a small provincial city compared with other urban centers of these empires. And yet, for Muslims, Christians, and Jews throughout the world it never lost its importance as a focal point for ritual observance, memories, and above all, for religious thought and aspirations.

For followers of the three religions, one of the practical expressions of the centrality of "celestial" Jerusalem has always been that some of their number lived within the confines of "earthly" Jerusalem, as long as the rulers of the land did not expressly forbid it. Religious sentiment no doubt accounted for the presence of

Christians and Jews in Muslim Jerusalem, but they were, nonetheless, ordinary people who engaged in social and economic activities within their own communities and maintained contact with the rest of the population in and outside the city.

There would be nothing particularly remarkable about the statement that Jerusalem was populated by ordinary people were it not for the fact that we are accustomed to visualizing earlier epochs as essentially one dimensional, so that details are blurred and nuances obliterated. This book will attempt to bring the picture closer to the reader's field of vision. From a dense accumulation of individual dots all viewed from a given perspective, as in the technique employed for satellite transmission, a multidimensional picture emerges. The reconstruction of a historical tableau can be achieved in precisely the same manner.

To penetrate deep into complexities, it is essential to focus one's sights on a single subject. The decision to study Jerusalem's Jewish community, then, is the result of an arbitrary choice that implies no value judgment. Needless to say, the majority of the residents of sixteenth-century Jerusalem were Arabs and Muslims. In the daily conduct of the city's life they were the group that most influenced its character. Their story has not yet been told in full, nor has that of Jerusalem's Christians, at first a smaller minority than the Jews, and later a larger one. Only after the stories of these two communities have been told will we have a complete history of the city's inhabitants at the time.

A great political upheaval took place in the Middle East in the sixteenth century, when Palestine—like Syria, Egypt, and parts of the Arabian peninsula—came under Ottoman dominion. This marked the inception of an era that continued for four hundred years, and during it patterns of government and administration were established that essentially remained in force until the beginning of the twentieth century. Moreover, most of the sixteenth century—the periods of Selim the First and Suleiman the Magnificent—was considered the golden era of the Ottoman Empire. Palestine then was not a separate administrative unit; its various districts (*sanjaqs*)—Safed, Nablus, Gaza, Lajjun—and Jerusalem too were all subordinate to the governor of Damascus. Through most of the century Jerusalem's population was larger than that of other Palestinian towns, but even at its peak of fifteen thousand, Jerusalem was small compared to Istanbul, Cairo, Aleppo, or Damascus. And yet, for the Ottoman conqueror, Jerusalem had far greater significance than many of the larger cities. The Temple Mount with its mosques not only was an important ritual center but also was closely associated with various events in the life of the Prophet Muhammad.

In the second quarter of the century and the decades immediately following, the rulers in Istanbul initiated many projects designed to strengthen and develop Jerusalem. A wall was built around the city, and its gates were locked every evening. A vigorous building program was begun: neglected markets and shops were renovated and repaired; the water system, which had fallen into disrepair during the decline of Mamluk power, was reconstructed and expanded; important endowments (*waqf*) were established to support scholarly activities and maintain Muslim institutions. The result was a steady growth of all the elements of Jerusalem's population.

The splendid era of growth and development did not last long. After some fifty years, in the last third of the century, there were perceptible signs of the Ottoman Empire's decline, and Palestine too suffered. It was no longer safe to travel the roads; commerce was adversely affected; officials began to be more interested in lining their own pockets than in maintaining the welfare of the citizenry. Military units stationed in Jerusalem's Citadel began to meddle in economic life, thereby undermining their military readiness. In brief, development came to a standstill, and people left the city in growing numbers. As fortunes changed and Jerusalem entered a period of decline that was to continue throughout the following centuries, its Jewish residents, who had flourished during the good years, suffered greatly. By the close of the sixteenth century the trends affecting the city's Jewry had already assumed the form and direction they would take in later years. Thus, I have chosen to conclude this work as the 1500s come to an end.

The concerns, form, and norms of Jewish life at that early time also remained essentially unchanged until the beginning of the modern era. What sources of information are available for studying the milieu in which the Jews lived and for learning what went on inside the Jewish community under Ottoman rule? Descriptions of the status of religious minorities, Jewish and Christian, can be found in books of Muslim laws and religious traditions. Despite their stereotypical formulations, volumes of the Jewish Responsa offer information about some of the actual problems raised and thus provide useful information for students of history. Descriptions written by travelers (occasionally a Jew or Muslim, but most often Christians) in a variety of languages offer abundant, if not always dependable, information. Arab chronicles and Muslim biographies, although relatively few, transmit inside information in the words of people describing their own society. Another source is the archives of European consulates, as well as letters written by European merchants who either lived in or traded with the Levant. These contain a wealth of economic information as well as tidbits about other spheres of life.

The major drawback of these sources is that the picture evoked by Muslim texts remains largely hypothetical, and texts written by European Christians or Jews tend to convey a biased description with details adapted to fit the author's purposes. Most of these descriptions were written by people of foreign origin, culture, and language. There is thus fairly good reason to doubt their credibility, and even their originality, since their authors necessarily had to draw upon the words of others, or rely on their own powers of invention. Authoritative sources, such as the official archives kept by European delegations, record only the aspects of events that were of specific interest to the home countries; and even such sources were almost nonexistent in the Arabic-speaking provinces during the sixteenth and seventeenth centuries. In the past thirty years Ottoman-Turkish archives containing a great store of information that is most important for compiling the administrative history of various provinces in the empire have been made available for scholarly research; but their references to the Jews and other religious minorities are relatively few.

As a student of Ottoman Palestine who has experienced the shortcomings of all the sources mentioned above—and who had nothing to match the rich Genizah archives and the monumental tableau for earlier Mediterranean society drawn by Goitein—I was intensely excited to encounter a very old, hitherto untapped source, the *sijill* volumes in the archives of the Muslim court. For hundreds of years in each administrative center throughout the empire—including Jerusalem, of course—the Muslim court kept careful daily records of all proceedings and judgments. The Muslim judge, the kadi, also recorded the many instructions, orders, and decrees that arrived from Istanbul, and in his capacity as notary public copied into the records the various permits and appointments received by his city and district. The Muslim court was not only a religious entity for Muslim believers but also the sole official legal body in the land. As such it adjudicated matters concerning individuals and groups, criminal and civil law, legacies and endowments, price fixing and currency exchange, as well as countless other issues involving all spheres of life.

As religious minorities, the Jews and Christians maintained their own internal legal systems; but being part of the society and economy of the Muslim state, they were bound by many of the orders and decisions issued by the Muslim court. In addition, Jews and Christians voluntarily came to the kadi for rulings in matters that touched on members of other religions and also in matters concerning the people of their own community. One can now turn to these court records for contemporary descriptions of incidents, events, and problems, recorded in Arabic, the everyday tongue, and sometimes in the official language, Turkish. From these thousands of closely written pages, the interested reader can glean vast quantities of information about each of the groups that made up Ottoman Palestine's society. The archives of the Muslim court in Jerusalem, preserved undamaged in the court offices, mirror the way of life of the Jewish community and reveal many aspects of that life that have heretofore been entirely unknown or could only be surmised. From the myriad details in these records I have attempted to reconstruct a picture of the manner in which the Jews of Jerusalem lived during the first century of Ottoman rule—something that could not have been done previously. This book is just a beginning; one can only hope that this work will be the forerunner of extensive research into the Jerusalem Jewish community's life in later centuries and in other centers under Ottoman rule.

A few years ago Yad Ben-Zvi published my first work based on the *sijill* registers: *Ottoman Documents on the Jewish Community of Jerusalem in the Sixteenth Century* (Jerusalem, 1976), in which I used only twenty-five Turkish-language decrees selected from the archives. I have since read through the eighty-four heavy tomes that cover the sixteenth century, but have not touched the several hundred volumes that deal with the following centuries of Ottoman and even post-Ottoman rule. These all await the searching eyes of scholars.

I began to accumulate the material for this book in 1968, shortly after learning that the Muslim court archives were extant in their entirety in Eastern Jerusalem. It was with some hesitation that I approached the heads of the Muslim Council for permission to do research in the archives. They allowed me to be the first Jew and the first Israeli to read through consecutive volumes of the court archives. I wish to express my deepest gratitude to them. I am also grateful to the late Shaykh Ḥilmī al-Muḥtasib and the late Shaykh Sa'īd Ṣabrī for their inestimable assistance as I took my first steps in the terra incognita of the *sijill* volumes. I am greatly indebted to Shaykh Sa'd al-Dīn al-'Alamī and Kadi Ibrahīm Ṣabrī, now Mufti and Kadi of Jerusalem, and their devoted team of assistants and officials for their patience, tolerance, courtesy, hospitality, and tireless readiness to help uncover the secrets of the past. These are men whose intellectual stature enabled them to rise above political difficulties and emotional obstacles and assist an Israeli to delve deeper into the history of the region we inhabit and the land in which we all were born. May this act of theirs be an omen and symbol for the future.

The original version of this book was written in Hebrew and published in 1982 by Yad Ben Zvi, Jerusalem. I am indebted to this institution for encouraging my research and for having contributed toward defraying part of the cost of its translation. I am grateful to Shirli Shpira, who undertook the task of translation into English and whose thoughtful remarks helped me further elucidate various points, and to Sylvia Farhi in Jerusalem for having painstakingly typed the first drafts of the manuscript. The final version was prepared during the academic year 1982–83 when I was a Member at the Institute for Advanced Study, Princeton. I benefited widely from my stay there, and most particularly from the wise advice and learned comments of Bernard Lewis on both general and particular aspects of this book. To my wife, Amalia, who had to bear the strains and inconveniences brought about by my research and writing, I offer this book as a token of gratitude.

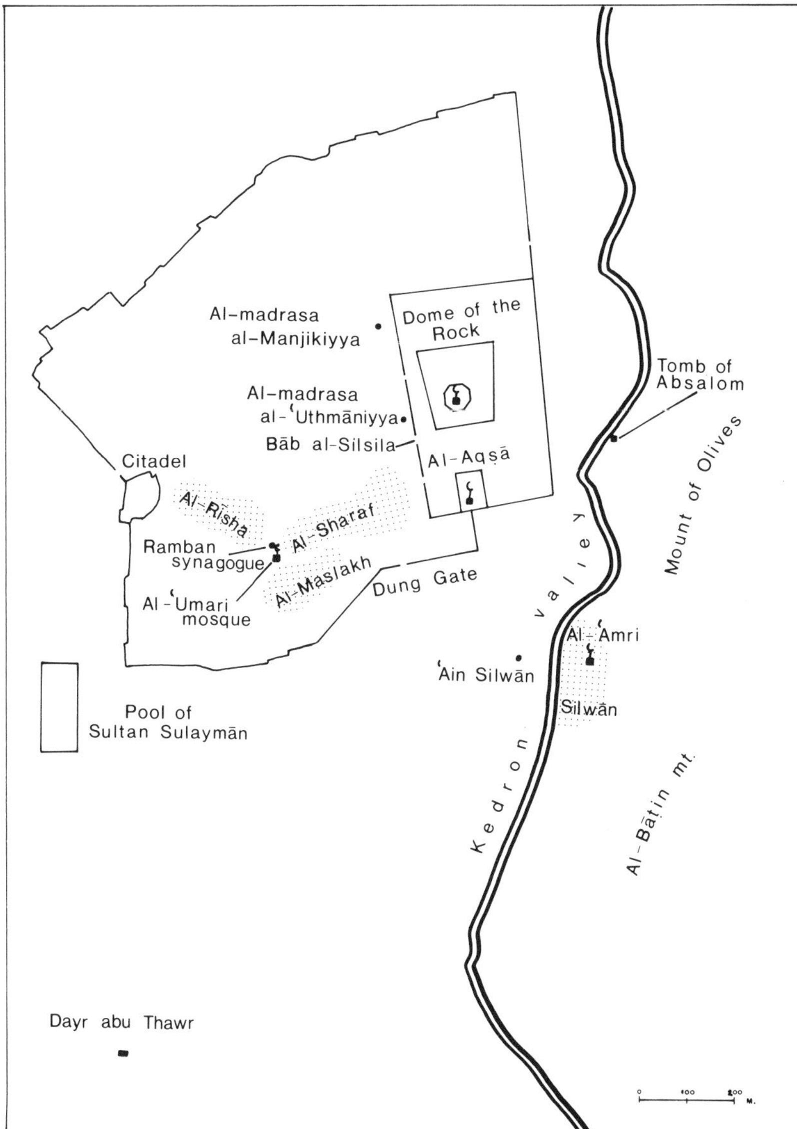


*Jerusalem in the Sixteenth Century*

O N E

# *Jews and the Authorities*

IN ONE of its basic precepts, classical Islam described the world as divided into two parts: "the abode of Islam" (*Dār al-Islām*), that is, those territories under Islamic rule; and everything beyond, "the abode of war" (*Dār al-Ḥarb*). The inhabitants of these two subregions were also regarded as different from each other: the first group was predominantly Muslim, while the second was alien. This view of the world was not confined solely to theoreticians; it was in force in Jerusalem during the sixteenth century. In June 1560 a Venetian Christian referred to as a *musta'min*—a non-Muslim inhabitant of *Dār al-Ḥarb* who requested and received a temporary safe conduct within the confines of the Islamic state—applied to the Kadi of Jerusalem for a change of his formal status to that of resident alien. This is how he presented his case: "he requests to be in the *Dār al-Islām*, under the protection of the All-Powerful Sultan . . . and to live in Jerusalem, and that the *jizya* tax be levied from him annually, like the other [non-Muslim] inhabitants living there who are under protection (*Dhimma*) . . . and he will not return to *Dār al-Ḥarb*."[1] For a non-Muslim to reside in the Ottoman Empire was regarded as a privilege, precisely as Islamic law prescribes, and it entailed paying the annual poll tax, the *jizya*. This particular Christian wished to enjoy such a privilege. Being alien by origin and newly arrived, he wished to terminate his status of temporary *musta'min* and become a permanent *dhimmī*. He would thus avail himself of the benefits that fell naturally to Christians born within the confines of the empire, who were numbered among its inhabitants and citizens and referred to as "protected persons." Jews, like Christians, belonged to this general category, to which the overall term *al-Dhimma*, or *al-Dhimm*, was generally applied.

The use of this term did not specify merely that these people were different; it also implied that they were somehow alien. It testified to the division between masters, who can command privilege, and those to whom privilege is granted. Furthermore, the distinction was neither conceptual nor philosophical. The term *Jew* or *Christian* as adjective or noun was used precisely like the term *Muslim*, without any implied value judgment or other substantive distinction. However, there is a further indication that the Jews were not perceived as merely another category of residents but rather as a group whose association with Jerusalem was less than that of their Muslim fellow citizens: whenever a person was mentioned by name alone, this sufficed to indicate that he was a Muslim, whereas others were singled out, for instance, as "So-and-so the Jew." In addition, a Muslim was referred to as "So-and-so of Jerusalem" or simply as "So-and-so"; but whenever a Jew was mentioned, he was "So-and-so the Jew, resident in Jerusalem," or "who has settled in Jerusalem," a phrase referring to *al-Mustawṭinīn*, persons who had applied for and been granted permission to adopt the city as their *waṭan*—their place of residence and native land.[2]

In this way, the Jew's link to Jerusalem was referred to as less direct, less unequivocal, less natural than the Muslim's. There was nothing derogatory or prejudicial in the use of the term *al-Mustawṭinīn*, nor did it apply to Jews alone. It could refer equally to any Muslim who had recently taken up residence in Jerusalem but who had been born elsewhere within the empire. In contrast to such a Muslim, however, these Jews, like their fathers before them, were born in Jerusalem and yet were considered strangers.

Religious affiliation, though important, was not the only criterion for grouping population. In the sixteenth century, and even subsequently, a line of demarcation was also drawn between the townspeople, or subjects, and the rulers, who had come from afar and who had at their disposal another foreign element, the army units they commanded. Complaints about the disorderly behavior of members of the ruling class referred to many incidents in which various townsfolk—not Jews or Christians alone—had suffered injury of some sort. Whether inside Jerusalem or in the outlying villages, everyone became acquainted with the heavy hand of the rulers and their followers. In mid-March 1589, for example, there was a flood of complaints against the governor's officers and men, who were "robbing the Muslims and the Jews and the Christians," a phrase that accurately expresses the variety, the relative numbers, and even the order of importance of the different demographic groups.[3] Throughout the first half of the sixteenth century, the Jews were the second-largest community in Jerusalem; it was only at the beginning of the 1560s that the Christians rose to second place numerically.[4] (Since this phrase was written near the close of the 1580s, one might expect it to have put the Christians in second place.) It is at any rate significant that all three groups are mentioned by name. Whenever reference was made to the local population, as distinct from their rulers, or to economic classes, members of the various communities were always distinguished from one another by religion. Religion represented the most legitimate frame of reference from any point of view. For the Jews, of course, this leads to the question, was this millet?

The term *millet*, denoting the system of autonomous organization of the Christians and Jews under the Ottomans, is familiar to anyone who has studied the Jewish presence in the Ottoman Empire. Hamilton A. R. Gibb and Harold Bowen, in their comprehensive work *Islamic Society and the West*, list three groups of *millet* that existed in the Ottoman Empire until the end of the eighteenth century: Greek Orthodox Christians, Armenian Christians, and Jews.[5] They were uncertain of the validity of the information at their disposal concerning the *Dhimmis*, feeling that their weakness lay in excessive reliance on secondary sources, and this observation of theirs with regard to both the term *millet* and its conceptual framework is borne out by the extensive documentation of the *sijill* of Jerusalem. In sixteenth-century Jerusalem the *millet* did not exist for the Jews, or for any of the Christian communities. In this respect the city differed not at all from other parts of the empire. Use of the Arabic term *millah* (religious community) is rather rare; furthermore, when it was mentioned in the Muslim courthouse, it was used in reference to the Muslim community, not the Jews or Christians. When a Christian approached the Hanafi kadi, asking him to conduct his wedding in conformance with the tenets of Islam, he asked him to do so "in ways of the Hanafi Millah." In other words, *millet* meant the Muslims, and not any of the other groups. The collective noun employed when referring to Jews or Christians was *ṭaifa*, *ṭāʾifa*, or the plural *ṭawāʾif*.[6] Only as late as the nineteenth century was the term *millet* used in the sense given above, and it was only then that the concept of a single community embracing all the Jews of the empire emerged and became historically valid.

In earlier times one of the most important characteristic forms of Ottoman local administration was the religious community grouped around its place of worship or headed by its man of religion. Was this grouping applicable to the Jewish *ṭāʾifa* of Jerusalem, where, as in some other important cities such as Salonica, Izmir, or Istanbul, Jews were living in several quarters and worshipping God in several synagogues, or were they organized into a single community? How far was this community related to other Jewish centers in the empire? Whether or not there was a superstructure of communal-sectarian organization, might an autonomous form of internal organization have existed within the Jerusalem Jewish community? And, above all, what was the nature and quality of life for the Jews of Jerusalem at the beginning of the Ottoman period?

These questions and their like are the main concern of this book. But, to return to the problem of whether or not the institution of *millet* was in existence, it is useful to outline some of the principal features of the pattern of relations between the Jews of Jerusalem and the various Muslim authorities. The community's external relations all involved the comparatively confined local circle of Jerusalem, with its governors, its judges, and people. True, the community had some contact with outside parties. As a rule, the Jews took their requests and complaints to the governor of Damascus, whose jurisdiction extended to Jerusalem, and to the "Noble Threshold" of the palace of the sultan, whose aid was sought in times of trouble and hardship. In response to such appeals the authorities would reply to the applicants or request the governor of Jerusalem or the city's judge to investigate the matter and rectify whatever was amiss. At times Damascus, the provincial capital, took the initiative, inquiring in Jerusalem whether the community had misbehaved, as, for example, by systematically evading the *jizya,* or poll tax, due from each of its members. Outside intervention in such matters was, however, limited and far from usual; and negotiations always were conducted through local officials of the judiciary or government. In other words, during the sixteenth century there was no system of institutional connections, whether horizontal (between communities in neighboring cities) or vertical (from the center of the empire to the Jerusalem community). Directives and demands from above, or explanations and payments from below, were always channeled through the local governor or the local kadi. The Ottoman Empire thus maintained no centralized system whereby all its Jewish communities were subject to a single authority such as a chief rabbi or some other functionary.[7]

That being the case, how were the Jews regarded by the surrounding Muslim society? Did it relate to Jews as individuals or as a group? And if the Jews were perceived as an entity, how were they referred to? Records of approaches by Jews to the various authorities, and hence the replies they received, mention them by name; that is, they originated from or were addressed to individuals. This is not surprising, since matters involving specific cases and individuals had to be presented in concrete form. But these issues were also related to the community as a whole. An incident that casts light on one important aspect of this situation occurred in August 1563. As part of the restoration and development initiated by the Ottoman regime, some of Jerusalem's markets were renovated and enlarged. The old vegetable market (*sūq al-khuḍar*), in a state of dilapidation at the close of the Mamluk period, underwent a series of renovations and consequently became known as the New Market. The official in charge of the market on behalf of the al-Ḥaramayn al-Sharifayn religious trust—the beneficiary of the income from the property—decided to let its forty stalls to all comers. A long list of names is registered in the records of the law court, where each tenant had to appear to record the formal act of renting his shop. The names are of Muslims, Jews, and Christians, and the document that details these transactions concludes, "And the aforementioned shops were [let] equitably to the tenants previously mentioned . . . to each community (*ṭā'ifa*) thirteen shops, except for the Muslims, to whom fourteen shops were [let] . . . he called to witness each of the communities of the aforementioned lessors, that it vouch for and guarantee its members in all matters of the rentals due from them and concerning them."[8]

Thus, although the shops were let to individuals, each being responsible for the property and the rent money, the transaction was made with due consideration for their communal affiliations. A quota of shops was laid down in advance for each community, which was regarded as a single entity, but the authorities did not intervene in the method of their allocation within the communities. Furthermore, the shops were divided into three identical portions and granted equally to the Muslims, the Jews, and the Christians, although the Muslims were an absolute numerical majority. The Jewish community was given an equal opportunity with regard not only to the number of shops but to the terms of the rental and the amount of rent charged. However, 40 being a number that does not divide equally into 3, the extra shop was allocated to the Muslims. After all, the person in charge of the whole operation was a Muslim, the income was intended for the Muslim religious trust, and the society and the state were Muslim. This small exception however only emphasizes the rule of equal economic treatment of Jew and Muslim.

Legally, the Jews were most definitely regarded as one community; this view arose from the prevalent concept of *ahl al-dhimma*, which granted legal rights to non-Muslims. Among the Christians, the authorities recognized additional subcategories (Greek Orthodox, Armenians, Copts), but this was not the case with the Jews. The sultan, the local kadis, and the general public all knew that the Jews did not constitute an undifferentiated group. The distinction between the Rabbinicals (*rabbān*) and the Karaites (*qarrā*) was an accepted fact, socially, ideologically, and on purely legal grounds. Thus, for example, the Karaites maintained their own separate religious trust, which was recognized as such by the Jerusalem authorities. There were also subgroups of Jews based on country of origin—the Ashkenazi, the *Musta'riba*, who spoke Arabic, the groups adhering to various Sephardic communities, and so on. But although these distinctions were obvious in everyday life and in communal organizations, the Jews were treated as an undivided community. This situation appears to have been acceptable to both sides: the rulers did not find the differences among the Jews as profound and fundamental as those dividing the various Christian sects, while the Jews, who were strict in upholding the differences among themselves, preferred to present a united front when dealing with the authorities.

One of the clearest and most unequivocal expressions of this view of the Jews as a single community was the way the *jizya* was collected. Whereas the Christians were required to pay according to sectarian division, the tax was demanded of the Jewish community as a single entity. The number of Jews subject to this tax was determined in advance on the basis of lists drawn up and confirmed by both the kadi and the community, but it was the latter that provided the information for their preparation. Over the years, the number of Jews living in Jerusalem fluctuated, and it is very doubtful whether the Jews reported their numbers in full. The authorities, who suspected, and perhaps even knew of, attempts to minimize the reporting of Jewish residents, tried to correct the shortfall in taxes by increasing the number assessed. However, this could not be done arbitrarily and unilaterally, since existing procedures made the community responsible for reporting personal and demographic changes. Since this tax was imposed within the framework of religious law, the Shari'a, it could not simply be made a general levy: as the name *poll tax* implies, payment was to be rendered according to the number of heads. Consequently, even though the Jews were suspected of not reporting their numbers in full, the investigations by the kadi, on the instructions of the central government, were conducted through community channels. This was, of course, more than just a way of upholding the traditional legal norm; indirectly, it also reinforced the status of the community as an administrative unit. As a result, the Jews were able to find ways of misleading the authorities; and while they did from time to time report changes in the list of those liable for the tax, they generally did not change the total number. Among the Christians, in 1595 the authorities were able to exploit internal dissension to obtain evidence from members of the community concerning a significant number (15) of Christians who were liable for *jizya* but had evaded payment by means of false returns submitted by their community leaders. In this way "they injured the Christian community and caused them financial loss," in the words of the report submitted to the kadi.[9] But among the Jews—no strangers to disputes and quarrels—there is no evidence of any cases of informing. The cohesiveness of the Jewish community seems to have exceeded that of other communities in Jerusalem.

In addition to perceiving the Jews as a single communal entity, the Ottoman authorities also allowed that community to conduct its own affairs. Some aspects of the autonomous conduct of Jewish communal life, though not reflected in descriptions or other evidence in contemporary material, can be assumed to have existed: for example, internal taxes, a system of mutual assistance, or regulations and covenants known from later periods that no doubt existed in the sixteenth century. Available evidence depicts a communal leadership wielding authority in various spheres of life, of institutions intended for the protection of the individual and the community, of the individual's concern and even responsibility for other members of the community. The authorities did not intervene in the life of the community, not merely because they had no wish to, but also because such intervention was superfluous. Their perception of the Jews as a single entity, reinforced communal cohesiveness.

The perception of the community did, however, entail certain disadvantages. The government too held the Jews responsible for one another. If some injury befell one of their number, the community was required to assist in finding the culprit. There are a number of accounts of attempts by the city's rulers to enforce this requirement, but the following case is the most instructive. Toward the end of 1551, a grave dispute arose between the leader of Jerusalem's Jews, shaykh al-yahūd Ya'qūb ibn Ḥayim Fallāq,[10] and the other dignitaries of the community. Believing he had been wronged, Ya'qūb sought ways of wreaking revenge on the other dignitaries, going so far as to threaten that if they did not make peace with him, he would poison himself. He added, "I will die, and so cause the Jews such great troubles that they will not know how to overcome them, and will be unable to pay the fine (*jarīma*) for it."[11] The Jews reported this to the kadi in an attempt to prevent repercussions in the event of Ya'qūb's death. The kadi acknowledged their position, issuing an official document to that effect.

There were no extraordinary apprehensions about the well-being and safety of Jews, although records exist of assaults in broad daylight on Jews as well as Christians and Muslims. At times, the assailant's identity was known, and there were even witnesses; at other times, the victims submitted their complaints to the kadi without being able to bring any form of corroborating evidence. But the greatest threat to security was nocturnal attack. Even though night watchmen (*'asas*) patrolled the streets of Jerusalem, the Jews seemed to consider themselves more vulnerable than their neighbors to assault. The Jewish community was the only one to hire additional watchmen to guard the synagogue, the shops, and their houses.[12] The Jews' fears were not groundless: cases in which Jewish-owned buildings were broken into, or Jews were robbed and even injured, confirmed the pressing need for these guards. The reason for these crimes was probably both economic and social, stemming from the common belief that the Jews were less secure than their neighbors. The Jews reacted by organizing their self-defense—not by taking up arms themselves, for which they had neither permission nor training, but by hiring Muslim watchmen.

The leaders of the community were not content with guaranteeing security from attacks by outsiders. The community itself contained men and women who broke the law. In an attempt to reform them, the community employed various methods of persuasion and social pressure, but these did not always suffice. In such cases, the leaders of the community would approach the kadi and request his help in applying more drastic sanctions. Some years before his dispute with the community, Ya'qūb Fallāq dealt with one such case. On March 12, 1541, he arrived at the Muslim law court accompanied by the chief rabbi of Jerusalem and other dignitaries, and they told the kadi about one of their congregation who had gone mad. For some time now, they related, he had been acting violently toward other Jews, even endangering their safety. They requested the kadi's permission to confine him to his own or some other house, where he would be given medical treatment until he was restored to his senses.[13] Denial of an individual's liberty was permissible solely with the judge's consent; only when he gave it could the community leaders apply such restraints against one of its members. This authority was not restricted exclusively to the deranged; sane persons could also pose such a threat that their removal became necessary. On March 10, 1593, the shaykh al-yahūd and the community leaders complained to the kadi about a Jew from Safed who had been living among them for some time. By his misbehavior, they claimed, he not only caused direct harm to the other Jews but also brought about troubles with their neighbors. The kadi was therefore requested to "order him to depart from amongst them and return to his town of origin." The community leaders had probably tried to reform the man, or even asked him to leave the city. Having failed, they turned to the Muslim judiciary, whose powers of enforcement were greater.[14]

These two cases, which occurred within a span of fifty years, clearly portray the cooperation between the communal leadership and the Muslim state's judiciary and government authorities. Not only did the former gain the latter's approval in principle to conduct their own affairs; they even obtained effective official assistance in enforcing their authority whenever this became necessary. However, these two episodes were unusual in that they involved unruly Jews and required intervention by the Muslim authorities. Jewish autonomy usually was expressed less violently. Without any outside intervention, the community itself attended to the marriage of its members and arranged for the burial of the dead in cemeteries cared for by the heads of the community. Gravediggers were appointed by the authorities on the recommendation of the community.[15] The hospital (*bimāristān*) in the Jewish community cared for Jewish patients until they were cured. The community also ensured that the estates of departed Jews were passed on to their heirs "according to the customs of their religion."[16] And of course the synagogues and institutions for teaching and study were managed by the Jews themselves. All these were distinct expressions of Jewish autonomy, which was recognized in principle by all concerned and maintained in practice throughout the sixteenth century. The responsibility for all these institutions was entrusted to the communal leaders: the shaykh al-yahūd, or "elder of the Jews"; the rabbi of the congregation, who bore the Hebrew titles *dayan* or *hakham* (*dayyān* or *ḥākhām*); and other dignitaries. All these enjoyed the full support of the authorities in the discharge of their duties and the administration of the community; but they were also held responsible, for better or for worse, for judicial, financial, social, and administrative matters.

Clearly, then, Jerusalem's Jewish community was autonomous and maintained an internal organization. Even though the term *millet* was not used, and there was no umbrella organization or integrated system across the empire, an institution of this kind did exist in practice.

T W O

# *Population of the Jewish Community*

ASCERTAINING the population of Middle Eastern cities during the Ottoman period is difficult, primarily because of the dearth of statistics. The first modern population census was taken in the late nineteenth century.[1] Before that, the deteriorating empire could not, or did not try to, verify the number of residents under its rule. Chronicles of the Ottoman Empire in the sixteenth, seventeenth, and eighteenth centuries are primarily descriptive; official Ottoman documents are almost entirely devoid of demographic data; and representatives of European powers rarely attempted to assess the size of the population under Ottoman rule. When they did so, they based their conclusions on data accumulated at irregular intervals.

The information we do have has been gleaned primarily from descriptions written by European Christian travelers, who occasionally gave the population figures for the places they visited. These travelers exercised absolutely no objective criteria, however, and their writings on the whole are characterized by generalizations. Hence, the numbers cited in their books confront anyone attempting to make use of them with numerous methodological and practical hurdles.[2]

This general paucity of data extends to the religious minorities in Palestine. Interested as those European travelers may have been in the Christians or the Jews of Palestine, they nevertheless failed to record precise, or even reasonably dependable information about the size of these communities. Their references to the Jews or Christians in the cities of the empire in general, and of

Palestine in particular, were either blurred by generalities, copied from works of earlier travelers, or interpreted in the light of personal impressions, and thus yielding highly improbable figures. Muslim chroniclers and travelers, who would have been more familiar with the local population and could have filled in some of the gaps left by the Europeans, on the whole revealed no particular interest in the religious minorities, or if they did, they also spoke in broad generalities. Jewish sources too—letters from natives of the area and descriptions of journeys by Jewish pilgrims from Europe—offer little enlightenment.

A quantitative history of the final days of the Ottoman Empire does exist, and there is some data about the empire's earliest days. In the course of the fifteenth and sixteenth centuries the Ottoman government conducted population and land surveys, the *taḥrīr*, in various provinces for purposes of taxation. This was not census taking in the modern sense, as only family units or households (*khāne*) were recorded, a practice that significantly reduced the accuracy of the data. In Palestine such surveys were taken several times during the sixteenth century, and most of the results have been preserved.[3] Since the Christians and the Jews, "the protected people," were mentioned explicitly and separately, it is possible to chart major statistical trends in the demographic development of these particular communities. The prime difficulty here is that some of the records have been lost. Sixteenth-century survey registers of Jerusalem are available, though, contain summaries of four periods between the years 1525–1563.[4] No official summaries have remained from the last third of the century. This is unfortunate as well as frustrating in that it thwarts the reconstruction of a complete picture of at least one century. Statistics pertaining to the final years of the century are available for other Palestinian towns, and a survey was taken at the end of the century in the Jerusalem district as well. But as for Jerusalem itself, only the first part of the record is extant in the Ankara archives, and those statistics refer only to the Muslim population.

Therefore, one seeking to learn the size of the Jewish or Christian community in Jerusalem at the end of the sixteenth century must seek sources other than the *taḥrīr* registers. It is reasonable to assume that the original version of the *taḥrīr* was sent to Istanbul, while a copy remained in the province itself, either with the governor or at the law court with the kadi. The governor's archives have not been found, but those of the kadi are intact and do contain some such registers, a volume of which I found in Jerusalem. That volume is identical to the original that is now in Ankara, and contains the record of the survey of 1562–63/970 A.H. In order to fill in the missing facts about the size of the Jewish community in the last third of the century, I had to go through all the volumes of the sixteenth-century court records. While their statistical information about the Christian community is limited, there is a great deal of data in these volumes concerning Jerusalem's Jews. Thus, I eventually acquired additional data that to a significant degree filled in the missing links.

## *Population Changes in the Jewish Community, 1525–1563*

The first survey in Jerusalem was taken not immediately after the Ottoman conquest but some eight years later, in 1525–26/932 A.H. The new rulers apparently needed time to become acquainted with the local population and to organize the administrative apparatus. The city's inhabitants, unfamiliar with the foreign conqueror, also needed time to adjust, and in some cases time to come back to the city from wherever they had taken refuge. Many of the Muslim residents had fled the city, or at least evaded the survey. Thus, in the first survey the Jews numbered more than 20 percent of Jerusalem's population. In the following survey, taken in 1538–39/945 A.H., life had returned to normal, and consequently a large amount of growth was recorded in the population as a whole, and particularly among the Muslims. The minority communities also grew, but relatively more slowly than the Muslims, who almost doubled in number. As a result, the Jews dropped to approximately 15 percent of Jerusalem's population, despite the fact that the Jewish community itself had grown by more than 10 percent: as against 199 households (*khāne*) in 1525–26, the *taḥrīr* register of 1538–39 cites the names of 224 heads of Jewish families and 19 bachelors.[5] Fifteen years later, in 1553–54/961 A.H., there was still a large influx of Muslims into the city, accounting for the increase of 70 percent in the Muslim population. The growth of the Jewish community was smaller—

an increase of 45 percent—though less so than in previous years. In absolute numbers the Jewish community had increased—the records now including 324 families and 14 bachelors—but the Jews represented only about 12 percent of the total population.

To this point the Jewish community had grown steadily, primarily as a result of immigration. The following survey, however, shows a change in this trend: for the first time since the Ottoman conquest there was an obvious decline in the number of Jewish residents in Jerusalem. In 1562–63/970 A.H. only 237 Jewish families and 12 bachelors were counted. In other words, the community had shrunk almost to the size it had been at the end of the 1530s. This reduction in the number of Jewish inhabitants paralleled the decline in Jerusalem's population as a whole, although the other components of the population dropped in relatively small proportions—the Muslims by 2 percent and the Christians by 7 percent—while the number of Jews decreased by approximately 25 percent.

In the first half of the sixteenth century the Jews were Jerusalem's largest minority group. Then, during the 1540s the number of Christians in the city grew until they almost equaled the number of Jews. In the 1550s the relative strength of the two minorities changed. Although, according to the 1562–63 survey, the number of Christians was smaller than in the previous survey, the greater decline in the number of Jews had not only reduced their relative proportion of the population to about 9 percent but had also deprived them of pride of place among the minorities. During this period the population of Jerusalem as a whole was on the decline, but this trend did not affect the steady growth in relative strength of the city's Muslim population. Their numbers had increased to 80 percent of the population in the 1562–63 survey, from 66 percent at the beginning of Ottoman rule. From a demographic standpoint, Jerusalem was becoming more Muslim and less Jewish. Table 1 shows a breakdown by religion of the population of sixteenth-century Jerusalem, according to available survey figures.[6]

Family size is an important factor in determining the size of the Jewish community. Because of the Ottoman method of counting and recording, the only statistics available to us are those of family units. To arrive at a reasonable quantitative estimate, these

Table 1. Population of Jerusalem in the sixteenth century, according to Ottoman survey returns.

| | Jews | | | Christians | | | Muslims | | | |
|---|---|---|---|---|---|---|---|---|---|---|
| Survey year | 1 | 2 | 3 | 1 | 2 | 3 | 1 | 2 | 3 | Total population |
| 1525–26 / 932 A.H. | 199 | 1194 | | 119 | 714 | | 616 | 3696 | 3 | 5607 |
| 1538–39 / 945 A.H. | 224 | 1344 | 19 | 136 | 816 | 68 | 1168 | 7008 | 109 | 9364 |
| 1553–54 / 961 A.H. | 324 | 1944 | 14 | 303 | 1818 | 138 | 1987 | 11,922 | 156 | 15,992 |
| 1562–63 / 970 A.H. | 237 | 1422 | 12 | 281 | 1686 | 144 | 1933 | 11,598 | 204 | 15,066 |

*Source:* A. Cohen and B. Lewis, *Population and Revenue in the Towns of Palestine in the Sixteenth Century* (Princeton, 1978), pp. 92–94.

*Note:* Column 1 under each heading indicates the number of households, column 2 the number of family members, and column 3 the number of individuals living alone.

must be multiplied by a given coefficient. Studies made of other provinces in the Ottoman Empire have used coefficients ranging from four to seven persons per family. I have used six, a high average which tends to give rather higher round numbers. These figures, however, make allowance for the percentage appended to the calculations of some scholars who used lower figures but added a margin for error.[7] Although Jewish *khāne* units may have been smaller than Muslim families, for it is generally assumed that many of the Jewish residents of Jerusalem were old people who came there to die, careful perusal of the lists of names in the *taḥrīr* and other population records demonstrates that there were in fact many large families in the Jewish community. I believe that there is thus no reason to apply different statistical criteria to the Jews. Moreover, many Jewish families included two wives, and not necessarily because one was barren.[8] This fact further justifies the use of six as the coefficient.[9]

## *Distribution by Residential Neighborhood*

The population count in Jerusalem was taken to facilitate effective tax collection. Population was figured not by the overall number of taxable persons but by the name of each family head. Since the survey was conducted by neighborhood, its results not only give a picture of the size of Jerusalem's Jewish community but also tell us where the Jews lived. There was no such breakdown in the first survey, taken when the Ottoman rulers were still feeling their way. But in the second census and all others thereafter, the Jews were registered as separate groups in the neighborhoods in which they resided. From these lists it is clear that no official Jewish quarter existed in Jerusalem in the sixteenth century, although there were such quarters in several other cities in Palestine.[10]

The Jews lived in three sectors: the Rīsha and Sharaf quarters, which had a mixed population, and Maslakh, which was not formally referred to as a quarter but was rather a neighborhood in which only Jews lived. Maslakh was apparently located between Rīsha and Sharaf (in the 1562–63 survey it is called Wusṭā, or "middle") and adjacent to the slaughterhouse from which it derived its name. Since it is not mentioned in any other connection, it may be assumed that it was contiguous with the other quarters. Although distinguished by its Jewish character, it was not called "the Jewish quarter" but was considered only another residential neighborhood of the Jewish community.

At the inception of Ottoman rule the largest concentration of Jews was in Rīsha, where they represented more than 50 percent of all residents. In 1538–39 there was a similar number of Jews in Sharaf, but there they represented only a quarter of all residents. In the middle of the century the number of Jews increased in varying proportions in the three areas (45, 25, and 75 percent, respectively, in Rīsha, Sharaf, and Maslakh), but the largest Jewish concentration was still in Rīsha. In the meantime, the Muslim population of Rīsha was increasing at an even higher rate, so that here too the Jews became a minority (some 45 percent of all residents), while in Sharaf they were still about one-quarter of the population. The survey of 1562–63 reveals a drastic change: the number of Jews in Maslakh had fallen to about one-half and in Rīsha to about one-third of their former numbers. Only in Sharaf was the trend toward an increasing Jewish population, for some Jews had moved there from other quarters, while others had left the city altogether, owing to political persecution, religious harassment, and various economic difficulties, among other factors.[11] These same troubles also appear to have been the reason behind a growing tendency among the Jews to congregate in one neighborhood. Living together fortified their sense of security and ensured their proximity to houses of prayer. Moreoever, it was probably no accident that they chose to live in the Sharaf quarter, which was nearer than the others to the Temple Mount and the Wailing Wall. Table 2 shows the distribution by neighborhood of the Jewish population of Jerusalem, according to the survey figures.[12]

In the course of the century Muslims also moved into the so-called Jewish neighborhood, an area not formally defined, as were the three neighborhoods mentioned earlier. In fact this neighborhood was such an amorphous concept that there were even different interpretations as to its exact location. The character of the neighborhood became less exclusively Jewish as Muslims moved into it, but it was still called the Jewish neighborhood, and until

Table 2. Distribution by neighborhoods of the Jewish population of Jerusalem during the sixteenth century.

| | Neighborhood | | | | | | | | |
|---|---|---|---|---|---|---|---|---|---|
| | Sharaf | | | Maslakh | | | Rīsha | | |
| Survey year | 1 | 2 | 3 | 1 | 2 | 3 | 1 | 2 | 3 |
| 1526–26 / 932 A.H.[a] | — | — | — | — | — | — | — | — | — |
| 1538–39 / 945 A.H. | 85 | 510 | 9 | 43 | 258 | 4 | 96 | 576 | 6 |
| 1553–54 / 961 A.H. | 107 | 642 | 3 | 79 | 474 | 3 | 138 | 828 | 8 |
| 1562–63 / 970 A.H. | 146 | 876 | 1 | 40 | 240 | 6 | 51 | 306 | 5 |

*Source:* A. Cohen and B. Lewis, *Population and Revenue in the Towns of Palestine in the Sixteenth Century* (Princeton, 1978), pp. 81–90.

*Note:* Column 1 under each heading indicates the number of households, column 2 the number of family members, and column 3 the number of individuals living alone.

a. The results of the 1525–26 survey are not broken down by neighborhood but rather give total figures for the Jewish community of 199 households and 1194 family members.

the end of the century was generally considered distinct from the Muslim neighborhoods. For example, as late as 1594, when the heads of the Jewish community wished to get rid of a Jew who had converted to Islam and was a source of contention, they requested the authorities to "let him leave their neighborhood and go to live in one of the Muslim neighborhoods."[13]

It should finally be noted that in all population counts Jerusalem's Jews were differentiated only by neighborhood. No survey—neither the *taḥrīr* nor the court registers—lists the Jews by any other category. Theoretically, the existence of the various neighborhoods might indicate concentrations of Jews by place of origin, but this was not the case. There is no hint in any source of such differentiation, and Jews who belonged to one congregation were found to be homeowners or even lessees in other neighborhoods. Moreover, in surveys taken during the same years, it is specifically noted that Jews from Safed not only belonged to separate congregations but lived in separate neighborhoods. A similar picture emerges from descriptions of the Jews of Salonica at the time. Furthermore, in Salonica not only was residence in a *maḥalla*, or neighborhood, a mark of belonging to the congregation; each of these congregations paid taxes to the authorities in accordance with a list submitted to the community.[14] Thus, for purposes of taxation at any rate, each congregation, and thus each neighborhood, was considered a legal entity. In Jerusalem, however, the names of all Jewish taxpayers in the city appear on one list without any breakdown into congregations. The authorities did not differentiate among groups of Jews.

## *Jizya Tax Lists, 1560s–1570s*

Islamic religious law, the Shari'a, provided for a poll tax, or *jizya*, to be levied on non-Muslims (*ahl al-dhimma*) living within the jurisdiction of the Islamic state. Every free man, healthy in body and mind, was obligated to pay this tax. Women, children, the elderly, the crippled, the insane, slaves, and poor people with no source of livelihood were exempt from the *jizya*, as were foreigners, on condition that they not settle permanently in the state.

The *jizya* was collected in two ways: as a lump sum (*maqṭū*ʿ) imposed on the non-Muslim community or from individuals (*ʿalā al-ruʾūs*).[15] In Jerusalem the *jizya* was collected from the Jews and the Christians as an individual poll tax. Yet, there was no direct contact or negotiation with each taxable member of the community. An overall quota was fixed in accordance with the number of individuals obliged to pay, and the community was required to pay this sum in a single remittance. The quota did not appear as a lump sum, but was a compilation of the individual names registered in the survey. The lists of names were rarely checked from one survey to the next, and the previous list served as the basis for the annual tax assessments. In practice, the tax was collected from legally obligated individuals: the head of the household for the family unit and each bachelor. According to the Shariʿa women, children, and the elderly did not pay taxes. Adult males who had been married but no longer were probably reverted to the category of bachelor and as such remained taxable.[16]

The traditional Islamic legal approach to taxation differentiated among three rates: high, intermediate, and low. The taxes levied in Jerusalem, therefore, seem to be an exception: there, everyone paid the lowest rate—80 *akçe* (90 *akçe* at the end of the century), valued at one gold piece. The revenue was sent to the imperial treasury via the treasury in Damascus, with this exception: *jizya* revenue from eighty-five Jews of Jerusalem was earmarked for the religious endowment (*waqf*) of the Dome of the Rock of the Temple Mount, and from the middle of the century on, it was regularly directed there.

As we have seen, the survey of 1562–63 showed a significant decrease in Jerusalem's population, which reflected the drop in overall population that began in midcentury. Lacking data for population counts taken later in Jerusalem, we can only draw an analogy from other Palestinian cities where population clearly declined from the middle to the end of the century. It may be assumed that this applied to Jerusalem as well, an assumption reinforced by the first, and only extant, part of the survey taken in the city in 1596–97/1005 A.H. This survey shows that toward the end of the century, the Muslim population shrank even more. This, of course, can hardly be regarded as sufficient proof that the number of Jews also decreased. Indeed, during the same period in Safed the Muslim population decreased while the number of Jews grew. Moreover, the fact that the number of Jews in Jerusalem began to fall early in the 1560s does not necessarily mean that the decline continued. It is an established fact that at the end of the seventeenth century the Jewish community of Jerusalem was somewhat smaller,[17] but the decline need not have been a steady one. Only from the records of *jizya* payments can the size of Jerusalem's Jewish community, or at least its growth trends, be studied and assessed.

Five years after the last survey, taken in 1567–68/975 A.H., a list was drawn up of all the Jews in Jerusalem who paid their *jizya* tax there. This list, unlike the *taḥrīr* registers, did not differentiate between heads of families and bachelors, though the number of bachelors listed among the Jews had always been very small. Ninety Jews appeared on the list.[18] (These would have been in addition to the eighty-five Jews whose *jizya* tax was paid directly to the *waqf* of the Dome of the Rock.) Hence, the number of Jews who paid the *jizya* that year was 175. In five years the recorded Jewish population had been reduced by another 25 percent. This sudden decrease was one reason why the authorities ordered a new list to be compiled, for the Ottoman treasury suspected the Jews of evading taxes by submitting incomplete and inaccurate tax rolls.

This was not the first time the *jizya* records were checked and brought up to date. In 1547 the *defterdar* of Damascus, the authority in charge of financial matters, instructed the kadi of Jerusalem to reexamine the lists of *jizya* revenue paid by Jews and Christians for the previous five years. The inspection showed that "there was an addition of five [Jews] to the previous year's list." On the basis of five additional people for each of the past five years, the community was assessed retroactively for another 25 *jizya* units to go to the *waqf* of the Dome of the Rock.[19] The following year once again the lists of Jews were thoroughly examined; 14 were found to have died, and their names were struck from the records.

The Ottoman rulers were not the only ones to question the reliability of the official statistics with regard to Jerusalem's Jewish community. The new figures, although smaller, soon became invalid owing to the continued rapid decrease in population. A few years after the survey of 1567–68 the Jews themselves complained to the *defterdar* of the province of al-Shām, who had authority over tax collection throughout Syria and Palestine. They protested that in the previous survey their names had been recorded by the official in charge (*kātib al-wilāya al-Qudisyya*) in two separate lists: 90 men whose taxes were earmarked for the state treasury (*al-khāṣṣ al-sharīf*) and another 55 whose taxes were allocated to the *waqf* of the Dome of the Rock (*Ḥaram al Quds*). These lists, the Jews claimed, were padded: some of the people recorded were not permanent residents of Jerusalem but pilgrims or transients who later returned to their places of permanent residence (*awṭān*);[20] others had died. 'Alī bey, who was in charge of collecting the *jizya* revenue in the Jerusalem district (*liwā'*), continued to demand that the community pay its recorded share. The trustee (*mutawallī*) of the *waqf* of the Dome of the Rock also insisted that the *waqf* be paid the amount that had been fixed in the past. The Jews claimed that they were unable to pay the *jizya* for 175 people, and that the basis for such a figure, as demanded by the latter two officials, was unfair.

Ḥasan Efendi, the *defterdar* of Damascus, with whom this complaint had been lodged at the time of his visit to Jerusalem at the end of September 1572, instructed the kadi of Jerusalem to conduct a new survey of all Jews who were permanent residents of the city and all others living among them. Kadi 'Abd al-Qādir Efendi appointed one of his assistants, Luṭf-Allāh ibn Mawlānā Shams al-Dīn Khalīfa, to perform the survey. 'Alī bey, who was normally responsible for the feudal cavalry the *sipahis*, of the district and bore the title Mir Alay, accompanied Luṭf-Allāh, probably to ensure the accuracy of the count. 'Alī bey's presence was bound to guarantee reliable results, for the lower the number counted, the more income he lost. But the two officials were not satisfied with the public act of counting and recording the names of the Jews; to verify their findings they put the people entering and leaving the synagogue under clandestine surveillance. The description in the court protocol gives no clear explanation of exactly how this was done, but it is altogether clear that this was not a casual act. The two men came to the synagogue secretly and checked the names on their list "one by one, many times" until "nobody [else] in addition to these was found."[21]

The results of this meticulous count showed that the Jewish community in Jerusalem had diminished by 60 men since the previous census ten years before—a reduction of one-third—and the tax was reduced accordingly to 60 *jizya* payments instead of 90 for the state treasury and 55 instead of the alleged 85 for the *waqf* of the Dome of the Rock. Notwithstanding the positive picture this incident gives of relations between the authorities and the Jewish community, the fact remains that there was a steady decline in Jerusalem's Jewish population throughout the 1560s and during at least the early years of the 1570s.

## *Jewish Population Surveys, 1584–1587*

In their complaint to the *defterdar* the heads of the Jewish community had cited two reasons for this decrease in population: first, some temporary residents had departed, and second, some members of the community had died. In deference to the rulers, and above all out of fear of imperial power, no mention was made of a third reason: Jews who had originally been permanent residents of Jerusalem were now leaving the city, in some cases for good. In fact, the phenomenon was not specific to the Jews. In the mid-1580s the governor of the Jerusalem district appears to have oppressed the city's residents cruelly, respecting neither property nor persons. "Many residents of the province (*wilāya*), Muslims, Christians, and Jews, have fled, and many others are planning to flee," was the description that reached the authorities.[22] This general statement was accompanied by examples taken from the relatively small Syrian Christian community. I have found statistics that confirm the oppression of Muslims as well, and we can assume that the Jews were affected too. Nevertheless, a comparison of the findings of 1572 with those of 1584 does not suggest that the Jews were fleeing the district. In 1584 / 992 A.H. the heads of the Jewish community, apparently doubting that the fiscal authorities would accept their *jizya* list as accurate, took the unusual step of submitting to the kadi a detailed statistical breakdown. Only after he had compared this list with the *jizya* tickets they had given him did he officially confirm that there were indeed 60 *khāne*, exactly the number recorded 12 years earlier. This count included only those families "whose *jizya* [went] into the state treasury."[23] To this number must be added those whose *jizya* was paid regularly to the *waqf* of the Dome of the Rock, whether 85—the quota in effect throughout most of the century—or 55—the reduced quota fixed at the time of the 1572 survey. Whichever the case may have been, the statistics show that, despite oppressive conditions and reports of widespread flight from the city, during the period between 1572–1584 the number of Jews not only did not decline but may even have increased.

Although the number of Christians in Jerusalem continued to fall steadily until the end of the century, as far as can be gathered from records of the century's last two decades, this decline provoked no questions from the authorities, nor did it arouse their suspicions. With the Jews, however, things were different. Their small number, and relatively small *jizya* remittances, time and again elicited interest and concern.

In 1586–87 the Grand Vizier Sinan Pasha ordered a careful investigation with respect to the Jews only, demanding a list of all those who were obliged to pay the *jizya* tax. The order of the sultan that reached there, the *wālī* of Damascus wrote to the governor of Jerusalem, stated that the number of Jews living in the province of Damascus was not known. Many of them were not listed among those liable to taxation, and with respect to those who were listed, there was no indication as to which of the three rates established by the Shari'a they were to pay. To ensure that the treasury would suffer no loss, a high official, Bakr Cha'ush, had been sent from Istanbul to Damascus to supervise the accurate registering of the Jews. He then appointed a deputy in Damascus, a *kātib*, or official, named Muṣṭafā, whom he sent to the main cities of Palestine—Nablus, Jerusalem, and Gaza—to carry out the investigation. This time no conspiratorial methods were employed. The Jews were called upon to report to the registry official within three weeks of his arrival in the city. Explicit instructions were issued. "[The members of] this community are to be kept under surveillance, carefully watched. Each Jew found is to be listed separately, clearly, and in full detail—name, appearance, shape, characteristics and all distinctive physical marks. A document (*tadhkara*) is to be filled out for each of them which will state, following my order, the [amount of the] *jizya* to be levied on him in accordance with the Shari'a." Only after remitting payment would each Jew be given proof that he had paid his debt. By thus analyzing and recording as many identifying details as possible, by making the obligation personal, and withholding acknowledgment until the tax had been paid in full, the authorities hoped to create a situation in which the Jews would be "unable to devise [further] evasive tricks."[24]

Indeed, at the end of July or beginning of August 1587, about a year after the matter had been brought to the grand vizier for his ruling, Muṣṭafā prepared a list of the Jews living in Jerusalem. He made use of the Shari'a court to verify and check the information transmitted to him. First he went over the list of the 85 Jews in the *taḥrīr* register whose *jizya* was earmarked for the *waqf* of the Dome of the rock. Then he inspected the names of the 60 Jews whom the community leaders had cited three years before as owing *jizya* to the state treasury. After he had eliminated those who had died or left, the resulting list included only 51 people. In other words, it was absolutely clear that the number of Jews in Jerusalem had not grown; indeed, the size of the community had again shrunk by 15 percent, and in the course of a very short time. Moreover, it emerged that "most were there as pilgrims (*ziyāra*) and were not permanent residents (*mutawaṭṭin*)." However, these people were considered inhabitants (*sākin*) and not merely pilgrims, they were taxable. Little was gained by the new count. "Those living [in Jerusalem] have become very poor," concluded the report. The new list appended to the summary report did not even differentiate among different economic levels; everyone was considered poor. Occupations were not even recorded. Next to each name was only the man's age and a brief physical description. Several conclusions may be drawn from an examination of the names. Men of 60 and boys of 15 had to pay the *jizya*. It is rather surprising that only five men of 60 are named; men over 60 may have been exempt. Among the others listed were two 55-year-olds, 12 men in their forties, 13 in their thirties, ten in their twenties, and eight below the age of 20. One person's age was not given. The relatively large number of young people is also surprising, but as the ages of those not included in the *jizya* list are unknown, it is difficult to generalize. It seems reasonable to assume that there was a larger number of elderly people than the *jizya* records indicate. Nevertheless, the relatively large number of people below the age of 50 permits us to conclude that among the Jews of Jerusalem at the end of the sixteenth century there were many fairly young people, able to maintain a relatively stable community. In addition, though the survey gives no surnames, it does record father-son and fraternal relationships. The records show that more than half of those counted belonged to eleven extended families, attesting to a large degree of cohesion within the community.[25]

Only the Jewish community's share in the *jizya* revenue meant for the state treasury was subjected to this careful check. By the mid-1580s the share earmarked for the Dome of the Rock was once again being figured on the basis of 85 families, and not the reduced figure of about ten years earlier.[26] It cannot be determined exactly when this return to the earlier figure came about. It is clear, though, that the authorities based it not on any real increase in population but rather on the assumption that past records had been falsified, and that the Jews had "concealed [their incomes] and appropriated them for themselves and thus tax revenues were unjustifiably and irretrievably lost to the treasury."[27]

The population decrease of the second half of the sixteenth century was particularly evident during the 1560s and beginning of the 1570s. The trend then tapered off; indeed, the latest data available indicate rather surprisingly that it may even have been partially reversed. Closer scrutiny, however, shows that the spurt of growth apparent at the end of the series is not an expression of an accurate count, such as was taken in the year 1572, but the result of the cancellation of the authorities' agreement and a return to the earlier figure of 85 *khāne* whose returns would be paid to the Dome of the Rock. All these steps were taken in order to overcome perceived doctoring of statistics on the part of the Jews and consequent cheating on their tax returns. Objective examination of the data indicates not an increase but a drop from 60 to 51 *khāne*, suggesting that midcentury population trends did not change until almost the end of the century.

## *True Size of the Jewish Community*

At this point it is useful to pose a number of questions concerning the reliability of the various statistics available. What kept the Jewish community from objecting to the raising of the number of households to pay the Temple *waqf* from 60 to 85? What is the meaning of the central government's conspiratorial manner of counting the Jews? How accurate are the *taḥrīr* data, and to what extent can these surveys be considered a true reflection of the size of the Jewish community in Jerusalem?

It is hard to overemphasize the importance of the statistical data contained in these registers about the Jews and other citizens of Jerusalem. They are a unique source of inestimable value, and one that unfortunately does not exist for later centuries. Nevertheless, some skepticism must be applied to the *taḥrīr* data, especially the statistics about the religious minorities. Charles Issawi has raised doubts based on a retrospective view of later data.[28] Doubts also arise concerning the accuracy of the reports transmitted by the Jewish community and the ability of the authorities to keep a reliable count of minorities.

By comparing the names that appear in each survey and checking them against those on other lists, it is possible to determine the reliability of the *taḥrīr* data. Comparing these names, however, presents difficulties. First of all, some names were recorded incorrectly, either because of the clerk's ignorance or his unfamiliarity with non-Muslim names. Second, family names were not used; throughout the century people were listed as So-and-so, son of So-and-so. Occasionally, an additional designation appears, derived from occupation, place of origin, or lineage—"the blacksmith," "the baker," "the shoemaker," "the Kurd," "the Egyptian," "from Safed," "the Cohen," "the Karaite"—but there are relatively few of these descriptions, and they are unsystematically employed. Also, the absence of diacritical voweling frequently misleads the contemporary reader no less than it did the scribe or copier of an earlier day. All of this notwithstanding, there are in the lists of Jews, some names that appear successively in two and even three surveys. Some one-quarter to one-thirds of the first names that appear frequently in their Arabic form, which differs somewhat from the original Hebrew form—Ya'qūb, Yūsuf, Ibrahīm, Isḥāq—can be identified in combination with the name of the father, although on the whole they reappear only once, and not always with systematic regularity. Some other first names that are often repeated appear in the *taḥrīr* in very distorted form, while about half are mentioned in only one survey. And among the first names that appear less frequently in the *taḥrīr*, an even smaller number of full names—that is, names in conjunction with the name of the father or with a descriptive attribute—are repeated.

There are three possible explanations, beyond the obvious one of errors and inaccuracies, for the relatively limited number of repeated names. There may have been a very rapid turnover of people, with the Jewish community consisting of a tiny permanent nucleus around which a transient multitude came and went. Or perhaps the names were not by and large authentic but were rather invented by the community's leaders to fulfill a tax quota. Finally, the community may have been larger than the total number of names indicates, but with different names being recorded each time. It does not seem likely that the survey listed more Jews than were living permanently in Jerusalem, for the community would have protested. In fact, as we have seen, such protests were made, but only in connection with the *sijill*, not the *taḥrīr* surveys.

To what extent are the names credible? Is it possible that the community was practicing a deception? For answers I extracted from the records of the Shari'a court the names of all Jews involved in litigation in the sixteenth century. Most of the names are legible, for the clerk, by the very nature of his work, was obliged to be more accurate than the *taḥrīr* clerk. And, too, he was a local official, to whom the names, and even some of the people, were familiar. Nevertheless, the clerk sometimes recorded only a first name, making it impossible to draw comparisons.

Obviously, only some of the names that appeared in the *taḥrīr* would also appear in court records. Still, even with this limited sample, it was possible to conclude that the names in the *taḥrīr* records were not fictitious but did in fact designate people who were then living in Jerusalem. Although the correlation is not complete, the conclusion is equally valid with respect to each survey and to many of the names. On the whole the correlation is higher in the later surveys, wherein sometimes more than half the names can be verified by the second source. There are, of course, difficulties in authenticating certain names. For example, 25 people whose first name was Ibrahīm do not appear in the census record for 1553–54/961 A.H. but do appear in the *sijill* registries as having lived in or near Jerusalem that year, and some of them even attended the law court either just before or shortly after the survey.[29] Then again, the 1553–54 survey lists 22 people named Ibrahīm—or Ibrahām, which is almost identical with the Hebrew Abraham—who were not on the court registry at all. At first glance, the correlation might seem almost perfect, but in actual fact the discrepancy between the two lists is much higher than 10 percent. For greater accuracy most of the Ibrahīms listed in the survey are identified by father's name as well, and the same pertains to the *sijill.* Thus, comparison shows that in 1553–54 there were many more Jews named Ibrahīm in Jerusalem than that year's survey shows.

In the following survey too (1562–63) some 10 percent of those included do not appear in the courthouse lists, while six of those listed in the *sijill* were not recorded in the survey. Almost all of them are clearly identified by father's name. A similar picture emerges from a comparison of other first names as well, suggesting a uniform trend within the Jewish community as a whole.[30] There is no apparent pattern governing the exclusion of names from the *taḥrīr* registries. For examples, some of those expressly mentioned as "distinguished men and elders of the Jewish community"[31] in the 1562–63/970 A.H. lists can be fully identified in the *taḥrīr* registry of that year. All in all, it is possible to identify more than half of them as having been listed in that survey.[32] This situation is true of other censuses as well. Thus, it is clear that most of the wealthy and influential members of the community did not evade their obligation to be recorded. However, there were some Karaites—a small minority sect within Jerusalem's Jewish community who were certainly not considered an elite —who managed to keep their names off the lists of the city's Jews, while other Karaites are listed simply as Jews, with nothing setting them apart in any way. In general, then, the names appearing on the lists are verifiable, and they represent the various social and economic groups within the Jewish community.

An overall statistical examination—of the correlation between the numbers of Jews appearing in the *taḥrīr* and in the *sijill* court records provides additional information. In the years prior to the survey of 1553–54/961 A.H., more than a hundred names that had not been mentioned in either of the two previous surveys appeared in the *sijill*. This is a considerable number, but then the first survey was less inclusive and accurate than the following ones, and the discrepancy may arise, at least in part, from its shortcomings. It is possible, however, to identify with certainty more than 60 Jews living in Jerusalem in 1553–54, most of whom were mentioned in the *sijill* court records as property owners, merchants, or residents of the city, who did not appear on the survey lists that year—a discrepancy of about 20 percent. In the decade following we find the names of at least 60 more unregistered Jews, and in 1562–63, when another survey was taken, the names of more than ten Jews omitted from the *taḥrīr* count appeared in the *sijill*. In all these cases the record speaks explicitly not of transient visitors but of permanent residents.

To clarify even further the question of the correlation and reliability of the *taḥrīr* data it is worthwhile to check the end of the series to determine the degree of accuracy of the two counts recorded in the *sijill*, although they do not appear in the *taḥrīr*, in the years 1572–73 and 1587. It is hard to doubt the accuracy of the *sijill*. Not only do many of the names clearly designate family relationships, but ages and physical descriptions are also included. Even toward the end of the century, in the list of law cases of 1587, the names are found of ten Jewish residents of Jerusalem who were not included in the count.[33] Then again, there is no record of the names of the 85 Jews whose taxes were earmarked for the *waqf* of the Temple Mount. Theoretically, at any rate, they might all have been included in the list of 1596–97, part of which has not been found.[34]

The preceding population survey, taken in 1572–73 / 980 A.H., however, is complete and accurate. Not part of the *taḥrīr*, this was a count solely of Jews and was recorded in the *sijill* registry by the court clerk; therefore there were almost no errors in the names. To what degree is there a correlation between this list and the *taḥrīr* survey taken ten years before? Some Jews who appeared in court before and after but not during 1562–63 were referred to as residents of Jerusalem. This means that in the actual year of the survey the list reflected only part of the demographic picture.[35] About thirty-five names had appeared even before this year in connection with various other affairs in Jerusalem. From a comparison of the names in the 1572–73 survey with those of 1562–63, it is obvious that half of the Jews named in the later *taḥrīr* list were not included at all in the earlier one. In other words, even if we eliminate an additional 10 to 20 percent of the 1572–73 names as inaccurately recorded or erroneous owing to incomplete earlier records, at least a quarter to a third of the Jewish residents of Jerusalem in 1572–73 had not been registered in the official survey of 1562–63. This is a significant number of people, and because of the relatively small time lapse between the two surveys, the discrepancy can be explained only partially by high turnover. Actually, the explanation lies in part in the simple fact that there were more Jews in Jerusalem than were reported to the authorities.

There is no reason to doubt the essential reliability of the *taḥrīr* surveys. The large number of names that can be verified against the *sijill* cancels out the possibility of the wholesale introduction of fictitious names. It is also hard to conceive of a hypothetical situation in which a large segment of the people, including leaders, would have been registered in the *taḥrīr* while other names were freely fabricated by the Jewish community. It is also clear that there were years in which many Jews in Jerusalem were not counted at all. It may well be that some of them were pilgrims from other provinces or visitors from other cities in Palestine and were not listed in Jerusalem because they paid the *jizya* in their home communities. Some of them, relatively new to the city, may have either enjoyed the status of *musta'min* or benefited from the assumption that they would pay their taxes to their previous place of residence. All evidence, at any rate, leads to one conclusion: the Jewish community of Jerusalem was larger than would appear from the official statistics—at least 20 percent larger.

This discrepancy justifies the government's charges that "the number of souls in the Jewish community . . . is not known," that their *jizya* taxes were not being paid as required, and that "they stubbornly object[ed] to" the *jizya* assessment altogether and "concealed and appropriated [these incomes] among themselves."[36] The Jews were not being harassed because of their religion or because of prejudices concerning their honesty and loyalty. The officials' accusations were by and large reasonable, and the Jews knew it. Indeed, even the increase from 60 to 85 families obliged to pay taxes to the *waqf* of the Dome of the Rock fell short of accounting for the disparity between the tax assessment and the actual number of Jews in Jerusalem.

The *jizya* taxes were also fair in that they were paid at a uniform rate, the lowest of the three provided for by Muslim law. The Jews of Jerusalem were not all poverty stricken; by any objective standard at least some of them could have been held liable for the intermediate or even the high *jizya* levy. Yet, not a single Jew paid more than the lowest *jizya* rate. Nevertheless, in the course of the century there was a significant increase in the rate levied on everybody: from 60 to 80 *akçe* for both Jews and Christians in the first decade in which the survey was taken until at least the middle of the century, 90 *akçe* for all in 1593–94/1002 A.H.,[37] and possibly throughout the entire reign of Murad the Third (1574–1595). In 1595–96/1004 A.H. the levy was 92 *akçe* for Christians and 104 *akçe* for Jews. When Sultan Mehmet the Third ascended the throne in 1595, additional fees raised the total *jizya* for Christians to 164 *akçe* and for Jews to 214 *akçe*.[38] The increase was due primarily to the change in value of the *altun*, the gold currency on the basis of which the *jizya* was calculated. By the end of the century a wine tithe had been added to the *jizya* paid by both Jews and Christians.

Once the tax rates were fixed, the sultan insisted that they be collected accordingly, and whenever a complaint reached him about an attempt to collect more than was due, the officials involved were warned to desist.[39] Rigorous tax collection was understood to be the privilege of the ruler, who had to adjust the rates to make up for the overall decline in the value of money. Nevertheless, the heavier burden imposed on the Jews probably represents an attempt to make their remittances consistent with their numbers. This would account for the frequent and futile attempts to correct the lists of the Jews only, and to draw a distinction between the *jizya* rates of Jews and Christians.[40]

## *Summary*

The Jewish community in Jerusalem did not conduct an independent census of its members, nor did it record the pilgrims who came to the city, as certain of the Christian sects did. The main sources of information about the size of the Jewish community are the population surveys taken by order of the Ottoman ruler for the purpose of collecting the *jizya*, or poll tax. There is ample proof that throughout the century the Jews paid the *jizya* regularly and in full. Despite the steep rise in the rate of payments, not a single complaint was entered against the inflated assessment. Since the community was looked upon as "very poor,"[41] the poll tax was collected from all of its members at the lowest rate. The community was expected to coordinate collection of the payment from its individual taxable members, although the community as a whole may have assumed the burden of the poor.

Tax levies were based on information accumulated by representatives of the ruling authorities, and the Jews tried in every way possible to minimize the number of names reaching those

Table 3 Jewish population of Jerusalem, sixteenth century.

| Survey year | No. persons according to survey | Actual no. persons[a] |
|---|---|---|
| 1525–26/932 A.H. | 1194 | 1330 |
| 1538–39/945 A.H. | 1363 | 1630 |
| 1553–54/961 A.H. | 1958 | 2350 |
| 1562–63/970 A.H. | 1434 | 1720 |
| 1567–68/975 A.H. | 1050 | 1160 |
| 1572–73/980 A.H. | 690 | 830 |
| 1584/992 A.H. | 870 | 1040 |
| 1587/995 A.H. | 816 | 980 |

*Source:* A. Cohen and B. Lewis, *Population and Revenue in the Towns of Palestine in the Sixteenth Century* (Princeton, 1978), p. 94; vol. 47, pp. 104–105; vol. 55, p. 207; vol. 68, pp. 4–5, 9–11, 13–14.

a. Survey figures corrected by approximately 20 percent.

authorities. Some people left Jerusalem while the survey was taking place. Community leaders paid the tax collectors to compromise over lower population figures.[42] As a result, both the *taḥrīr* census and the *jizya* counts reflected only a partial picture of the Jewish community. Although the authorities continued to use the *taḥrīr* figures as a basis for tax assessment from the Jews, again and again they tried to revise their records.

There was also a steady, real decline in the size of the community, beginning in approximately the middle of the 1550s and continuing at an accelerated pace through the sixties and seventies. At the end of the 1570s and beginning of the 1580s the decline slowed, and there was even a new spurt of growth, but the numbers fell again in the middle of the eighties, when there was a resurgence of local oppression. The brief reversal in the statistical trend may have resulted from an increased influx of settlers.

Just as in the first half of the century the Jewish community in Jerusalem grew along with the rest of the city's population, so the community was affected in the second half of the century by the processes of decline and contraction caused by the degeneration of the ruling power. Table 3 illustrates the effects of this decline on the size of the Jewish community. By the end of the century there were fewer Jews living in Jerusalem than at any time since the Ottoman conquest.

THREE

# *The Leadership*

THE Jewish community in Jerusalem, like its counterparts in other cities in Palestine and in the empire as a whole, was far from homogeneous. Tradition, country, and even city of origin were some of the criteria that broke the community down into subgroups. Some of these distinctions were known to the rulers as well and found a number of institutionalized expressions; for example, a separate *waqf* existed for Karaite sect. But although the government differentiated among Christian subgroups, they made no such distinctions among the Jews, who were looked on as a single, inclusive entity.

## *The Shaykh al-Yahūd*

To deal with various issues of interest to both ruler and subjects, the Jews appointed a spokesman for the entire community. The official title of this head of the community was shaykh ṭā'ifat al-yahūd, or shaykh al-yahūd, "elder of the Jewish community," or "elder of Jews" in Jerusalem, referring not only to the city but to the subdistrict (*nāḥiya*) and even the district (*sanjaq*) as well, though the Jews who lived in the *nāḥiya* (subdistrict) of Hebron—which meant essentially Hebron itself—were not subject to his authority. There were no Jewish communities in the villages of the Jerusalem district.

The shaykh al-yahūd was appointed by the kadi of Jerusalem

at an official public session of the religious court. The appointment was backed by the request of certain Jews, who came to the court in person. According to the writ of appointment, the shaykh was authorized to "study and deal with the affairs of the Jews," a mandate that embraced many and various matters. In some of the appointments the wording was more precise: the man was appointed as "elder and spokesman (*mutakallim*) for them"—that is, for those who specifically approached him, and for "the rest of the community of Jews that is in Jerusalem." His major responsibilities were fiscal. The leader collected taxes imposed on the members of his community and was even responsible for remitting them to the authorities. The community was required to make these payments—called variously *'awā'id 'ādiyya*, *kilaf 'urfiyya*, or *gharamāt 'urfiyya*—collectively. The head of the community apportioned the amount among the members, distributing the tax burden according to each individual's economic situation. When complaints arose about the distribution of the tax burden, the kadi did not pass judgment but rather instructed the shaykh of the Jews to behave "with an attitude of equality toward [the members of] his community," and particularly to treat "the rich and the poor as befits their situation." The head of the community was also in charge of marriages and burials. He did not, however, have exclusive authority, and in each case had to get the kadi's express confirmation in advance. This was in no way intended to limit his personal authority but was meant solely to ensure the payment of taxes and other expenses involved in the kadi's formal approval for each marriage, and to guarantee that when a Jew died without heirs his property was transferred to the general treasury (*bayt al-māl*).[1]

An examination of the public activities of the shaykh al-yahūd as actually practiced indicates that he was responsible for a variety of additional matters. He collected the *jizya* tax from the community and transmitted it in full to its destination, even if some of those who were taxable had not actually paid. Later, he would collect from the members of the community whatever he had laid out from his own pocket; if they refused to pay their debt, he would appeal to the kadi, who then would help elicit payment by force. He reimbursed the community for money collected illegally. He hired and paid night watchmen to guard the Jewish neighborhood against thieves. The shaykh al-yahūd received and distributed new coins allocated to the community and oversaw the implementation of various economic regulations, such as the purchase and selling of grain or production of cheese. He was responsible for community officials and institutions. Overseeing the baking of bread, the ritual slaughter and the sale of meat, and of course the proper functioning of the synagogue were all within his province. Putting up financial guarantees for the debts of individual Jews or the community as a whole and also helping to collect debts; summoning a representative of the kadi to a dying person's bedside to record his property; reporting deaths; contracting for the right to receive the legacy of Jews who left no heirs (*bayt māl al-yahūd*); removing irresponsible or immoral men and women from the community and from the city—all these and more were functions of the shaykh al-yahūd.

The entire complex of relationships with governmental and legal authorities was thus conducted through the head of the Jewish community, who was considered responsible for administrative and economic affairs, for the maintenance of social and legal order, and for security and welfare. His prime authority was administrative, his main activities forming a link between the ruling authority and the members of the Jewish community. To the extent that he exercised his executive authority, he did so in the name of the ruler and with the approval of the kadi. As the intermediary between the Jews and the governing authority, he helped the authorities implement policies concerning the Jews, while making it possible for the Jews to conduct their community life without interference.

The shaykh al-yahūd was appointed for an unlimited period of time: only once, at the close of the century, did I find an instance of the shaykh's term of office being limited in advance, in this case to five years.[2] There were a few isolated cases of a man serving in this capacity for one year only, and some men were appointed to the office a number of times at various intervals; Shamwīl ibn abi Jūkār, for example, served several times at the beginning of the 1550s, the beginning of the 1570s, and the end of the 1580s. It is clear that when a shaykh al-yahūd was replaced after a short period of time it was because the community found him inadequate. Usually, though, he bore the mantle of authority for many years.

Of 11 shaykhs who held office in the course of the 70 years under review, Shamīlā ibn Yūsuf held the post for six years (1566–1572), Yūsuf ibn 'abd al-Karīm for eight years (1558–1566), and Ya'qūb ibn Ḥayyim Fallāq for 14 years (1537–1551). It is interesting to point out that this last lengthy incumbency came during years in which the Jewish population of Jerusalem, and in fact the city's population in general, had reached its peak.[3]

Although the shaykh was appointed by the kadi, and transacted most of his business with representatives of the Muslim law court, he was not an official of the government. Not only was he looked upon as the representative of the Jews, but he also received a steady salary and various expenses (*kharj wa-'ujra*) from the Jewish community. This was an official arrangement, and even after he ceased to hold office, the community was obligated to pay any debt it owed for his term of office.[4]

There were others in the community who, although given no formal appointment, in practice fulfilled various leadership functions. Apart from the shaykh al-yahūd two other Jews were sometimes referred to as "the two shaykhs of the Jewish community"; in 1551–52 these were Ibrahīm ibn Ya'qūb and Yūsuf ibn Yahūdā, and in 1565–66, when Shamīlā ibn Yūsuf began his six-year incumbency, Salamūn ibn Mūsā and Isḥāq ibn Ibrahīm were mentioned. Sometimes others were called *mashā'ikh*, or "elders" of the Jews—three during 1553–54 and 1574–75 and as many as seven in 1572–73. In the two latter cases the name of the formally appointed shaykh was included among them. Additional titles that reappear frequently throughout the century are head (*ra'īs*, two of them *ra'īsān*, and more than two *ru'asā*), spokesman (*al-mutakallim*, two *mutakallimān*, and more than two *mutakallimīn*), authorized agents (*wukalā'*), elders of the Jews (*akābir al-yahūd, kubarā' al-yahūd*), and notables (*a'yān*). Two or three people generally bore each of the titles, although on occasion there were ten *mutakallimīn* (in 1559–1560) and even sixteen *a'yān* (1563–64). Sometimes the shaykh al-yahūd himself was included in the list of the elders of the Jews: for example, Ya'qūb Fallāq in 1537–1550, during which time he held the high office. At other times a former shaykh appears as one of the heads and spokesmen both prior to and for many years after his appointment as shaykh: for example, Yūsuf ibn 'abd al-Karīm from 1555–1591, who served as shaykh al-yahūd from 1558–1566. In at least one case (Salamūn ibn Mūsā Shullāl, 1555–1575) not only was the man spokesman and shaykh for many years, but his father too had been referred to in 1550 as one of the "elders of the Jews."

These examples demonstrate that the office of shaykh was often held continuously for many years, although with the participation of others whose names and roles varied. In the last quarter of the century this pattern remained in force. The title spokesman appears with respect to the same men over many years: for example Yūsuf ibn Sha'bān, 1583–1597, and Ma'īr ibn Ibrahīm, 1583–1600, both wealthy cloth merchants. Also, several members or descandants of the same family were included among the heads of the community. This continuity invested the position with even greater prestige and weight. These leading families wielded power in the community over many years. Members of the Shullāl family, the most outstanding example, had served as the heads of Jewry, or *nagids,* in Mamluk Egypt. Shullāls were looked upon as leading members of the Jewish community in Jerusalem in the generation of Rabbi Yitzḥaq Hakohen Shūllāl, immediately after the Ottoman conquest, and some of them were still bearing the burden of leadership in the late 1570s. Salamūn ibn Mūsā Shullāl is one example.[5] He and his maternal uncle Ibrahīm ibn Hilāl are mentioned among the leaders of the Jewish community during the 1550s, 1560s, and 1570s. Serving alongside Yūsuf ibn 'Abd al-Karīm for many years were his brothers Ibrahīm and Yahūdā, whose sons Da'ūd, 'Abbūd, and Shamīla joined them from the mid-1580s until the end of the century. The Ibn abi Jūkār family also held key positions in the community for many years. The fact that out of a myriad of names there emerged a stable core of a few families who were accepted by the people, and therefore by the rulers, as effective leaders implies an element of conservatism in the Jewish community with wealth and influence concentrated in the hands of relatively few individuals. Over the course of many years, this conservatism was the foundation of stability in a society prone to upheaval, constant change, and untold political and economic hardship.

It is difficult to distinguish a division of responsibility among the various officeholders. A study of the names of men in actual charge of the annual *jizya* tax collection within the community shows that the shaykh al-yahūd performed this function, but—with the approval of the kadi and agreement of the community—he was assisted by one or two other influential figures. The obligation to report deaths devolved sometimes on the shaykh and sometimes on the "two heads of the Jewish tribe." Hiring guards for the Jewish neighborhood was done by the shaykh al-yahūd together with other "representatives of the Jews." For important legal hearings, such as those touching on rights to the synagogue building and its immediate surroundings or the leasing of the cemetery on the Mount of Olives, three, six, and occasionally as many as ten Jewish elders, the shaykh al-yahūd among them, were summoned and appeared. There were even times when they were held in detention because of the community's debts. In money matters among Jews—such as appointing fund-raising emissaries, allocating the contributions they brought back with them, and receiving and allocating other contributions that came to Jerusalem from the disapora—prominent personalities in addition to the shaykh were repeatedly made responsible.[6]

The picture that emerges is of a collective leadership that headed the community and had incontestable authority over the Jews. However, since this leadership was to a great extent amorphous, at least in the eyes of the ruling authority, it was convenient for the latter to look upon one of these men as the main representative. The shaykh al-yahūd was the only one of the leading figures who was considered a functionary of the Jewish community and who in that capacity received a wage. He was, so to speak, first among equals.

While serving his term, the shaykh al-yahūd continued his normal occupation, although, of course, he had to devote a great deal of his time to public affairs. To help him carry out his duties he was assisted by a secretary (*kātib*) "for all matters connected with the Jews living in Jerusalem, such as the *jizya* and other financial affairs, as well as associated matters." The secretary was not only a technical assistant; he was invested with real authority by the shaykh. The dignitaries of the community coming to the kadi to request his approval of these two appointments declared that "they would obey both of them and not rebel against their word in whatever they would do."[7] Obviously, the secretary's work afforded him broad experience in managing public affairs and thus helped prepare him to serve as shaykh al-yahūd in later years. For example, Ya'qūb ibn Barūkh al-Ḥāmī, who was the *kātib* in 1595–96, became shaykh al-yahūd from 1598–1600.

## *The Dayyān*

The dayyān, or religious judge, wielded authority in certain aspects of legal affairs, mainly marriages and burials, that fell within the province of the shaykh al-yahūd.

Not only the Jews but the Muslim court as well and all official documents used the Hebrew word in its Arabic form, even maintaining the stress on the final syllable: *dayyān, al-dayyān.* In many matters the dayyān's authority paralleled that of the shaykh, so close coordination was necessary. It was essential that the shaykh approve the dayyān's appointment, but the dayyān was not subordinate to him, nor did he act as his functionary. A candidate for the post was recommended to the kadi by the community's dignitaries, and the kadi's approval gave the appointment legal validity. When the dignitaries approached the kadi, their definition of the authority to be invested in the dayyān was that he would "inquire into [and pass judgment on] their affairs as exemplified by his predecessors in this role."[8] It may reasonably be assumed that it was the rabbi of the Jewish community who bore the title of dayyān. As the hebrew word *dayyān* implies, he was meant to hear and pass judgment on disputes that surfaced among the Jews and deal with matters of personal status, or, in the words of the Responsa "to deal with and resolve every issue coming before him, concerning the one or the many, concerning marriage or divorce."[9] The ruling authorities did not interfere in these matters.

The dayyān was described several times in the Muslim court as being responsible for performing weddings.[10] Nevertheless, in each case he had to receive permission to perform the marriage ceremony and a written document from the kadi to that effect. This was the kadi's way of securing his fee—the marriage tax, or *resm-i nikāḥ*—in return for his signature on the document. As a means of ensuring the dayyān's cooperation in this matter, he was held subject to fine or punishment if he failed to report as required.

When a new dayyān was to be appointed, the Jews declared before the kadi that he would also serve as their spokesman (*mutakallim*).[11] Indeed, this was not merely a figure of speech. A study of the activities of the various dayyāns indicates that they were looked upon as among the distinguished personalities of the community. They dealt with such affairs as preserving order and security within the community (imposing house arrest on a Jew who went mad, for which the dayyān would surely have had to get official confirmation, or banishing a demented Jewish woman); assuming responsibility for dispensing legacies; representing the Jewish community in the Muslim court; representing the community when there were attempts to infringe on the established rights of the Jews to the synagogue or cemetery; managing the assets of the Jewish *waqf;* and so on. In a few cases the dayyān engaged in teaching and in the management of public affairs. There is at least one instance of a dayyān who was the ritual slaughterer, and another, Kamāl ibn Mūsā, 1570–71, who was a physician.[12]

There was not always only one dayyān for all the Jews of Jerusalem. Isḥāq ibn Isḥāq ibn Da'ūd, known as *mūlīnā* (*mawlānā*?) was "dayyān of the Ifranj Jews" in Cairo, which indicates a differentiation between the Sephardic and the Ashkenazic dayyān. Yāsif ibn Ya'qūb, called "the Egyptian dayyān," held that office in Jerusalem at the end of the 1550s. Possibly the same differentiation between Sephardic and Ashkenazic was applied in Jerusalem too.[13] The dayyān Isḥāq of Demascus (*al-Shāmī*) declared that he and his group (*huwwa wa-jamā'atuhu*) represented the Syrian Jews, and apparently even the Sephardic Jews, in a broader context.[14] There are also indications that the authority of the dayyān did not hold for the Karaite sect in Jerusalem. Sometimes there is mention of *al-dayyān al rabbān,* or "the Rabbinical dayyān," as distinguished from the "Karaite dayyān," and in one instance Isḥāq ibn Ya'qūb ibn Ḥayyim is pointedly referred to as "dayyān of the community of Rabbinical Jews."[15] During certain years the names of several dayyāns appear, and sometimes a Jew who served as dayyān for a few years is mentioned subsequently in connection with another serving simultaneously: for example,

Yūsuf ibn Ibrahīm alone in 1540–1550 and in 1547–48 with Isḥāq ibn Ya'qūb ibn Ḥayyim; Yūsuf ibn Ibrahīm in 1551–1560 and with Nassīm ibn Faraj in 1552 and Salamūn ibn Yūsuf a year later.[16] In 1560–61/968 A.H. two dayyāns were specifically mentioned—Da'ūd ibn Zamīrū, also Damīrū, and Yūsuf ibn Ya'qūb al Miṣrī.[17]

Da'ūd ibn Zamīrū, in Hebrew Rabbi David ben Zimra, known as Radbaz, came to Jerusalem from Egypt in the mid-1550s. He served at first as rabbi and dayyān, having received written approval from the heads of the Jewish community. However, when he had sat in judgment for a few years without having been officially appointed by the local authorities, the deputy to the kadi (*nā'ib*) and the governor forbade him to remain in office. He was beaten and harassed until he agreed to pay a large sum of money for his freedom. The authorities reacted so strongly in this case not only out of acquisitiveness (the Radbaz was known to be fabulously wealthy) but because of the affront to the orderly conduct of government. Nevertheless, since the community wanted him as dayyān, even after he had been attacked and financially penalized, he was given the official appointment. From 1560 on, though, the Radbaz remained the only dayyān, for the other one had died, and he continued to represent the community at least until 1564.[18]

When the full court sat, several dayyāns were certainly members, but when the dayyān is spoken of in the singular, the reference is to the man or men appointed to the post by the kadi. (The distinction between Jews of Sephardic and Ashkenazic origin brought about the appointment of separate dayyāns to whom the rulers gave official approval.) Here, too, as in the case of the shaykh al-yahūd, little importance seems to have attached to the exclusive use of the title or even to establishing formal degrees of importance among its bearers. However, just as among the Muslims the Hanafi kadi was chief among equals, so the highest Rabbinical dayyān was surely considered first among his colleagues, and by the same token the Sephardic dayyān was regarded as more important than his Ashkenazic colleagues.

Two other posts must be mentioned: the Jewish community's cantor and its ritual slaughterer. Mention to the former appears incidentally as part of the name of a Jew recorded by the Muslim court scribe exactly as he heard it, probably without knowing its meaning: Ibrahīm *al-Ḥazzān* or *al-Ḥazzān al-Ḍarrīr*, "the blind cantor," who sold a house he owned to another Jew.[19] The slaughterer, *al-Dhabbāḥ*, is mentioned several times as a participant in debates concerning slaughtering and Jerusalem's meat supplies. There was also a person with no official title who occasionally served in the specific capacity of recorder of marriages, a job that fell within the basic realm of responsibility of the dayyān or shaykh. In early July 1557 the Hanafi kadi permitted the Jew 'Ānū ibn 'Azar to perform marriages "according to the custom of his religion" after receiving the Muslim court's separate approval for each ceremony. This was to be over and above his job as *kātib*, which was his occupation "customarily until now," on condition that he reveal to the authorities the amount of money he was paid for carrying out his various functions.[20]

## *Community Leadership and Collective Responsibility*

The dayyān, who was supposed to pass objective judgment on internal affairs among Jews, also appeared from time to time before the Muslim kadi and other governmental bodies. He assumed no personal responsibility for the deeds of any member of the community. When the authorities termed him "responsible," they meant responsible for affairs of the community as a whole and not for those of any single individual. With the shaykh al-yahūd the situation was different: he bore general responsibility and from time to time also served as guarantor for individuals. The institution of guarantor (*kafāla*) had two forms of expression, one arising out of specific problems and the other being systematic, inclusive, arising from the needs of the rulers. In the first instance Jews were asked to find a guarantor, for example for a debt they owed to a Muslim or Christian. The creditors, looking for maximum security, were not always satisfied with just any guarantor but asked that the shaykh al-yahūd put up the security. Sometimes it was the Jew who wanted the shaykh to represent him before the kadi.[21] But over and above the many cases in which the shaykh al-yahūd served as the authorized agent (wakīl) or guarantor (kafīl), he was also the guarantor of the community as a whole in their dealings with the rulers.

It is pertinent to refer at this point to the theme of collective responsibility in Muslim society. Beyond each adult's individual responsibility for his actions, beyond the responsibility of the family head for his *khāne*, there was the responsibility for the neighborhood, which fell to the neighborhood elder (shaykh *al-maḥalla*, shaykh *al-ḥāra*). His responsibility extended to everything that happened in his neighborhood and to all the households in it. Not only was he concerned with the proper functioning of the neighborhood; he also had to bring its residents before the kadi or governor whenever he was asked to do so.[22]

In addition, certain neighborhood dignitaries (*aʿyān*) were granted responsibility for a given group of local inhabitants. These people, some ten to fifteen in number, are always referred to as "the dignitaries of such-and-such a neighborhood." In the case of the dignitaries of the Christian community and those of the Jewish community (*aʿyān* [*wa*] *akābir ṭāʾifat al-yahūd*),[23] their responsibility lay in the context of the religious community rather than the neighborhood. Whenever members of the community were summoned to either the kadi or the governor, these dignitaries had to see to it that they appeared "as [is the case with] the people of the neighborhoods."[24] A kind of network of responsible dignitaries was thus created that was meant to encompass the entire community, supervise it, and impose collective responsibility on it.

The system that functioned among the Jews and Christians was probably rooted not only in the cohesiveness of these communities but also in the fact that the people were not settled in a single neighborhood. The Jews, as we have seen, were distributed among two or three neighborhoods, and although they probably lived close to one another, from the standpoint of the formal division of the city they were in effect under two or three different neighborhood shaykhs. Not a single Jew appeared in the list of dignitaries of those neighborhoods; they were considered a unit unto themselves. It was therefore more efficient from the standpoint of the rulers to consider the community leaders, particularly the shaykh al-yahūd, responsible for their people, rather than the heads and shaykh of the neighborhood. Indeed, the shaykh al-yahūd and the other Jewish community leaders "were the guarantors of the rest of their coreligionists who lived in Jerusalem." Such guarantee would receive further validity when it was endorsed by the shaykh of the neighborhood. Responsibility was shared by the head of the neighborhood and the head of the Jewish community held true in the opposite direction too. In 1543 the shaykh of the al-Rīsha neighborhood obligated himself to be responsible for "everything that would appear in or disappear from the neighborhood." Since many Jews resided in this neighborhood, the obligation was undertaken not only before the kadi but in the presence of the shaykh al-yahūd, who endorsed the promise.[25] In 1556 the Muslim shaykh *al-maḥalla* of the al-Rīsha neighborhood tortured a number of Jews. The Jews asked the kadi to fire him and he did so, replacing him with another Muslim the Jews had recommended for the post.[26]

In the course of the century the importance of the institution of shaykh *al-ḥāra* gradually diminished; while the shaykh al-yahūd became fully responsible ("face and body," *wajh wa-badan*) for all the Jews of Jerusalem.[27] With that it should be noted that toward the end of the century one also finds a shaykh of the Jewish neighborhood (shaykh *maḥallat al-yahūd*). On the face of it this may seem redundant; but the Jewish neighborhood did not replace the existing neighborhoods, nor was it an entity in addition to them. It was a compound of houses and courtyards within the boundaries of the al-Sharaf neighborhood, possibly extending into parts of the al-Maslakh and al-Rīsha neighborhoods as well. This was the major, although not the only concentration of Jews in Jerusalem. Because of the steadily waning importance of the shaykh *al-ḥāra* on the one hand and the government's view of the Jews as subject to the shaykh al-yahūd on the other, by the middle of the century the former had ceased to be responsible for what took place within the confines of the Jewish neighborhood. Since the Jews hired the Muslim watchmen for their section, the al-Sharaf shaykh could divest himself of responsibility for the security of the Jewish neighborhood, maintaining that it was a separate entity outside the scope of his authority. The growing number of Jews in that neighborhood during the second half of the century made the security problem there more pressing at a time when the shaykh of the neighborhood could have done very little to reassure them. Eventually they hired a shaykh *maḥallat al-yahūd*, or Muslim overseer of the guards, to attend to these matters. Issues of public safety aside, the shaykh al-yahūd, with the assistance of the heads of the community, continued to be responsible for the Jews whether they lived in the *maḥallat al-yahūd* or outside it.[28]

## *Secular and Religious Authority*

On the whole, the responsibilities of the head of the Jewish community were secular, although the distinction between religious and secular in that time and place was not great. It is interesting to note that many cases described in the *sijill* registries are not the kind that required the attention of a judge or religious functionary but rather concerned administrative or financial matters or other affairs of mundane import. For adjudicating disputes between Jews and for overseeing ritual slaughtering there were special officials, and only rarely did the head of the community serve in one of these capacities. Nor was the head of the community necessarily a rabbi. In the many references to the holders of the office of shaykh al-yahūd, none are called rabbi, as are other members of the community. Many followed other vocations before, during, and after their appointment: *sayrajānī* (oil presser), *barādi'ī* (saddle maker), butcher, spice dealer, soap merchant, shopkeeper. Ya'qūb Fallāq, referred to as a dealer in soap after his incumbency, specifically undertook not to conduct marriages or burials while serving as shaykh al-yahūd. That is, although he was perceived by the members of his congregation to be a religious authority, not even when he was involved in a serious dispute with the community and needed all the support he could get did he profess to be a rabbi or scholar of the law.

In the final years of the century the rabbi began to emerge as the person also responsible for the community. In 1595–96 when Baṣal'īl (Rabbi Betzalel Ashkenazi), who was referred to as *khākhām* ("wise man," in the Islamic world a term equivalent to *rabbi*), died before his time, leading public figures came before the kadi to say that they did not want to appoint another in his place. If "something arises that affects the kadis and others responsible for Islamic affairs, why, they would deal with everything that the *khākhām* had dealt with, instead of him." The secular authority invested in the rabbi in this case may well have stemmed from the personality of the man himself. Rabbi Betzalel Ashkenazi dealt with many routine community affairs, but under subsequent leaders the community maintained the duality of functions. For example, two years later, although the *khākhām* Ibrahīm ibn ʻAmrān was among the dignitaries of the community, he was not serving in an official position. The people asked that another Jew, Khalīfa ibn Shiḥāda, be made responsible for public affairs, and their candidate was approved. By the last year of the century the rabbi had become even more firmly entrenched as the head of the Jewish community. ʻAṭā Allāh was appointed as the "*khākhām* responsible for them." The Jews would do "nothing without his knowledge," and he could impose whatever financial burdens on them they were able to carry.[29]

Throughout most of the century the head of the Jews was not looked upon as a rabbi but was in fact a secular leader who also had authority in religious matters. Toward the end of the century a change began to take place. First, a rabbi emerged among the dignitaries of the community. Second, he was appointed by the kadi as *khākhām* of the Jewish community. Third, another rabbi was appointed to replace him in the same capacity. It is clear that by the end of the century the religious aspect of leadership was becoming increasingly important.

## *Social Differences within the Leadership*

Although the shaykh al-yahūd was the formal embodiment of the Jewish community's leadership in its relations with the rulers, the component parts of that leadership were quite heterogeneous. The small Karaite sect in Jerusalem maintained several separate institutions, including a *waqf*, but they had no separate shaykh. Despite the sect's separatist tendencies, the rulers looked upon the Karaites simply as Jews. The *jizya*, for example, was collected from them as part of the Jewish community's share, and not separately as in the case of the various Christian sects. The Karaites were subordinate to the shaykh al-yahūd and the other heads of the Jewish community. Although no Karaite was ever appointed shaykh, the sect was represented among the community's leadership, the overwhelming majority of which was nevertheless not

Karaite but Rabbinical. Two such leaders were 'Abd al-Karīm ibn 'abd al-Laṭīf, the Karaite physician, who served from 1559–1560, and Ibrahīm the Karaite, 1563–64.[30] Within their group, of course, the Karaites had a leading figure who may even have been chosen informally to represent them with the heads of the community; but they were a tiny sect within a large Jewish public, and this was the only representation granted them.

Within the community itself, a distinction was made between Ashkenazic and Sephardic Jews, and a further group identity was based on cities of origin. Such perpetuation of community identity was found throughout the Ottoman Empire in the sixteenth century. The practice was particularly widespread in large urban concentrations of Jews, who could thereby ensure the minimum attendance of ten men, a *minyan*, for prayers in a congregation of common origin, or could maintain a separate synagogue. The Ottoman *taḥrīr* surveys, which listed many such congregations in Safed, were much less accurate with respect to the Jews of Jerusalem, whom the officials recorded only by residential neighborhood. Yet, here too, separate congregational loyalties were undoubtedly preserved, and some evidence can be cited to that effect. Sometimes, with respect to individuals, a descriptive adjective attached to the name of a man or woman indicated geographic origin: Iskandrī, Malṭī, 'Ifranjī, Rūmī, Siknājī, and so forth. Sometimes there was specific identification by place of residence or apparel: for example, Lāwī ibn Shamwīl al-Fāsī from Morocco, who leased a house from the shaykh *al-maghāriba*, the head of the Muslim community, who was originally from North Africa, or Isḥāq ibn Ibrahīm, who was put on trial because he wandered around outside with phylacteries on his forehead ("a knotted leather strap tied between his eyes") and in answer to the kadi's question explained that "this is how they behave in their country in North Africa." At other times there is even explicit reference to the ethnic group: "the community of Ashkenazi Jews" (*Siknājī*), or the hospice of "al-aman, who are a congregation among the Jews."[31]

As far as can be learned from the recurrence of these various descriptive titles in the court records, they were very prevalent in the 1530s–1550s, later becoming less common. Until the end of the century the records show the existence of separate communities, or at least a continuing sense of separateness. Such indications, however, become increasingly infrequent, with the general descriptions (Rūmī, 'Ifranjī) almost entirely disappearing but the more specific ones (Istanbūlī, 'Adanī, Maghribī) still fairly prevalent. This evidence may indicate a gradual weakening of the frameworks of relationships throughout the empire. The appointment in the early 1590s of Rabbi Betzalel Ashkenazi as responsible for all the Jews of Jerusalem is an example of the willingness of the Ashkenazi Jews, who were the minority, to accept a Sephardic rabbi as the community head. This explains why he tried to abolish the then accepted practice of separating Sephardis and Ashkenazis, and why he went to the trouble of introducing a regulation that provided for the Ashkenazi Jews to undertake part of the general financial burden, which they had left to others until then.[32]

The weakening of ties within the larger, separate groups of Jewry should under no circumstances be construed as evidence of assimilation within the general Jewish public. In Istanbul, for example, although the Sephardis were a clear majority, the Ashkenazis continued to maintain their particularity. The distinction was fading steadily, however, and eventually the Ashkenazis were forced, after fire devastated their homes, to leave their neighborhoods and mingle with the other Jews. It may reasonably be assumed that in Jerusalem, too, in the absence of external pressures, the Ashkenazis continued to preserve their separate neighborhood, leaders, and customs.

The leadership of the Jewish community gave a certain representation to the different groups: there were dayyāns who were Damascene (*Shāmī*) or Cairene (*Miṣrī*), a shaykh al-yahūd from Hamat (*Ḥāmī*). Other influential public figures were Sulaymān ibn Yāsif the Yemenite (*Yamanī*), Isḥaq ibn Murdakhay and Ibrahīm ibn Mūsā the North Africans, a Moroccan (*Maghribī*, *Gharbī*), and so forth. Nevertheless, on the whole there was a single leadership for all the Jews, with the shaykh al-yahūd perceived by both the official authorities and the Jewish community to be the head of the Jews.

I found only one exception to this rule: the Jews of Aman (*al-yahūd al-aman*), who were looked upon as a subgroup within Jewry (*al-aman hum ṭā'ifa min al-yahūd*). Throughout the century *Amanī* is appended to the names of various Jews. The appellation might, of course, have its source in their place of origin, although I have not located a place of that name. There are, however, some indications that the word is a distortion of *Alamān*, or "German."[33] In 1551, when Ya'qūb Fallāq was shaykh al-yahūd, two of these Jews appealed to the kadi to appoint a spokesman over all the members of their congregation (*ṭā'ifa*) who lived in Jerusalem, as "had been customary in the past." The kadi did not make a formal appointment, but the fact that he confirmed and registered the candidate was tantamount to an appointment. Immediately after this he recorded another document in which he validated the agreement between Ya'qūb Fallāq and Sulaymān ibn Aṣlān, "the two shaykhs who are over the Jews in Jerusalem": Fallāq would not interfere in the financial or general affairs of the al-Aman congregation, while Sulaymān would represent only the latter. Thus, at least until midcentury there was a group within Jerusalem's Jewry that was an exception to the general rule in that it had its own separate shaykh. By the final quarter of the century, however, not only was there no further mention of the shaykh al-aman, but from time to time Jews bearing the title al-Amanī appear as part of the Jewish community's collective leadership. They still maintained their particularity, as did the Maghribis, Yemenites, and other Jewish ethnic groups, but they were undergoing a process of integration into a broad, inclusive Sephardic society.[34]

The possibility exists that Amanī refers to Karaite Jews, although there is no evidence to this effect. The people's names do not seem to be Karaite. And when Karaites are mentioned in juxtaposition with the rest of the Jews, the latter are usually referred to as Rabbinical. In the absence of further clarification, it seems more likely that al-aman is a synonym, inaccurately written, for German, thus meaning Ashkenazi Jews. Certain of their institutions reinforce the view that this group may be regarded as a separate unit: they maintained a sort of hospice for the poor and sick ("*bimāristān* of the Jews in Jerusalem") which offered a roof to lonely, impoverished women and was called *ribāṭ al-aman* or *dayr al-aman*, the same names used by parallel Muslim or Christian institutions.[35] This view is further confirmed in a court judgment, dated end of August 1612, according to which there was a separate spokesman recognized by the kadi for the "Ashkenazic Jewish community." Thus, at the beginning of the seventeenth century the community still existed, was differentiated from the Sephardic public, and was even recognized as separate by the ruling authorities.[36] Attempts to force the Ashkenazis to shoulder part of the general financial burden were unsuccessful; after the death of Betzalel Ashkenazi, the heads of Ashkenazi Jewry even abolished the regulation he had instituted for that purpose.[37]

The heads of the community differed in terms of occupation as well as origin. The fact that some of them belonged to the same family suggests that they followed similar vocations: for example, Shamwīl ibn abi Jūkār and his brother Mūsā were butchers, while Salamūn ibn Mūsā Shullāl and his uncle Ibrahim ibn Hilāl were spice dealers (*'aṭṭār*).[38] In addition, there were Shamwīl ibn abi Jūkār, a butcher who during the 1560s also dealt in cheese and watermelons; 'Abd al-Karīm ibn 'abd al-Laṭīf (1559–1560), who was a physician, as were Salamūn (1563–64) and Kamāl ibn Mūsā (1570–71); Mas'ūd ibn al-Fattāl (Naftalī?), who was a dealer in precious metals throughout the 1560s; Yahūdā ibn Mūsā, a locksmith during the 1570s; and Yāsif ibn Sha'bān and Ma'īr ibn Ibrahām, cloth merchants during the last quarter of the century.[39]

Economic status also varied accordingly: a physician or a dealer in precious metals was undoubtedly more affluent than a locksmith. To some extent, holding a responsible position in the community required wealth. In 1600–01 Ma'īr ibn Shamwīl al-Maghribī complained that the shaykh al-yahūd and other heads of the community had appointed him as their rabbi "according to their vain, futile ways," in the hope that they would thus make him stand security for the debts of the Jewish community. He refused to assume such financial responsibility, claiming that he was impoverished.[40] It seems unlikely that the kadi would have been willing to accept a guarantee, financial or otherwise, from an indigent person, and the heads of the Jewish community were asked from time to time to defray such debts. Moreover, there are many indications that in at least some cases there was a correlation between the high social standing of the community leaders and their economic status. Some of them are referred to as owners of houses, rooms, or plots of land. Others leased significantly large sources of income such as the *bayt al-māl* of the Jewish community; that is, they had the right to manage the property of a Jew who died without heirs. When Yūsuf ibn Ya'qūb Karkuz, the Egyptian dayyān of Jerusalem, died in the middle of August 1560, his death was noted among the important events of that year, and a list of his possessions was drawn up.[41] The heads of the Jewish community, or the dayyān's heirs, were careful to conceal from the authorities the amount of cash the deceased had had in his possession, but the list does mention 139 books and 26 manuscripts, various types of cloth and fabrics, carpets, copper utensils, a necklace of precious gems, and so forth.[42]

Although the Jewish community surely looked upon the rabbi as its spiritual and religious authority, when it came to relations with local officials, the Jews preferred to be represented by people of firm social and economic standing. Internal frictions and tensions undoubtedly existed, but they were almost always contained within the community and were not permitted to detract from the image of unity projected to the rulers, and accepted by them.

## *Internal Dissension*

Despite the value placed on the outward appearance of unit, there sometimes arose disputes so severe that they could not be kept from the authorities. In 1585, when the body of a Ya'qūb ibn Yūsuf ibn 'abd al-Karīm was found, the heads of the Jewish community were summoned before the kadi for interrogation. Certain Muslims claimed that Ya'qūb, son of a former shaykh al-yahūd who had remained one of the dignitaries of the Jewish community in the last quarter of the century, was hated by the Jews and might have been murdered.[43] The very fact that such a suspicion was brought before the kadi indicates that the Muslims were aware of antagonisms in the Jewish community.

Ya'qūb Fallāq served as shaykh al-yahūd for some fifteen consecutive years, longer than any other Jew in the sixteenth century. In the course of this lengthy incumbency he was attacked and beaten by a member of his community (1543) and was even arrested because of rent the community owed to cover the lease of the cemetery on the Mount of Olives (1537). But these were only exceptional mishaps. The picture that emerges from the many volumes of court records that mention his name is one of a man intensely active in many aspects of life in the Jewish community of Jerusalem (*jizya*, slaughtering, marriages, burials, the synagogue, public order and security, community debts, guarantees, litigation).[44] The very fact that he remained in the post for so many years attests to his effectiveness.

By the end of 1551 discord had sharpened between Ya'qūb Fallāq and the rest of the Jewish leadership. Just what happened is not entirely clear, but one of the charges against him was that he embezzled public funds. A member of the community accused him before the kadi of having failed to transmit to the *subashi* (the officer in charge of law enforcement) all the gold coins he had collected as a marriage tax from the man. Ya'qūb denied the charge, but two Jews testified against him and he was found guilty.[45] The bringing of such a charge was both an expression of the deterioration of community relations and a spur to further deterioration. This was not the first time a Jew had gone to the Muslim kadi bringing charges against the official Jewish representative: a woman once accused Ya'qūb of taking control of her son's legacy. But that was in connection with a private dispute, not a criminal action involving one of the most important areas in which the shaykh al-yahūd functioned. Relations continued to deteriorate to the point where Ya'qūb was relieved of his high office.[46] The actual act of deposing the shaykh, like that of appointing him, was officially taken by the kadi after it had become clear to him that the shaykh al-yahūd was no longer able to represent his community.

Ya'qūb Fallāq first tried to change the verdict. He then threatened to kill himself in such a way as to make it appear that the heads of the Jewish community had murdered him, which could cause them much trouble and expense.[47] To avert such a disaster, four of the community's leaders requested and received from the kadi an official document to use in the event of malicious gossip in the future. They finally persuaded Ya'qūb to leave Jerusalem for good. Apparently there was so much unsavory evidence about his past that, had he been tried before the kadi, the Jewish community would have had enough grounds for a conviction. He therefore not only agreed to leave the city to avoid such an eventuality but also contrived to give the kadi the impression that his departure was of his own free will. It is possible that Ya'qūb had fled Jerusalem temporarily before matters were settled, for he never appeared for a court hearing.[48]

About a week later Ya'qūb's son Shamwīl came to the court and declared that his father had agreed to leave for Cairo within two weeks, after which time the son would join him. To give further credence to their promise, they agreed to pay a fine of 100 *sultani* to the mosque of the Dome of the Rock should they renege. In order to ensure that the family would leave the city, and perhaps also to prevent others from taking possession of their property in their absence, the family divested itself of everything it possessed. Aahārūn ibn 'Ilyā, referred to five years later as spokesman and at this time certainly already one of the community's leading personalities, bought a room that had belonged to Miriam, one of Ya'qūb's two wives, the bread oven, and half of a house that Ya'qūb had owned, also renting from him a two-story building adjacent to the slaughterhouse.

This arrangement was only temporary and was apparently intended to relieve certain financial difficulties. In the middle of 1553, about a year and a half after these events, Aahārūn sold the property back to members of the family. In the description of the transaction before the court there is no reference to an authorized representative of the Fallāq family, which means that members of the family themselves were present, having returned to Jerusalem and been granted rehabilitation. Ya'qūb Fallāq is not mentioned again as a public figure, although he engaged in trade during his last years. Shamwīl also returned to Jerusalem. He soon expanded his business ventures, becoming a spice dealer.[49] The property that was returned to the family was used as security to finance its business transactions. After Ya'qūb died in 1557, the property was again sold, this time to cover his debts.

## *Summary*

The Jewish community in Jerusalem maintained its particularity as a result of the merging of two systems. One was an internal set of regulations, consensus, and custom that governed the behavior of Jews among themselves. The other was an apparatus comprising functionaries who maintained the internal system while managing relations with the external world. To a great extent the Jewish community could enjoy its autonomy not only because of the Muslim rulers' tolerant attitude toward the *ahl al-dhimma* but also because of their willingness to recognize the leaders of the Jewish people. These leaders became an active part of the general administrative organization.

The rulers recognized the autonomous structure of the community and allowed it to manage its own affairs, within limits. There was no relationship between the heads of Jerusalem's Jewish community and the communities of other cities elsewhere in the empire. The community maintained connections with its counterparts in other provinces through traditional and economic ties that required no administrative association. The shaykh, the heads of the community, the dayyān, and others were bound to the community on the one hand and to the kadi and the governor on the other. The local government adopted recommendations submitted to it and did not interfere in the autonomous internal management of the Jewish community, and the Jewish leaders reciprocated by conducting all their affairs with and through the government's representatives.

The Jewish functionaries fulfilled managerial roles in the community. Their power was a function of their effectiveness. Their methods of exercising their authority were many and varied: on occasion the dayyān might beat a person who had disobeyed him, while the shaykh al-yahūd himself might be beaten by a member of the community who disagreed with him, though these were clearly exceptional cases.[50] As a rule the heads of the Jewish community guarded their constituents' interests and saw that there was no miscarriage of justice. They also found ways of circumventing and even deceiving the rulers, primarily in financial matters.

Both the shaykh al-yahūd and the dayyān-rabbi were considered the main representatives of the Jewish community.[51] Their functions and relative importance in different contexts were clearly defined. The dayyān was considered the decisive figure in the internal management of the Jewish community; but in dealing with the government the shaykh al-yahūd was of primary importance. Toward the end of the century it became important for the shaykh also to be a rabbi. Before that time the secular aspects of his task were preeminent. The leading public figure was not necessarily an older man. For example, Yūsuf ibn ʿabd al Karīm, one of the Jewish community's dignitaries until the end of the century, is mentioned in the survey of 1587 as about sixty years old. He bore the title *mutakallim*, or "responsible spokesman," and later shaykh al-yahud, when he was in his early thirties. It was the combination of wealth and a large, highly influential family that invested the shaykh al-yahūd with authority, both in the community and in the eyes of the rulers.

Group affiliation was also an important aspect of status, and among the many heads of the community were influential figures from various group backgrounds. Often two leaders would emerge from this group of dignitaries: the head of the Sephardic community and the head of the Askenazic community.[52] As a rule, the authorities appointed only one shaykh al-yahūd at a time, and as in their own affairs they were guided by the principles of Hanafi majority representation, so they would choose this shaykh from within the Sephardic majority. The rulers were nevertheless aware of the distinction between the Ashkenazis and Sephardis, as well as of the differences between the Karaites and the rest of the Jews. The attitude of the government reflected the actual composition of the Jewish community—a unified entity made up of distinctive individual elements.

FOUR

# *Legacies, Debts, and Financial Obligations*

ONE of the duties imposed on the heads of the various religious communities was to report deaths.[1] The shaykh al-yahūd was usually responsible for this task in the Jewish community. This requirement was based in the authorities' concern for the disposal of inheritances. The Shari'a had long since ruled that if a person was absent for a long time, or died and left no heirs, his property must be transferred to the Muslim public treasury, the *bayt al-māl.* It is not easy to determine whether the Muslims conformed fully to this rule, though such property of course went into their own treasury (*bayt al-māl al-Muslimīn*). But for the minorities, transmitting such property to the Muslim authorities meant relinquishing their own assets for the benefit of the alien Muslim public. The Jewish community hardly had a surplus of such assets, and were probably reluctant to comply. Thus, not only were the heads of the community required to report deaths; they were also obliged to pay a fine (*jarīma*) of 1000 *akçe* if they failed to do so.[2]

Despite these provisions and arrangements, the Jews found ways of retaining at least some of the assets. At the beginning of 1535 the man responsible for the *bayt al-māl* informed the kadi that a woman had died in the Jewish neighborhood and had been buried by the community; the death had not been announced publicly, nor had a burial permit been granted.[3] Such a permit was issued regularly by the officials in charge of the *bayt al-māl* (*bayt al-mālj̄ī*) in response to testimony submitted by the Jews. Since the Jews were apparently not trusted to give reliable testimony about their fellow Jews in this connection, the officials of the *bayt al-māl* would sometimes request corroboration by a Muslim witness before issuing the permit.[4] When, in March 1552, a Jewish woman died, the man in charge of the *bayt al-māl*—the *subashi* of the city at the time—accompanied by two shaykhs al-yahūd, went to record the property she had left. It was only after this usual procedure was completed that the *subashi* found out that the Jews had concealed part of the legacy. When he queried the heads of the Jewish community they explained that she had been a poor woman and had possessed nothing more than what they had recorded. A search was made, and more of the dead woman's possessions were found. They had been intentionally hidden. "Now," as the kadi ruled, "their [the Jews'] treacherous deception was revealed."[5]

To counteract this resistance, at the beginning of the 1550s a post was established for a superintendent of the *bayt al-māl* of the Jews. In 1553 the governor of the Jerusalem district to which the income from this source had been allocated gave the job to Muhammad, a Jew who had converted to Islam. He knew the secrets of his former community, was acquainted with the economic position of its members, and knew the means they used to avoid paying the *bayt al-māl.* He threw himself into the job with a fervor that was highly appreciated by the governor, though not by the Jewish community, unearthing money that Jews had appropriated and returning it to the *bayt al-māl.*[6]

In the second half of the century there were also Jews who were given responsibility for the collection of funds for the *bayt al-māl* of the Jews. The shaykh al-yahūd usually leased the income from the *bayt al-māl* of the Jews for an entire year and paid a fixed sum to whoever was entitled to this income. The recipient was generally the person in charge of the mosques (*nāẓir*) on the Temple Mount in Jerusalem and the Cave of the Ancestors in Hebron (*al-Ḥaramayn al-Sharīfayn*); sometimes he was the governor himself. In return he was authorized to collect the money for the *bayt al-māl* from legacies left by Jewish residents and even pilgrims (*mujāwirīn* and *wāridīn*) who had died without heirs. In this way the state treasury was assured of a permanent income. Additional power thus accrued to the shaykh al-yahūd, as well as income, though it may be assumed that this money went into the community's coffers.

Nothing obliged the authorities to award the lease of this income to the *shaykh al-yahūd;* indeed, the highest bidder usually won. For example, when at the beginning of 1561 Ya'qūb ibn Ibrahīm al-Sukkarī, a member of the Jewish community, offered to pay over 50 percent more than the shaykh al-yahūd had been paying, the lease was taken from the shaykh and given to his competitor. The heads of the community tried to thwart this transfer by refusing to guarantee the new lesee's remittances to the *nāẓir*, an essential condition of the contract. But Ya'qūb ibn Ibrahīm was not one to give in easily; he found a Muslim guarantor, thereby securing the appointment.[7] Generally speaking, the lease was granted to Jews; but in 1566 a Muslim offered 25 percent more than the amount a Jew had been paying until then for the concession, and the kadi appointed him for three years.[8]

The larger sums of money offered by aspirants to the position are an indication of the income they expected to make from the *bayt al-māl.* Essentially, the fluctuation in the rental rate reflected changes in the Jewish community's economic situation. When the economy improved, it was fairly certain that the income from legacies would increase. Thus, in the 1550s and the beginning of the 1560s, years in which the size and affluence of the Jewish community reached a high point, substantial offers were made for the concession. In the last quarter of the century, when the Jewish community began to shrink and its economic situation declined, the income that could be expected from the *bayt al-māl* of the Jews also declined, as did the sums of money offered for the lease. During the 1550s the lease cost 45 *sultani* per year; in 1561 the price rose to 70; in the middle of the sixties it fell to 40 and in 1566 again rose to 50; in 1581 the amount was still 50 gold coins, while in the final years of the century it fell to exactly half of that.[9]

The appointment of a Jew to be responsible for the income from legacies due the *bayt al-māl* put an end to some of the deceptions and evasions practiced by the Jewish community. But the Jews evolved a new way of dealing with this problem: a selective sharing of information with the person in charge of the *bayt al-māl.* A Jew who felt that his death was imminent would invite the man to meet him at his home or in the Muslim court. He would then declare all his assets and debts, and would see to it that everything was duly recorded in a formal document (*ḥujja*). By thus confirming his debts, real or fabricated, including those to his wife, he could ensure that his property would not be confiscated for the *bayt al-māl* but would be turned over as settlement for his debts to the creditors he had stipulated.[10] Thus, the person in charge of the *bayt al-māl* became instrumental in safeguarding Jewish property and ensuring that it would remain in the Jewish community and not pass into Muslim hands.[11]

Bequests to heirs presented an altogether different problem, which must be seen in the broader context of the autonomous management of internal affairs that the government permitted the Jewish community. In the middle of the 1550s the heads of the Jewish community in Jerusalem lodged a complaint with the central government in Istanbul: the kadis of Jerusalem were trying to force them to apportion the legacies of deceased Jews in accordance with the Muslim laws of inheritance, whereas they wanted to continue dividing legacies among the heirs in accordance with Jewish law. At the beginning of June 1556 the Jews were ordered to submit a formal legal agreement (*fatwā*) that they claimed to have to a judge for inspection. The judge of the case was the highest legal authority in Istanbul, the shaykh al-Islām, Abu al-Su'ūd. He ruled that the Jews should be allowed to behave in accordance with the laws of their religion, and that the kadis had no right to force them to behave otherwise. As a result, the kadi of Jerusalem ruled (January 4, 1558) that as long as a Jew did not explicitly request the allocation (*qisma*) of a legacy in accordance with Muslim law, nothing should prevent his following the tenets of his religion.[12]

The attempt by the Muslim rulers to settle the matter of unclaimed legacies coincided with the complaints lodged by Jews about the way in which inheritances were to be divided among heirs. It may be reasonably assumed that during the years of development and growth, the Muslim authorities attempted to transfer part of the property of deceased Jews into Muslim hands. The Jews learned to exploit the authorities to their own advantage in order to protect their property and their rights.

## *The Burden of Debt*

Jews in Jerusalem during the sixteenth century both lent and borrowed money for interest. Even when such transactions were undertaken between Jews, the lender would ask for collateral security. To make sure of his money, he would have the agreement recorded in the protocol of the Muslim court.

There are also many records of loans to Jews given by merchants, military or religious personnel, and other Muslims. A Muslim jeweler, for example, lent money in the 1530s to a long list of Jews: Rūbīn al-ʿaṭṭār, the spice merchant; ʿUbayd al-ʿaṭṭār; Mināḥīm al-qaṭṭān, the cotton merchant; Murdakhay al-najjār, the carpenter; Mūsā al-jawkhī, the cloth merchant; and others.[13] More questionable are the cases in which a Jew is listed as being in debt to government personnel or religious figures. The relatively high incidence of Jews indebted to kadis raises the possibility that some of these loans were simply an elegant form of extortion: for example, the debt of ʿAbd al-Laṭīf the Karaite, who owed 5400 *para* to the Shafiʿi kadi in Jerusalem in 1537–38; the debt of Yaʿqūb Fallāq, shaykh al-yahūd, who owed the Hanafi kadi of Jerusalem 24 gold *qubrusi* in 1545–46; and others.[14]

Jewish merchants were frequently inextricably involved in debt. A good example was Bella bint Shamʿūn, who bought and sold great quantities of apparel, fabrics, jewels, and pearls, until she was heavily in debt and was arrested for not honoring her obligations. When she claimed that she was unable to pay, despite having recently sold a house to a Jew for 40 *sultani*, the heads of the Jewish community put up security for her for another six months. Collateral was commonly given for money owed by fellow Jews, but there were also cases in which government officials offered their persons and property to the kadi as security for debts owed by Jews.[15] This reflected the close business associations between Jews and government and administrative personnel, and also the certainty of the latter that the Jews would be able to pay their debts.

There are also many examples of Muslim officials—primarily the district governor (*sanjaq bey*), the man in charge of the city's security (the *subashi*), and high-echelon military personnel (*si-*

*pahis*)—owing large amounts of money to Jewish merchants. In 1557 the governor declared himself to be in debt for more than 200 *sultani* for various fabrics he had bought from the Jew Ya'qūb ibn Awliyā. In 1560 a *sipahi* owed the Jew Ibrahīm ibn Zakariyyā more than 110 *sultani* on account of a loan. Two years later the same Jew entered a charge against the *subashi* 'Umar for money still outstanding in payment of various fabrics. In 1585 the representative of one of the *sipahis* deposited the jeweled sword of his master with the Jew Ma'īr ibn Ibrahīm as security for a debt of 100 *sultani;* other *siphais* had also declared themselves to be in debt to the same Jew for large sums. The highest amount recorded by a Jew was for a loan to the governor of Jerusalem, who in 1571–72 owed a Jewish merchant and his son from Damascus 1250 gold *sultani.* The governor mortgaged the bathhouse (*ḥammām*) he had built in Nablus to the Jew until he could pay the debt.[16]

There were also debts owed by the Jewish community as a whole to Muslim creditors. Although regarded as one entity by the authorities, the Jewish community—in the spirit of the traditional Muslim legal usage—could not contract a debt or any other legal obligation unless certain specific individuals acted on its behalf. Throughout the years the community had to make various payments to the authorities that required its leaders to take out loans. From the 1540s on, the court records show debts of gold coins owed by the heads of the Jewish community to Muslim religious figures or laymen. In some cases it is clear that these were legitimate loans, for example when money was owed to a Christian for various transactions. However, if it is doubtful that money given by Muslims to individuals were actually loans, it is even more unlikely that money given to the community as a whole was actually a loan.[17] Regardless of the true nature of these transactions, it is clear that the heads of the community usually paid these debts more or less on time and made sure that the payment was recorded in the kadi's books.

In the last decade of the century the picture changes. The records show ten thousand gold pieces sent by Kalsūn, the rabbi of the Istanbul Jewish community in 1593, for distribution among the poor Jews of Jerusalem. The size of the amount attests to the unprecedented increase in the financial burden borne by

Jerusalem's Jews.[18] During those years from time to time the heads of the Jewish community would come to the kadi and declare debts in their name, and in the name of the community as a whole, that were many times larger than those carried in the past. The debts were no longer reckoned in a few dozen pieces of gold but in several hundred. Here, too, the role of Muslim religious personnel as creditors is conspicuous: for example, 135 gold pieces were owed to the kadi 'Abd al-Ḥamīd, 345 to the *khādim* in charge of maintenance of the al-Aqṣā mosque. At the end of the century these debts appear with greater frequency, and the community's debts to several *waqf*s are also mentioned—primarily several tens of gold pieces in regular annual payments to the *waqf* of Abu Sayfayn, also called Khodāwardī.[19] As the century drew to a close, increasingly heavy financial burdens rested on the Jewish community, and in order to meet them the heads of the community assumed responsibility for ever larger loans. As the economic situation in Palestine deteriorated, in order to ensure the continuation of the privileges they had enjoyed, the Jews of Jerusalem had to pay ever larger fees to rulers and officials, for which they borrowed from the city's Muslims.

The main difficulty was not in finding people to lend money but in repaying the loans. The fact that the Jewish community's debt comprised many small amounts owed to many different creditors made repayment even more difficult, for the combined instalments amounted to a total that was disproportionately high. In April 1597 the Jewish community owed more than five thousand gold pieces "to many Muslim people," found it increasingly difficult to meet payments, and finally declared that it could not pay at all. Although the loans had been taken to defray the obligations of the community, this was not a recognized legal entity, at any rate not for purposes of borrowing money from individuals. The heads of the community personally assumed the responsibility for the public debt "in their own name and as guarantors for the rest of the Jews" (*al-'iṣāla* . . . and *al-kafāla*) and were called upon to pay the penalty. Five leaders of the community, among them rabbi Ibrahīm ibn 'Amrān, were taken into custody until they could pay off at least part of the debt. Although they were detained for some time, they were not treated as ordinary criminals. Eventually they complained to the kadi that the conditions of their detention prevented them from praying in public according to their custom, and forced them to desecrate the Sabbath. They asked to be moved to another building, called "the building of the cistern." The kadi feared that improving their conditions would reduce their incentive to pay the debt. The Jews showed him a ruling of the mufti of Jerusalem, which stated that "the kadi has the right to detain them wherever he sees fit, but in such a manner that fulfillment of their obligations will not be affected adversely." The kadi then approved their request and moved them into a sort of private jail.[20] The Jews eventually came to a settlement with their creditors and were freed.

About a year later, in March 1598, three of the heads of the community were arrested again, this time for the smaller sum of 105 *qurūsh* owed in the name of the Jewish community. Since they acknowledged their indebtedness, one must assume that this was only one of several financial obligations, and that it was the total burden that was excessive. Indeed, they stated at a hearing held later that "they have many debts and are unable to pay them." This time they were not put into the public jail at all but from the outset were incarcerated in the building nearby. Not satisfied by precedent, the kadi summoned the man in charge of the prison (*sajjān*) to report on the case in detail, and even sent his deputy to check the facts. When he was convinced that the place in which they were detained exerted "a sufficient measure of pressure," he instructed that the entrance to it be made smaller, for security reasons, and gave his permission to keep the Jews there.[21]

By April 1599 this debt had been paid, for at that time these community dignitaries were asked to make a down payment of 50 gold pieces on an account of 300 that they owed to Muslims. From these incidents a pattern emerges. In the last decade of the century the Jewish community owed various sums of money that its leaders found hard to pay back. The creditors sought the kadi's legal assistance. To exert pressure on them, the Jewish community leaders were imprisoned until they reached a partial settlement. This, of course, solved little more than the immediate problem. The roots of the difficulties remained, as did the search for ways to alleviate the burden.

How did the Jews defray their obligations? One way was

through contributions from abroad, such as the money sent by the rabbi of Istanbul. Envoys were sent to Europe and the East to collect money from Jews abroad. In 1597 one such envoy brought the leaders of the Jerusalem community 510 *qurūsh* collected in Venice,[22] and in February 1600 the Jew Ma'īr ibn Isḥāq came to Jerusalem from Morocco bringing contributions for the city's Jewry. He was issued a receipt stating that he had given them all that he had brought "from the West" and that there was no outstanding debt.[23]

Regular, fixed expenses (al-kilaf al-'urfiyya wa'l'umūr al-'ādiyya) were apportioned among all the members of the Jewish community according to their ability to pay. It is obvious from the testimony of some of the Jewish community's leaders, as well as Muslims who probably made the community loans in time of need, that the leaders who undertook the obligation for loans distributed the burden equally (*'alā al-wasaṭ*) among the rest of the Jews.[24] To relieve this constantly growing debt, the community asked Jews who were not permanent residents of Jerusalem to help defray payments. When Ma'īr ibn Shamwīl came to Jerusalem with his family at the end of the century as a pilgrim, the heads of the Jewish community persuaded him to remain with them and even appointed him rabbi, expressly promising that he would not have to share their financial burden with them. Once he had agreed, however, and was acting as rabbi, he discovered that he was being named as a guarantor for debts, and was also expected to make the same regular payments as the rest of the community. His attempts to hold his neighbors to their promise were unsuccessful, so he turned to the kadi, who handed down a ruling prohibiting the heads of the Jewish community from unjustly obliging him to pay their debts.[25]

In a similar incident, a rabbi from Morocco, Ya'qūb ibn Ibrahīm, and his family came on pilgrimage to Jerusalem, intending to stay a month. Thinking him a man of means, the community tried to shift part of their financial burden onto him, even registering him as a guarantor for their debts. Distressed, he appealed to the kadi, who forbade the Jews to demand funds from people visiting the city temporarily.[26] Even among the city's residents there were those who tried to evade payment of their share on the grounds that the principle of equal distribution was not a valid one. In these cases the kadi ruled that payment of one's share amounted to a personal debt.[27]

The very fact that in the last decade of the century there were unprecedented contentions within the Jewish community is an indication of the growing burden of debt they were carrying. Another dispute that took place at about the same time is of particular interest. At the end of December 1598 the Jew Isḥāq ibn Murdakhay came before the kadi and complained in the presence of the shaykh al-yahūd that the heads of the community were obliging him to bear a heavier burden of the community's debts and fees than the rest of his colleagues.[28] Soon after, Isḥāq ibn Murdakhay again appeared at court and reported that the heads of the community had been recording his name as a borrower and a guarantor on behalf of the Jewish community, sometimes doing so without his knowledge. He had nevertheless paid his portion of the debts. Now, he said, he was again being ask to pay a large debt, which he could not afford. To force him to pay, he had been arrested and kept in solitary confinement. When the heads of the Jewish community were called upon to discuss the matter, they explained that listing guarantors in this way was an accepted practice, and that Isḥāq, despite his objections, could afford to pay. Isḥāq's wife, they explained, was very wealthy, and he could pay his share with her money. The kadi did not accept this argument; he refused to regard the obligation as personally binding on Isḥāq's wife.[29] Isḥāq did not remain in jail for long. Claiming bankruptcy, he freed himself of the obligation to pay the debts. However, unable to face the consequences of bankruptcy and the controversy that arose over the dispute, he left Jerusalem, although his wife remained. In a last attempt to collect part of the debt, a few Muslim merchants, no doubt encouraged by the Jewish leaders, brought Isḥāq's wife to court for her husband's debts. The heads of the Jewish community testified against her. The kadi ruled that she was to be dispossessed of her houses. When she once again revealed to the kadi the details of her husband's dispute with these people, he reversed his decision and canceled the order to seize her property.[30]

The decline of the economy in Palestine was not the only factor in the increase of the financial burden on the Jews. The declining Jewish population of Jerusalem was also a factor, as was increasing governmental oppression. These hardships were unavoidable. But others were not, and in 1599 the Jews tried to change one of them: the high interest rates they were required to pay. A Muslim merchant had demanded that the heads of the Jewish community be forced to pay him at least 50 of the 360 *sultani* he had lent them. The kadi questioned the Jews, who admitted that they indeed owed the merchant money, but not nearly so much. They argued that most of the money he claimed was not for the amount of the loan but for interest. Four years previously they had borrowed 120 *sultani* from him, a debt they were prepared to pay, but not at an annual interest rate of 30 percent. The Jews argued that according to traditional Muslim law the interest being demanded of them was not only exorbitant but illegal, as the *Qanun-Name*, the codified version of criminal financial laws of Suleiman the Magnificent, explicitly stated that permissible interest for a loan is 10 percent.[31] They even submitted two rulings handed down by the mufti of Jerusalem, which stated that it is forbidden to ask for 30 percent interest on a loan. The only way to circumvent this prohibition, one of the judgments stated, was to use a legal fiction (*ḥīla*) whereby some object would be bought and sold between two parties, the difference in the buying and selling price being, in effect, the interest.[32] This judgment gave the kadi the right to determine if the arrangement had indeed been a legally permissible commercial transaction (*muʿāmala*) or an outright loan with interest, which was prohibited.

He found that the Jews had borrowed only 120 gold pieces, and that the Muslim had not even bothered to employ the subterfuge of making a fictitious sale. That being the case, he ruled that not only was the interest of 30 percent exaggerated but that the lender was not even entitled to 10 percent. If the Jews had already paid back more than the actual amount of the loan, he ruled, the surplus was to be returned to them.[33] It is not known if this judgment was actually carried out. The *sijill* volumes show that harsh decisions taken by the court could be circumvented either by ignoring them, or by having a different kadi reverse the judgment. Implementation is especially doubtful here, since the winners were Jews and the loser an affluent Muslim merchant. Nevertheless, the incident is illuminating. It tells us that the community was forced to borrow money at high interest rates, and that when it did not pay, the debt quickly swelled to huge dimensions. Although in this instance the Jews were able to turn Muslim law to their benefit, it seems probable that when the time came to ask for another loan, their Muslim creditors would take measures to ensure repayment that would be satisfactory to even the most fastidious kadi.

Although the 10 percent interest rate was the accepted rule, and was even provided for by law in Jerusalem, the law courts recognized interest rates as high as 15 to 20 percent.[34] Since Muslim law prohibited usury, the fiction of representing a loan as a sale was a common subterfuge in the sixteenth century, and not only with respect to repayment of loans. For instance, the Jews were obliged to pay a certain amount of money for the upkeep of a *waqf*, to which was added a further sum, referred to as interest, that would fall due within a year. In order to avoid the use of the term *interest*, the pertinent documents spoke of a fictitious sale. We know it was fictitious because at the end of May 1588 the kadi recorded the promise of the Jewish community leaders to pay 400 *qurūsh* to the *waqf* of *sanjaq bey* Khodāwardī, better known as Abu Sayfayn. This was a large sum, and all the heads of the community confirmed the obligation in the presence of the kadi and the *nāẓir* of the *waqf*. In addition to this amount, which they owed "on account of the previous *sijill*"—in other words, in accordance with the amount fixed in the past, which was considered the original debt—they were obligated to pay the additional sum of 60 *qurūsh* a year from then on. This additional 15 percent was not called interest but was described as the price of three lengths of cloth bought from the man in charge of the *waqf*. The ruling given by the kadi drops this fiction, making it clear that the reference is to interest. The man in charge of the *waqf* declared that he "had received from the aforementioned Jews interest (*ribḥ*) in the amount mentioned the previous year as determined in the document recording the business transaction (*mu'āmala*)." That the legal fiction existed and was regularly put to use to earn higher interest rates than provided for in the *Qanun* was a matter of general knowledge. However, the Jewish community was obligated to honor the practice unquestioningly, further increasing its financial burden.[35]

In summary, by the end of the sixteenth century the financial burden on the Jewish community was becoming unbearable. The Jews had to borrow large sums of money from their Muslim neighbors and consequently sank deeper and deeper into debt. They had to turn to their brothers in more prosperous communities for help. No distinction was made between the debts of Sephardic and Ashkenazic Jews at the time, though two hundred years later this distinction would force the Ashkenazis to choose between leaving Jerusalem or concealing their identity.

# FIVE
# *Religious Practice and Institutions*

ALTHOUGH the state and society in which the Jews lived perceived their Jewishness as a negative quality, their differences were tolerated, provided that the Jews did nothing to offend the Muslims or Islam. To prevent such offenses from happening, both the Muslim majority and the Jewish minority conscientiously supported the norms, practices, and institutions of Jewish life that set the Jews apart from the Muslim world.

## *Jews and Islam*

In sixteenth-century Jerusalem the Jews lived in their own neighborhoods and worshiped unmolested in their own synagogues, on the condition that they refrain from passing themselves off as Muslims, entering islamic holy places, or otherwise offending Islam, such as by reading the Bible aloud in public. Even the Jews who lived in Muslim sections of the city lived next door to one another, creating a separate Jewish neighborhood, so to speak. It was thus only natural that their voices, raised in prayer, should be heard outside the synagogue; but as long as this happened only in sections of the city with a relatively dense Jewish population, it caused no public disturbance.

Neighbors normally recognized individual Jews by face and by name, and the beard too was often an identifying mark. But to avoid all doubt, the Jews were required to wear a yellow turban (*'amāma*), yellow having been used in earlier generations to set the Jews apart in the Islamic countries. Removal of the turban or use of another color was considered an attempt to masquerade as a Muslim.[1] Women too had to use yellow in their clothing.

A Jew was marked as long as he was dressed, but when he went to the bathhouse and had to undress, how could he be set apart? He was issued different towels from those used by the Muslims, as he was inferior. Additionally, a Jew was required to "enter the bath house with a bell" around his neck to announce his arrival and warn the Muslims to hide their nakedness.[2]

These expedients were not meant to offend the Jews but merely to protect the Muslims from excessive contact or from violation of their holy places. In Jerusalem the most sensitive spot in this connection was the compound on the Temple Mount, where non-Muslims were forbidden to set foot. Anyone violating this prohibition was in great physical danger from the worshipers, and therefore the Jews did not dare trespass. However, mainly because of the special significance to the Jews of the Temple Mount, and to some extent because of the curiosity aroused by the stern prohibition, the site greatly attracted them, and some tried to get as near as possible, at least to see what was going on in the courtyard around the mosques. On May 4, 1551, six Jewish men and six Jewish women were brought before the kadi on charges of having gone up to the roof of the Ottoman college (*al-madrasa al-'Uthmāniyya*) and from there to the roof of the colonnade that borders the western side of the Temple Mount (*riwāq al-masjid al-aqṣā*).[3] The Jews, when brought to trial, were very arrogant in court, and one of them, Ya'qūb ibn Yūsuf, even dared—under the influence of the wine he had been drinking, as the record states—to raise his voice against the judges and claim that two religious officials, whose names he cited, had given them permission. The officials denied this, and separate judgments were then handed down. Each person was sentenced to a flogging, the sentence to be carried out at once so that it might serve as an "exemplary punishment" (*ta'zīr mithlī*) to other potential transgressors.[4]

There was only one way a Jew could overcome the assumption of inferiority: by converting to Islam. Every Jew could become a member of the majority group on condition that he accept its religion. The Muslims did not engage in missionary activity among the Jews, and of course within Jewry there were barriers that effectively prevented Jews from drifting into Muslim society. The temptation was there, though, and despite the many barriers, conversion to Islam was not unknown. I found references to at least fifteen men and two women who had converted to Islam at various times during the sixteenth century.

For a Jew to accept Islam was not a difficult procedure, and many more people than this may have been converted. The only formal act the convert had to undertake was to repeat a statement, and not necessarily in front of an official body. Some Jews preferred to do this with witnessses before the kadi, and descriptions of the ceremony have come down to us. The convert had to prove that he was not a minor and was responsible for his words and deeds. He would declare in a loud, clear voice that, freely and without compulsion, he recited the two declarations, originally called the two *shahādas:* "I declare and testify that there is no god but *the* God and that our Lord Muḥammad is his servant and prophet." He would go on to declare himself purged of any religion that conflicts with Islam, asserting that he had left Jewry ("I have gone out of the Jewish religion") and assumed the Islamic religion, and that Judaism and Christianity are false. He would swear to adhere to Islam and its prophet willingly as the way of truth and uprightness along which the prophet guided the believers.[5]

Converting to Islam meant removing the yellow turban and either publicly throwing it away or in the presence of the kadi selling it to a Jew.[6] This signified severance of the connection with Jewry. From that moment on, the person was called *muhtadī,* that is, one who has been led along the right path. Sometimes, although rarely, the convert would even change his name. Converting to Islam did not automatically mean leaving the Jewish neighborhood. Some converts stayed on, creating a source of friction. In one case the heads of the community came to the kadi and described the damage stemming from the constant tension between a convert and themselves. They requested that he be made to move away from "their neighborhood" to "one of the Muslim neighborhoods." The kadi complied, ordering the convert to leave and stop affronting the Jews.[7] The Muslim religious apparatus regarded conversion as an act to be encouraged. But, as this incident demonstrates, once the step was taken, it was not permitted to disrupt the normal order of things, even if this meant the kadi's siding with Jews against a Muslim.

Despite the religious and physical break involved in converting, not all connections with jewry were severed. At the end of the century a flour mill in the Jewish neighborhood was rented to two converts to Islam.[8] Sometimes it was the convert who was unwilling to sever old ties. A Jew who had converted on a vessel sailing from Egypt to Tripoli tried to return to Jerusalem as a Jew, but he was recognized by a man who had witnessed his conversion—Durmush from Qayseri, Anatolia. The convert was brought to court, where his conversion was reaffirmed, as was the fact that he was no longer free to behave as a Jew.[9] This was an extreme case, of course, which hints at the desire on the part of some Jews to have the best of both worlds. Although the act of conversion was a severe blow to the Jews, they remained in contact with the convert, sometimes even taking advantage of his good offices. For instance, when the Muslim court in Jerusalem cast doubt on the ritual purity of a slaughterer who had been away for some time, the Jewish community brought two converts to the kadi to testify that they knew the man from the time when they had been Jews and that his claim was correct. The kadi accepted their depositions, and the Jewish community was granted his reappointment.[10] The authorities also exploited the converts' background. In 1553 the governor of Jerusalem appointed Muḥammad, a Jew who had "honored himself with the Islamic religion," to be responsible for collecting the legacies of Jews who had left no heirs. Muḥammad knew the Jewish community and the subterfuges used to withhold such legacies from the authorities. He used this knowledge to collect large sums for the treasury.[11]

What factors motivated Jews to convert? The case of Muḥammad indicates an element of striving for social and economic betterment. A similar case was that of young ibn Ḥanān, who, immediately after converting to Islam, went to work for a wealthy fish dealer and in 1567 began to live in his house.[12] A woman might convert if her husband had done so, or if she wanted to marry a Muslim.[13] Although the convert was required to declare officially his disappointment with Judaism and the superiority of Islam, there is no evidence that purely ideological or religious reasons were really at the heart of the matter. Admitting the superiority of Islam over Judaism, as the convert saw it, meant only that he recognized the social and economic advantages he was likely to gain from embracing Islam. Apart from this motive, there seems to be no convincing reason for the convert's severing himself from his environment to become attached to a society that may have looked somewhat suspiciously on newcomers, even if converts were seen as having "honored themselves," in the words of the kadi, by becoming Muslims.

Despite the fact that the practical attractions of converting to Islam were stronger than the pressures to refrain from doing so, conversion nevertheless remained a marginal phenomenon. Although it casts light on some aspects of the relations between Jews and Muslims, conversion had no influence on the life and conduct of the Jewish community in Jerusalem.

## *Synagogues*

Although the Jews and their religion were considered inferior to the Muslims and theirs, no attempt was made to keep the Jews from practicing their religion—at least not when it came to official Muslim policy.

In practical terms, however, the religious difference was a source of some friction. In some measure this friction was inherent in human nature. But its immediate causes were the steady growth of the Jewish community in Jerusalem until the 1560s and the close proximity of Jewish and Muslim neighborhoods.

Jews recently arrived in the city tended to settle near their former countrymen, and sometimes even their former townsmen. One expression of this sort of group identity was to maintain the religious customs of the place of origin. This meant that the more Jews there were in Jerusalem, the more need there was for separate houses of prayer. As we have seen, although the Jews lived in what were called Jewish neighborhoods, predominantly al-Sharaf and al-Rīsha, they nevertheless lived in these areas among a Muslim majority. The proximity of Jewish and Muslim homes meant, among other things, proximity of synagogue and mosque: indeed, the main synagogue of the Jews, the Ramban synagoguge, was very close to the al-ʿUmari mosque.

Such proximity was not without precedent. In 1488, at the end of the *Mamluk* period, Rabbi Ovadia of Bartenora wrote that "in the courtyard of the synagogue, very near, is a dais and *mosqita* [mosque] for the Ishmaelites."[1] This closeness was a source of dissension even then, and at the end of the fifteenth century the synagogue was destroyed by the Muslim residents of the city.[2] A few years later it was rebuilt by permission of the Mamluk sultan, but it soon again became the focal point of disputes. At the end of the 1530s the governor of Jerusalem was informed that the Jews had, without permission, "renovated and built a new building at their synagogue." This report was accompanied by a detailed description: the Jews had broken through the west side of the building, built a stone wall next to it, and put new paving stones in the plaza leading to the building.[3] The district governor, Ḥasan bey el Muẓaffarī, sent his assistant and some professional builders to determine the extent to which the report was true. They were able to confirm all the claims. At the end of November 1540 the Shariʿa court was convened, and the heads of the Jewish community—the shaykh al-yahūd, Mūsā the dayyān, Mūsā the *jawkhī*, and Mūsā ibn Shullāl—were summoned to the session. They did not deny that there had been construction but maintained that the improvements had been made by Ibrahim Kastro a few years before, "in the time of Ballāl bey, the former governor of the Jerusalem district." That being the case, the governor took no steps against them.[4]

Renovation of the synagogue was an ongoing project. Some ten years later Shaykh Aḥmad al-Dajjānī claimed he had learned that the Jews had enlarged a small building located between the synagogue and the mosque, very close to the mosque. A delegation of religious dignitaries and the head builder (*miʿmār bāshī*) of Jerusalem went out to have a look and found that the southern side of the northern wall of the mosque courtyard had been renovated, while the wall of the structure located south of the synagogue and belonging to it was an old one and had not recently been repaired or rebuilt. Nevertheless, the Muslims insisted that the northern wall, once part of a small room (*ḥujra*), had been incorporated by the Jews into the building in the southern part of the synagogue yard. The Jews denied that they had appropriated property belonging to the mosque, maintaining that the small building in question, like the synagogue itself, had belonged to them since before the Ottoman conquest. To get at the truth, the kadi ordered the destruction of the northern wall. No evidence was found of a room or a foundation, proving that the wall was not connected in any way to the small building. The kadi then asked the Jews to prove their right to the synagogue and the small building south of it. Representatives of the Jewish community not only brought several Muslim witnesses to testify in their favor but submitted old legal documents to the court proving that the synagogue and the building had been theirs for many years. Accordingly, on June 10, 1549, the kadi ordered the rebuilding of the wall separating the 'Umari mosque from the courtyard of the synagogue.[5]

The incident was not an attempt to wrest the synagogue from the Jews; rather it was a concerted effort to decrease the area belonging to the Jews and add it to the mosque. Another far more drastic attempt was made to revoke the Jews' right to use the synagogue at all. In the middle of October 1540 a general order was sent to the governor of Damascus and to the various kadis throughout the province, asking them to determine whether any new synagogues had been established in their areas. All synagogues were to be abolished, "with the exception of their ancient synagogues," the continued use of these being permitted by the Shari'a.[6] An inspection was undertaken in Jerusalem, and several Muslims testified that the Ramban synagogue had been a stable (*'iṣṭabil*) until the Jews bought from its owner, Ibn al-Sharaf, and turned into a synagogue. The Jews, for their part, maintained that the building had been a synagogue for many years, having been used as such even before the Ottoman conquest. On October 27, 1542, the heads of the Jewish community submitted an official document to prove their claims.[7] That document was an edict issued by the Mamluk sultans on March 25, 1425, a date that established the antiquity of the synagogue. The authenticity of the edict was checked and confirmed, and it was accepted as binding.[8]

Seven years later, when the Jews were again asked to produce such evidence, they were unable to: the document had disappeared. The only evidence they could submit was the testimony of two Muslims to the effect that Yāsif ibn ʻAbd al-Karīm, one of the heads of the Jewish community, had claimed that the synagogue was bought by his forefathers from Ibn al-Sharaf and had been bequeathed from father to son ever since. This was not good enough for the kadi; he declared that if a document supporting this claim was not brought to him within a few days, the building would be confiscated and given over to the *bayt al-māl.* The Jews apparently managed to submit such a document, because they continued to pray in the Ramban synagogue for another forty years. Attempts were made to harass the synagogue personnel and worshipers, but the use of the building was not questioned.

Harassment of the worshipers took different forms. At the end of 1556, when the number of people attending the synagogue was particularly large, the *subashi* of Jerusalem tried to prevent the Jews from entering the building. Again the claim was made that the synagogue was new, and thus illegal, and the building was locked. When the Jews showed him documents proving the age of the synagogue, he agreed to open it again, but not until he had received 150 *sultani* from the beadle (*khādim*). The governor of the Jerusalem district did not immediately return the document to the Jews, an ill omen for the future, when the synagogue was closed because the Jews were unable to produce the original document proving their right to the building.[9]

During the 1550s some Jews were harassed because of the way they used their prayer shawls during prayer. In June of 1560 the *subashi* brought the heads of the community before the kadi on the charge that they were masquerading as Muslims. Some of their Muslim neighbors, he said, had informed him that before the Jews entered the synagogue they covered their heads with white shawls. He had even visited the synagogue and seen that this was true. The Jews explained that from ancient times they had followed the custom of dressing in their best clothes and covering their heads when they went into the synagogue, and that they even had official permission to do so. Some three years later the issue arose again when two local officials, the *muḥtasib* (inspector of the markets) and the *subashi,* tried to collect a fine from the community, again charging that during prayer the Jews draped white or checked shawls over their heads, rather than the yellow they were supposed to use. When the Jews explained that this was the traditional prayer shawl (*ṭaylasān*), any action that might disturb their use of it was forbidden.[10]

At the beginning of 1579 there was trouble over the same matter, when the *subashi* brought the heads of the Jewish community to trial on the charge that they were trying to look like Muslims "inside their synagogue." The Jews this time did not trust to an oral defense but showed the kadi a legal opinion (*fatwā*) passed by the shaykh al-Islām Abu al-Su'ūd Efendi, who was the highest religious and legal authority during the days of Suleiman the Magnificent. It stated, in the main, "They are not to be prevented from wearing the head covering of white cloth and wool during their prayer." To justify the precedent from the secular standpoint as well, they submitted a decree of the sultan, issued at the end of March 1554, enforcing the ruling of Abu al-Su'ūd. They also submitted to the court a judgment passed by a former kadi of Jerusalem that quoted from Hanafi legal texts describing this custom as one followed by the Jews for many generations. The kadi ruled that the Jews were not to be kept from carrying out this custom, and "their belongings [were] not to be removed from their synagogues" either as a means of exerting pressure or as punishment.[11]

In principle, these recurrent disturbances over a thirty-year period, were no different from other ways in which officials harassed Jews and non-Jews in order to collect large sums of money from them. The kadi, who was responsible for upholding the Shari'a, either at his own instigation or pursuant to instructions from Istanbul or Damascus would also check to make sure that this law was being implemented as far as the Jews and their houses of worship were concerned. He did not hesitate, as we have seen, to rule in favor of the Jews against Muslims, even the *muḥtasib* or the *subashi.* In the middle of 1576 the Jews complained that a local Muslim was annoying them during their Sabbath prayers by climbing onto roofs near the synagogue and "[drumming] over their heads," throwing stones, and affronting the women by performing obscene acts. The man denied these accusations in court, but he was warned in the harshest terms that if he disturbed the prayers again, "on the Sabbath, on Thursday or at any other time," he would be punished by flogging and a long jail sentence.[12]

In the main, the rights of the Jews to the synagogue, as well as to other property, were fully recognized. At the end of 1557, for example, when the Jews put in a request to repair the leaking roof, the kadi gave official permission.[13] In July 1561, twenty-four bound books were found in the house of the deceased Isḥāq ibn Yantūf, the 'Ifranjī. The heads of the Jewish community bore witness that they had been among the books endowed to the synagogue by members of the community and lent by the beadle to Yantūf. The rabbi of the community, the Radbaz, bore witness to the truth of this claim, and the books were returned to the synagogue.[14]

From the early 1580s pressure on the Jews increased. At the beginning of February 1580 the Jews complained that the *subashi*'s assistant, the *turjumān*, or interpreter, had tried to take some lamps out of the synagogue and that a Jew who had tried to stop him had been beaten.[15] The kadi sternly rebuked the man, and he never again bothered the Jews. Two months later, though, on the eve of the Sabbath, the synagogue was broken into, and many valuable objects were stolen. Since the main entrance was locked, the thieves entered through the chamber set aside for the women, which was next to the main hall. They broke the lock of the holy ark and stole everything of value from it: silver, implements, ornaments, altar covers, tapestries.[16] These two incidents clearly reflect the extent to which the synagogue, like the Christian church, was attractive to thieves, who sought the works of art and the valuables it contained.

From the standpoint of the Jewish community, mercenary officials and common burglars were not the source of the greatest concern: the major difficulty lay in the very location of the synagogue. The proximity of the synagogue to the mosque was a constant thorn in the side of the Muslim worshipers. Aḥmad al-Dajjānī, one of the great Sufi mystics of Jerusalem, spoke for the masses when he complained of the religious activities of the Jews as an unbearable provocation.

In the mid-eighties public tension increased, and pressure was again exerted not only to limit the right of the Jews to use the synagogue but even to evict them from it altogether. On March

11, 1585, the heads of the Jewish community were again summoned to the kadi to hear complaints submitted by a group of residents in the neighborhood that the synagogue was adjacent to (*mulāṣiqa*) the 'Umari mosque, that the Jews "raise[d] their voices and pronounce[d] profane words in the synagogue every day, morning and evening," thereby doing great harm to the Muslim worshippers by preventing them from praying with pious devotion. The petitioners requested that this synagogue be closed: "prohibiting [their use of it] will [bring about] advantage to the Muslims."[17]

At bottom these complaints returned to the familiar claim that the synagogue was new and therefore illegal. The court again examined the situation. They first examined the minaret, the prayer tower on the northern side of the mosque, and found it to be an old structure surrounded by a small building attached to the mosque, its opening facing the synagogue courtyard. This building was held by the Jews. The head builder of Jerusalem, who conducted the examination, reported to the court that the small building attached to the mosque was relatively new, having been constructed later than the minaret. He reported that there was another long room, which, like the small building, opened onto the synagogue courtyard. To the south it was attached to the mosque, and to the north to the synagogue. The opening of a cistern used for storing rainwater was in the northern wall of this room.[18]

When the examination had been completed, the Jews were asked to bring in the edict from the Mamluk period that in 1542 had served as the basis for the kadi's ruling on the synagogue. They could not produce the document. Maintaining that it was in Egypt, they requested and were granted a month's grace in which to retrieve it. In the meantime the Muslim neighbors again brought up the claim that the building had been a stable, quoting the kadi Sa'd al-Dīn, who was over a hundred years old. Concerning the cistern, the administrator of the 'Umari mosque declared that it had belonged to the mosque in the past. Thus, two separate issues had emerged. First, there was the matter of the right to use the synagogue at all, which depended upon the question of how long it had been used for that purpose. Second, there was the problem of the small structure between the synagogue and the mosque. During the following year, 1586, it was again declared that this small building belonged to the mosque. The Jews were forbidden to use it, and by order of the kadi it was sealed. Only after the Jewish community repeatedly appealed to the kadi was the matter again examined. On November 16, 1586, the kadi reversed his decision, and the Jews were allowed to use it again.[19]

Before long, trouble arose again over the synagogue building itself, and by the final months of 1587 the Jews had been forbidden to use the Ramban synagogue by order of the district governor.[20] (This prohibition has been erroneously dated to 1586,[21] but even at the end of the following year the order was not considered absolute or final.) The Jews managed to get a *firman* from Istanbul that ordered an investigation to be carried out as to the factual grounds on which the synagogue had been closed and required the kadi to ensure that the rights of the Jews would not be violated. This intervention seems to have been achieved through mediators in Istanbul, who went so far as to argue that closing the synagogue might cause "the community referred to . . . to exile itself from Jerusalem."[22] Within half a year the *firman* was no longer in effect. On April 8, 1588, the kadi of Jerusalem issued an explicit order: the Jews were to be prevented from entering the synagogue, and under no circumstances were they to be permitted to pray in it.[23] The closing of the synagogue became final after the intervention of various influential religious figures in Jerusalem, including the kadi and the mufti and testimony from residents of the neighborhood near the 'Umari mosque, as well as from its various functionaries (the *khādim*, *mu'adhdhin*, and *'imām*). The report submitted to the kadi asserted that the Jews were "infidels" who disturbed the serenity of the Muslims' prayers. It was claimed that this disturbance could not be prevented by technical means because the two houses of worship were too close, to each other, in effect sharing a wall.

The actual closing was done in an orderly fashion. The community was permitted to remove the sixty Torah scrolls and put them in various homes for safekeeping.[24] The door of the synagogue was locked and sealed. Yet, decisive as these various steps were, the issue continued to trouble the authorities. The Jews applied pressure in Jerusalem and Istanbul to get the building opened again, and they attempted to mobilize the support of influential religious figures, but without success. In January 1589, for example, another specific and detailed ruling was sent by the sultan to the kadi of Jerusalem, supporting him in his opposition to all attempts to reopen the synagogue.[25] At the end of 1595 and again at the end of 1596 the kadis of Jerusalem reiterated the fact that the synagogue was closed to Jews, and it remained closed until well into the seventeenth century.

Even after the Ramban synagogue had been closed, the Jews continued to pray together. During the years when the synagogue functioned regularly, it had not satisfied all the groups of Jews in Jerusalem. Accordingly, minyans of ten men or more had begun to gather in private homes to pray. To prevent new synagogues from being established, at the beginning of the 1540s the sultan explicitly prohibited such gatherings throughout the province of Damascus. This order was easily circumvented at first, when the Jews prayed in private homes. But these meeting places gradually became institutionalized with the addition of a *mizraḥ* wall (the decorative plaque on the synagogue's eastern wall), the holy ark, and permanent ornaments, or "pictures," as they were called by contemporaries.

This process of institutionalization did not take place in all cases. The Jews were aware that the sultan would not welcome such a development. In 1581, when they petitioned him for permission to continue praying in one private house, they assured him that they were not offending anyone with their prayers and that they had not hung pictures[26] or made a *mizraḥ* or a holy ark.[27] The Sultan affirmed that if what the Jews told him was true, they were not to be prevented from praying there.[28] Six years later, when attempts were made to close the Ramban synagogue, the Jewish community called it "the ancient synagogue." In earlier years, when it had been the only synagogue, there had been no need to give it an identifying adjective.[29] When the Ramban synagogue had been closed, attempts were also made to keep the Jews from worshiping in other synagogues in Jerusalem. They asked the kadi again to record in the court books the Sultan's edict permitting them to pray in private homes, and in 1591, 1594, 1595, and again in 1599, this confirmation was granted.[30]

In the year 1599 the Ottoman regime took another step toward coming to terms with the institutionalization of new synagogues. On the first Sabbath of the month of April 1599, the kadi of Jerusalem visited one of these synagogues. When he came into the house and found "men and women engaged in reading the Bible out loud," he asked who had given them permission to turn the house into a synagogue. The Jews made no attempt to deny their actions, and even gave the name of the Jew, Salamūn ibn Ifrayyim, who had established it. We do not know who this Salamūn was and by what authority he acted, but his name appears in the list of Jerusalem's Jewry in the final years of the century. The Jews also showed the kadi the sultan's order permitting them to use the house, provided they did not install permanent fixtures. Although the kadi found "things that are specifically for synagogues," and even noted that the prayers could be heard outside the building, he nevertheless did not forbid the Jews to continue worshiping there but merely recorded the facts in the court protocol.[31]

The kadi's behavior in this case implies that he was largely reconciled to action that was essentially contrary to accepted official norms. While the authorities, under pressure from local residents, had ordered the closing of a synagogue that had functioned for many generations, other places of worship—synagogues for all intents and purposes—were permitted to function and undisturbed. Beyond obvious explanations such as bribery, very likely a contributing factor, the prime reason for the distinction was that the Ramban synagogue, so close to the 'Umari mosque, had been too persistent a provocation to the Muslims.[32]

Although many of the distinctions within the Jewish community began to break down toward the end of the century, the separate synagogues remained. In 1596 five Jews, with Rabbi Ibrahīm ibn 'Amrān leading them, broke into another Jew's house and appropriated four of the Bible scrolls from the Ramban synagogue that were being kept there.[33] This act was perpetrated for the sake of their own synagogue. These newly formed congregations were permitted to flourish, since the Muslims understood that the Jews, and the Christians as well, must be allowed to conduct their "idolatrous ceremonies" as they wished. Although the main synagogue was closed down by the authorities, they had no intention of ending the normal functioning of Jewish religious life. If this did not entirely conform with certain instructions from the capital, practical considerations and mutual interest were stronger than abstract principles and even than antagonisms between the majority and the minority.

## *Burying the Dead*

The burial of the community's dead was in many respects a significant event. People gave thought to their right to be buried in the Jewish cemetery and to the disposal of their property. The cemetery as an institution—its size, location, and the conditions of its maintenance—was also of utmost importance.

Because space was limited within the city's walls, all burials took place outside. Jews, no matter where they lived, wanted to die and be buried in Jerusalem because of its sanctity and because of the belief that the resurrection of the dead would start there. In relative terms, more Jews were buried in Jerusalem than Muslims or Christians. The growth of Jerusalem's Jewish community during the first half of the century, as well as the influx of Jews who came there to die, increased the demand of Jews for burial grounds. They were particularly attracted to an area east of the Temple Mount which, according to tradition, had been a cemetery from the time of the kings of Judea. One indication of the increasing importance of Jerusalem's Jewish cemetery is that the matter was debated in the Muslim court with growing frequency, and the debates were recorded in exceptional detail. Problems associated with their cemeteries engaged the attention of the Jewish community and were aired in court more often than any others. Judgments handed down in this connection were long and most detailed.[1]

The Jewish cemetery (*maqbarat al-yahūd, turbat al-yahūd*) was on the Gethsemane lands (*arḍ al-jismāniyya*), which, according to Christian tradition, lie opposite the Golden Gate of the Temple Mount, on the western slope of the Mount of Olives. These lands were part of the *waqf* endowed for the upkeep of the college (*madrasa*) named after Ṣalāḥ al-Dīn al-Ayyūbī (*al-madrasa al-ṣalāḥiyya*). At the inception of ottoman rule the boundaries of this *waqf*, established on July 25, 1192,[2] were reconfirmed by the kadi of Jerusalem, first on June 4, 1534 and again on August 9–18, 1537. It encompases a very large area, including all of the Mount of Olives up to the al-ʿIsawiyya lands in the north, the ruined monastery of Abu-Dis, ʿAzariyya and Ṭūr Zaytā in the east, the Kedron valley, Mount Zion and Mamilla pool to the south, and in the west the lands of the Nestorian monastery and the road leading to the ʿOfel. Before the Ottoman conquest the Jews had leased part of this large area for a cemetery, and they continued to use it after the conquest. The earliest description of the area of the cemetery dates from the middle of 1532 and notes that "the boundaries of this area distinguish it from the others": to the south the open space (*ḥarīm*) in front of the eastern spring of Siloam (ʿAyn Silwān),[3] which is at the bottom of the valley to the western slope of al-Bāṭin mountain (Mons Offensionis); to the east a stone fence that separates it from the area called "land of the mulberry tree" (*al-Tūta* or possibly *al-Tawba*), held by one of the residents of Silwān; to the west the road leading to Jerusalem and to the southern spring of Siloam (ʿAyn Silwān),[4] the southern end of which is the ruined stone wall north of the road to Gethsemane; from the north the stone bridge at the crossroad that is in the lower part of the valley, and its western end the bed of the Kedron stream.[5] It emerges from a later description that the old boundaries of the cemetery were in the south and east, while the details given for the western and northern boundaries indicate that these were the new ones.[6] Thus, the cemetery was at first developed from south to north. It is immaterial whether the distinction *old* and *new* refers to the years before and after Ottoman conquest or the years immediately afterward, up to 1532. A more general description of the cemetery area fixes it within the following boundaries: "in Wadi Jahannam [the Kedron valley] outside of Jerusalem, south of the city wall and east [of it], north of the eastern spring of Siloam and south of the bridge at the crossroads, which is west of the Tomb of Absalom (Ṭarṭūr Firʿaun)." In the middle of 1560 the eastern border of the cemetery is described in rather greater detail: "the al-ʿAmri mosque [on the Mount of Olives, not to be confused with the mosque within the walls that has the same name, although it is pronounced slightly differently] and the road leading to the Tomb of Absalom (Ṭarṭūr Firʿaun)."[7]

Although it is difficult today to locate some of the landmarks cited in descriptions written hundreds of years ago, there is no doubt that everybody then knew exactly what area was being referred to. This may not have been due so much to demarcation lines as to the fact that by that time it was already full of Jewish graves. Despite its importance to the Jews—and indirectly to the Muslims, who were in charge of it—the burial area was only a small part of the *waqf* of al-Ṣalāḥiyya on the Gethsemane lands, and this was only one of the *waqf*s of Jerusalem.

The boundaries of the area merit extensive discussion. At the time, the area of the cemetery was relatively small and, unlike in earlier years, it extended on both sides of the Kedron valley. In the words of a French traveler who passed through in 1532 "the Kedron valley . . . is a cemetery for the Jews on one side and the other of the river bed."[8] Documentation exists that marks out more precise boundaries: from south to north between the spring of Siloam and the bridge. It is hard to determine the boundary on the west, but it seems to have been up the slope of the Temple Mount west of the river bed.[9] Eastward the boundary ran along the lower western slope of the Mount of Olives to the roadway leading to the bridge, and it was in this direction that the cemetery expanded. This is implied in a judgment handed down in the mid-1550s, during the period of greatest population growth among the Jews of Jerusalem. It was charged that the al-'Amri mosque "was near [the Jews'] graves" and recently the Jews had begun to bury their dead "in the al-'Amri mosque . . . in its walls and fences"—that is, within the area belonging to the mosque. The Jews denied this, despite the testimony of witnesses who pointed out a cave inside the mosque courtyard that had allegedly been used for this purpose. The kadi instructed the Jews to stop using the place, even ordering them to take their dead away, "and they removed some of them."[10] This was not an easy task, and quite likely the Jews were slow to carry out the order. Emptying the cave went on for more than two years. In April 1552, when the last graves were being removed, the cave collapsed and one of the diggers, Mūsā Zaqilmān, was crushed to death.[11] Today, although the al-'Amri mosque exists east of the Kedron, on the slope of the Mount of Olives—not to be confused with the mosque southwest of the opening of the Siloam tunnel outlet—it is hard to determine the location of the cave. The increased demand for burial sites during the middle of the century motivated the Jews to expand the cemetery to the east on the slope of the Mount of Olives beyond the al-ʿAmri mosque and possibly even across the road. But formally, throughout the century the boundaries of the Jewish cemetery did not change.

All of this area was leased (*'ijāra ṣaḥīḥa*)[12] to Jews to be used for burying their dead. They were also explicitly granted the right to use the stones found there, apparently for making tombstones. The kadi Shams al-Dīn Muḥammad ibn al-Jawharī granted the lease for a thirty-year period beginning in *maliye* year of 940, that is, the spring of 1534.[13] The lessees were three representatives of the Jewish community: Yūsuf ibn Mūsā, Malkī ibn Yahūdā, and Mūsā ibn Hayyim. They agreed to pay 2250 silver *qiṭʿa* in the month of Rajab every year. When the kadi handed down a ruling with respect to a period that would begin two years later, he did so knowing that until then the Jews would continue to use the same area in accordance with an earlier lease that apparently had been in force as far back as the end of the Mamluk period.

The distinction between *old* and *new* is not clear from the wording of the lease. *New* may refer to the expansion of the cemetery that took place when the agreement was made, or perhaps to an area that was added at the end of the Mamluk period. It may be that the wave of immigration into Palestine, particularly to Jerusalem, after the expulsion of the Jews from Spain required an enlargement of the cemetery. In practical terms, this would have meant bribing the Mamluk authorities during the last ineffectual days of their rule. Or it may have been easier to buy the support of administrative and religious functionaries during the first years of the newly established Ottoman government. Unfortunately, no *sijill* volumes remain from those days, just as there are none for Mamluk times, so it is impossible to answer this question.

Since the cemetery land did not belong to the kadi or even to the court, by what right did he rent it to the Jews? The land was part of the *waqf* of the *al-madrasa al-Ṣalāḥiyya*, and therefore could be leased only by the person in charge of the *waqf*. Shams al-Dīn, the kadi, disposed of the lease only after receiving permission from the *mutawallī* responsible for the *waqf*. Not everyone, however, felt that with this the definitive word had been said on the subject. 'Alī ja'ūsh ibn Shaqrā, who was granted a *timar* fief from which to collect taxes in the Jerusalem subdistrict, lodged a complaint before the Sublime Porte. He maintained that as his *timar* included the lands of Silwān village, he was entitled to the income from the cemetery. Not only was it within the bounds of the village, he claimed, but some of the burial plots, at least those in the Kedron valley, were actually on land that belonged to the village. Since this land was used to bury the dead, it could not be cultivated, and both the village and the *timar* holder himself were thus directly affected. Since the annual rent for those plots was 100 *sultani*, he demanded that the Jews pay him the tithe on this amount. Maintaining that they had paid everything they owed to the al-Ṣalāḥiyya *waqf*, the Jews refused to give him anything. He then charged that not only was he not being paid, but that the amount paid the *waqf* was entirely unsuitable. He claimed that the lease was nullified because a legal judgment of the Istanbul mufti, Abu al-Su'ūd, specifically provided that if a concession is leased (*'ijāra*) without adequate recompense (*'ujrat al-mithl*),[14] it is invalid (*ghayr ṣaḥīḥa*).

The Sublime Porte instructed the governor and the kadi of Jerusalem to investigate these claims carefully and settle the dispute. In mid-September 1550 representatives of the Jewish community were summoned to court to present their case. In their defense, they submitted the document establishing 2250 silver *dirhams* as the annual rent. They also submitted a later document stipulating the value of that sum in gold. In this same document one of 'Alī Ja'ūsh's predecessors had declared this sum to be appropriate (*'ujrat al-mithl*) in the case under review, confirming that the lease was therefore valid. The kadi then turned to the prosecution. Muslim witnesses testified under oath that the rent of the cemetery was worth 100 *sultani* a year. They justified the relatively high sum "because of the burying and the deep digging [for purposes of burial], which defiles (*tanjīs*) the depths as well as the surface of this land, and also its continuous use [as a cemetery] summer and winter, spring and fall." The kadi accepted the claims of the prosecution, rejected those of the Jews, and obligated them to pay 100 gold pieces a year.[15]

This additional rent represented a significant financial burden, and the Jews began to seek ways of revoking the judgment. Eight years later they succeeded.[16] Aḥmad bey, who bore the title *kātib al-wilāya* (the person responsible for recording governmental affairs), arrived in Jerusalem for the purpose of recording official documents and bringing them up to date, primarily the city's *taḥrīr* records. Representatives of the Jewish community asked him to investigate the question of the cemetery, establishing its boundaries and fixing the legal amount of *'ujrat al-mithl.* Aḥmad bey appointed two high officials, Muṣṭafā bey Ketkhuda and Rustum Çelebi, to act in his name, and Jar-allāh al-ḥanafī, the chief kadi of Jerusalem, appointed a deputy, the Hanafi kadi Ḥusām al-Dīn, to act in his name. First they confirmed the cemetery's boundaries old and new. It is not easy to be specific about the landmarks they noted owing to the imprecise wording of the description ("road," "path," "remains of stone wall," and so on). It is clear, nevertheless, that the new boundaries increased the area. Moreover, there is definitive evidence that between 1532 and 1558 the cemetery was enlarged. The mulberry tree plot (*al-tūta*) that according to 1532 description of the boundaries belonged to Sulaymān ibn Sulaymān of Silwān twenty-five years later was referred to as having been his "in the past" but as being "now in the hands of the Jews" by legal lease. This plot, which cannot be located today, had been the eastern boundary of the cemetery, which means that in the course of the years the cemetery expanded eastward, up the Mount of Olives. This coincides with the description already given of the removal of Jewish graves from the vicinity of the al-'Amri mosque.

Once the boundary lines were marked, with the help of Muslim villagers from Silwān and its surroundings, the rental to be paid for the site had to be established. For this the government representatives brought in many expert witnesses: the commander of the *sipahis*, *Alay bey* of the Jerusalem district, several other *sipahis* from the Jerusalem and Safed districts, the commander of the Janissary unit of Jerusalem, and others. Their unanimous decision was that the appropriate compensation for leasing the entire area was 3½ *sultani*, with another 1½ *sultani* to be added as an act of grace to increase the income of the *waqf*. Thus, the Jews were to pay a total of 5 *sultani* a year for the lease of the cemetery. All these decisions were taken in the presence of the man in charge of the al-Ṣalāḥiyya *waqf*, Muḥammad ibn Jamā'a al-Kinānī al-Shāfi'ī. The decision was registered in the court records and confirmed by the head kadi of Jerusalem. From the standpoint of the Jewish community this was a complete victory.

A year later an attempt was made to upset this decision. The *sipahi* 'Ilyās Ja'ūsh, who in the past had had the right to collect the tithes of 'Ayn Silwān as part of his territory, demanded through a Jerusalem *sipahi* that for use of the cemetery the Jews pay him a tithe of 8 *sultani* for the year 1557–58. They refused, and hoping to force them to agree, 'Ilyās Ja'ūsh brought them to court, where the Jews submitted the ruling delivered by Ḥusam al-Dīn in 1558. The head kadi of Jerusalem was now 'Abd al-Raḥmān. After hearing the evidence, he ruled that the Jews were to continue to pay the *waqf*, in accordance with the judgment handed down by his predecessor.

Although the ruling in favor of the Jews was thus corroborated, the struggle over the cemetery did not end here. Some two months later several Muslim religious functionaries came to the court and testified before the Hanafi kadi, Shams al-Dīn, that 100 gold *qubrusi* per year were to be paid as rent for the cemetery. Among those bearing witness were the head of the Qadiri order in Jerusalem, the preacher (*khaṭīb*) of the al-Aqṣā mosque, the Maliki prayer leader (*'imām*) of al-Aqṣā, and a long line of the most distinguished religious dignitaries (*'ulema*) of Jerusalem. The Hanafi kadi ruled against the stand of the Jewish community (November 2–11, 1559). However, there is no evidence that the ruling was implemented.[17]

At this stage the Jews still managed to go on paying in accordance with their interpretation of the decisions. At the end of March 1560 the *sipahi* 'Ilyās Ja'ūsh demanded the tithe for the past three years' use of the cemetery. Just as he had seven months before, he now demanded eight gold pieces a year, the representatives of the Jewish community again insisting that they had to pay only five. This time, however, the Jews no longer maintained that the entire amount was meant for the al-Ṣalāḥiyya *waqf* and the judge therefore ruled that the *sipahi* was entitled to a tenth part of 15 gold pieces, obligating the Jews to pay him one and a half gold pieces, which they did.[18]

Although the Jews fought successfully, as the dispute dragged on their position was steadily weakening. About a month and a half after this last court session, the issue was again brought before Shams al-Dīn, although he had ruled on it only half a year before. Since no practical steps toward implementation had been taken, public pressure was growing. The list of Muslim witnesses who appeared before the court was much longer this time, many of them from the religious establishment: Shaykh Aḥmad al-Dajjānī,[19] the kadi's deputies from the various religious schools of thought (Maliki, Shafi'i, Hanbali), and others. Several additional public figures came as well, particularly people well acquainted with problems of real estate, the head builder of Jerusalem among them. They all testified that the rent was 100 *qubrusi* annually, and their testimony was accepted by the kadi, who made it his legal judgment (May 5, 1560). The judgment was also approved by 'Abd al-Raḥmān, the head kadi of the city, who gave instructions that action be taken to implement it.[20]

Another two months or so passed, and again the Jews' hold on the cemetery was questioned. This time the trouble was caused by the Shafi'i mufti of Jerusalem, who was also responsible for the al-Ṣalāḥiyya *waqf*. He maintained in court that it was illegal for the Jews to use the cemetery at all, since the entire area was within the boundaries of his *waqf* and he had never leased them the land. The representatives of the Jewish community acknowledged that this was true but submitted the document dated 1533–34/940 A.H. confirming that they had leased the land for thirty years from the superintendent of the *waqf*. But now another difficulty came to light: it emerged that Yūsūf ibn Mūsā, one of the three representatives of the Jewish community who had leased the plot at that time, had died long ago. Since the lessees had not leased the land as a legal entity but rather as individuals, the kadi ruled that one-third of the lease was canceled until the end of the period. He instructed the Jews on June 28, 1560 to cease using a third of the cemetery area.[21]

On the same day, he handed down another judgment, expanding on the entire affair.[22] Istanbul was behind his reexamination of the issue. The Jewish community of Jerusalem sent a representative to the Sublime Porte to press its claims, presenting them as follows: Jews had been burying their dead in the cemetery on the al-Jismāniyya lands since before the Ottoman conquest. The *mutawallī* responsible for the *waqf* had rented the area to them for 3½ *sultani* per year. When he had tried to raise the rent a number of different parties had intervened to bring about a compromise (*ṣulḥ*), and the rent had been raised to 5 *sultani*. Now the *mutawallī* was again demanding more and threatening "to remove their dead from the area" if his demand was not met. The Sublime Porte ordered (April 17–26, 1560) the governor and the kadi of the Jerusalem district to investigate the matter and arrive at a just decision.[23]

The district governor took the unusual step of appointing this personal representative to be present at the court sessions. Representatives of the Jewish community and the superintendent of the al-Ṣalāḥiyya *waqf* were also summoned to court. This *nāẓir* maintained that the Jews were holding an area of the cemetery unlawfully, and by his reckoning they owed him a total of 200 *sultani* for the years 1557–58 and 1558–59. The Jews countered that their use of the cemetery was entirely lawful. When the judge asked to see the original document proving their claim, they explained that they were unable to produce it but that a copy was included in the court protocol. They submitted this to him along with an abstract of the favorable 1558 decision. The superintendent of the al-Ṣalāḥiyya *waqf* submitted another document containing the ruling of September 1550. The kadi studied both documents and decided that the latter *ḥujja*, although earlier chronologically, was consonant with the Shari'a, while the document presented by the "Jewish infidels" contained many errors and legal shortcomings. First, he ruled that the Jews should not have turned to the *kātib al-wilāya*, since only the *mutawallī* of the *waqf* had the right to determine appropriate compensation. Second, the evidence concerning the five gold pieces was declared invalid, since it was not the outcome of a charge made by a legal claimant (*mudda' shar'ī*). Third, the claim that the *mutawallī* had leased the site for three and one-half gold pieces was ruled a lie, "as became apparent to the kadi." Furthermore, even if the *mutawallī* had agreed to a lower rent, his agreement was determined to be invalid, for a guardian has no right to surrender the rights of his wards. Fourth, he declared that at the hearing held by the *kātib al-wilāya* the Jews had not submitted any legal rent agreement issued by the *mutawallī* of the *waqf*. Fifth, even if the *mutawallī* had decreased the rent, he ruled that the original rental was still valid because the lessee had freely agreed to it. Sixth, he ruled that the evidence pertaining to additional payment took precedence over that pertaining to lower payment (*bayyinat al-ziyāda muqaddama 'alā bayyinat al-nuqṣān*). Seventh, he said that at the time of the hearing held at the initiative of the *kātib al-wilāya*, the *mutawallī* had to keep quiet because of his fear of the *kātib al-wilāya* and other cogent reasons. Eighth, despite the Jews' claim that they were obligated to pay 41⅔ *sultani*, they had continued to pay only five gold pieces annually; "their words," he ruled, "belied their deeds and thus contradictions arose in their claims." The kadi declared that the document submitted by the Jews was nul and void. Despite the fact that this same kadi, 'Abd al-Raḥmān, had approved and signed the document in the past, he now canceled his earlier approval, claiming that he had acted then with inadequate knowledge of all the details of the matter. He therefore obliged the Jews to pay 200 *sultani* to the *mutawallī*. After the kadi gave his ruling and debate was closed, probably in answer to some of the points he had raised, the Jews submitted to him the court ruling from the year 1532 attesting to the fact that they had leased the area for thirty years. When the kadi summoned the three Jews who had signed the lease at the time, he was told that one of them had died several years before. The superintendent of the waqf therefore again asked the kadi to cancel a third of the area leased "to prevent the Jews from using a third of the undivided commonly owned area (*mushā'*) of all the aforementioned lands." Once again the kadi handed down such a ruling.

The Jewish community had lost this battle, but they did not give up hope. The Jews sent an envoy to Damascus to ask Aḥmad Pasha, the governor of that city, to help in this protracted dispute. From the wording of the appeal to Damascus, it emerges that several of the heads of the Jewish community had been imprisoned for not having paid the rent stipulated by the kadi. In mid-August 1560, less than two months after the hearing, the *defterdar* of Damascus arrived in Jerusalem to divide the "feudal" estates among the various *sipahis* of the Jerusalem province. He also had instructions from the governor of Damascus to clarify the matter of the cemetery. Before the *defterdar* and the governor of the Jerusalem province, Qaytas bey, the Jews submitted the original thirty-year lease, a document establishing the rent at 41⅔ *sultani* per year, and the document issued during the visit of the *kātib al-wilāya* fixing the rent at five gold pieces.

A representative of the *waqf* argued that the first and second documents did not establish appropriate compensation and that the third document had been signed by the *mutawallī* against his will. The *defterdar* upheld the kadi's ruling, ordering the Jews to pay the one hundred gold pieces as a lump sum (*maqṭū'*), regardless of changes in the value of the land. The kadi did not demand retroactive payment from the Jews, although he arbitrarily nullified the legality of all amounts the Jews had paid until then. This final decision was taken on August 17, 1560 and was recorded once again the following year on June 29, 1561, apparently to counteract another attempt on the part of the Jews to challenge the judgment.

In the meantime, the *sipahi* of 'Ayn Silwān attempted to try his luck again, this time in the hope of deriving some personal benefit from the new ruling. As the person entitled to collect a tithe from all income of the village, he claimed that he was also entitled to a tithe of the rent money. With the support of the district governor the kadi ruled (July 4, 1560) that the request be granted. From 1559–1560 on, only ninety gold pieces would be paid into the waqf of al-Ṣalāḥiyya, while the remaining ten would be transmitted to the *sipahi* of 'Ayn Silwān.[24]

There still remained some three years until the expiration of the thirty-year lease, and during that time no other essential changes were made, although on August 31, 1560 the ruling with regard to the one hundred gold pieces was reconfirmed. The decision taken at the beginning of November 1559 was arrived at in consonance with the view of the residents of the neighboring villages (al-Ṭūr, al-'Azariyya, and Silwān), in addition to that of religious personnel and specialists in real estate. According to the testimony of all of them, since the cemetery had been leased to the Jews early in the 1530s, "the [real] value (*'ujra*) of the area was no less than the appropriate rent money (*'ujrat al-mithl*) [that was demanded in return for the lease]."[25] The change, therefore, was not in the sum demanded but in that factual endorsement was given retroactively that the rent could not be less than one hundred gold pieces.

It is interesting that in the copy of the original document (vol. 39, p. 98 of the *sijill*) this point is not mentioned at all, although there is a hint of it in the reasons given by the judge, 'Abd al-Raḥmān, for throwing out the claims of the Jews in June 1560. It is doubtful that this is an example of the wisdom of hindsight; it seems rather more reasonable to assume that the first version of the kadi's ruling was only a faulty summary of the judgment. The new summary was more complete. But why did the authorities return to the old papers? A fuller quotation from the judgment, although changing nothing in actual fact, was meant primarily to give the official stamp of the four religious schools, the Hanbali, Shafi'i, and Hanafi kadis now adding their confirmation to the original judgment, which before had referred explicitly only to the Maliki kadi of Jerusalem.

About a month after the last decision, on September 26, 1560, the court was convened to introduce a new amendment. After it was decided at the beginning of July that one-tenth of the rent money would go to the *sipahi* of the 'Ayn Silwān village, the district governor of Jerusalem, Qaytas bey, entered an appeal. He submitted a new version of the land registry, *al-daftar al-jadīd al-khāqānī*, which stated explicitly that the tithe of the al-Ṣalāḥiyya *waqf* income was part of the income (*khāṣṣ*) of the governor. The kadi invalidated the ruling he had passed in July, ordering that the tithe be given to the governor of the district.[26]

This decision did not change the fact that the cemetery was very close to the village of 'Ayn Silwān and to land belonging to it. Therefore, when a new siphai was given the income of the village, he too tried to get the tithe of the *waqf* income from the cemetery. The year after the last decision, on June 1, 1561, this issue came to court. The Jews objected to the *sipahi*'s claim, and the kadi again ruled that the cemetery was "not part of the Silwān lands." The Jews owed the *sipahi* nothing.[27]

The last episode in this lengthy affair was a session of the court on November 28, 1563. At this session the *mutawallī* of the al-Ṣalāḥiyya *waqf* declared that he had received a total of two hundred gold pieces from representatives of the Jewish community in payment for the lease of the cemetery for the years 1560–61 and

1561–62. The Jews confirmed this. Moreover, each side declared before the kadi that it had no further claims in this matter against the other, and that "each party cancel[ed] any dispute or difference he may have had with the other."[28] This put an end to the protracted arguments.

In summary, although the Jewish cemetery on the Gethsemane lands was the burial ground for Jews throughout the sixteenth century, it did not become a matter for public debate until 1532–1563. Three heads of the Jewish community had leased the cemetery, and two of them repeatedly appeared at court hearings on the issue. The third lessee had died, and so the kadi nullified the lease for one-third of the land. The community did not object, and it seems likely that this declaration had no practical significance. From the standpoint of the Jewish community, the leasing of the land was a matter of public concern, and therefore the hearings were attended not only by those who had formally signed the lease but also by many of the heads of the community.

The cemetery was leased to the community for thirty years. During the first twenty years the use of the cemetery was entirely uncontested, and the Jews gradually expanded its borders eastward, up the western slope of the Mount of Olives. In one case this expansion was stopped, as the cemetery began to encroach on the grounds of the al-'Amri mosque, but for the most part the Jews were able to enlarge the cemetery to suit the needs of a growing community. The fact that the Muslims did not exploit the charge of attempted expansion indicates that the acquisition of additional area was not particularly conspicuous. The main arguments concerned the amount of rent to be paid for the land. These arguments arose in the late 1550s, just as the Jewish population was reaching its peak. The period for which the land had been leased was also drawing to a close at this time, giving the guardians of the al-Ṣalāḥiyya *waqf* a strong bargaining position. The growing demand for higher rent was not due to the decline in the value of the money, which primarily affected the imperial silver coin, for the rent payments were figured in gold. The Jews paid 5 *sultani* through most of the period in question and were never asked to pay more retroactively. A more likely reason behind the increase is that, as Jerusalem developed, the value of the land outside the city's walls rose in response to the rising demand for agricultural produce. The *sipahi*s of the 'Ayn Silwān village, who were better aware of land values than were the governors of Jerusalem or even those responsible for the *waqf,* were the first to demand a higher rent, but in most cases they lost. The *waqf* and the governor of Jerusalem, however, won, and the issue was thus brought to the attention of the public time and time again. Three times the Jews initiated hearings in court on the issue of the cemetery. They were convinced that with the support of the authorities in Damascus and Istanbul they would be able to gain a favorable decision, even from the religious authorities in Jerusalem. This could be an indication of the self-confidence of the Jews, or perhaps of their faith in bribery. Otherwise it is hard to comprehend why they took these initiatives, for the position of the Jews was very weak, and the kadi arbitrarily nullified the documents they submitted.[29] Their arguments concerning the amount of rent were unsatisfactory at times and even contradictory. During the two lengthy hearings of the summer of 1560 they did not submit the original lease of the cemetery; they must have known that whatever documents they could submit would very likely be considered a weak basis to build their defense on. Even less convincing was their claim that the original rental was worth 41⅔ gold pieces while standing by the interpretation given at the end of 1558 to the effect that they were obligated to pay only 5 gold pieces a year. It is impossible to disagree with the kadi's ruling on this point.

The Jews, of course, were bound by law, custom, and the kadi's decisions. When their attempts to pay the smaller amount failed, they had to agree to pay the much higher sum. However, it should be remembered that there was never an actual attempt to stop the burial of the dead in that cemetery.[30] The demand for higher payment in return for use of the cemetery was related to the real value of the land, a value attested to by various local people and by experts in such matters. It should not be attributed to discrimination, although the increasing use made by the Jews of the cemetery doubtless pushed the argument to the fore. Once the rent of one hundred gold pieces was settled upon, no further increases were requested until the end of the century, and even the Jews ceased arguing about it.

When the period of the lease ended, the issue was not brought before the court. It is not clear whether the lease was renewed for another thirty years or for a shorter period, but there is no doubt that the bickering was finally over. It is also certain that the Jewish community continued to make use of the cemetery. The only time the issue came to court again during the sixteenth century was at the end of 1569, when two Jewish gravediggers promised the kadi that they would not dig any grave without the permission of the community's leadership.[31] Only in the final months of the century did the subject again come up for litigation. The superintendent of the al-Ṣalāḥiyya *waqf* brought charges against the heads of the Jewish community, claiming that since the day the previous lease had ended some five years before, the Jews had continued to bury their dead without any formal arrangement. They paid the man part of the rent, but they still owed him money. This time the Jews admitted their obligation and promised to pay the outstanding amount (April 9, 1599).[32] No one raised the rent, for the Jewish community had shrunk by then and its need for the cemetery had diminished.

Finally, it should be noted that the cemetery on the Mount of Olives was not the only one used by the Jews of Jerusalem. When dissension arose over that cemetery, the Jews leased additional areas on the other side of the Kedron valley, in the Ben-Hinnom (Jahannam) valley near the village of Dayr abu Thawr. The heads of the Jewish community also leased a plot on the slope of *Wādī* al-Shaqf, within the bounds of the land belonging to the village of the same name and with the approval of the village *sipahi.* This plot was probably not very large because the rent paid by the Jews for the tithe was 5 *akçe* a year, and for the burial permit, an additional *sultani* a year. The plot was part of an orchard, and there were fruit trees as well as a cave on it. Despite this, the land was leased on April 2, 1562 explicitly for the purpose of burying the Jewish dead in Jerusalem. The *sipahi* was to receive a special gratuity in return.[33] Two years later the heads of the Jewish community leased more land in the vicinity of the groves of the village of Dayr abu Thawr for six years at 29 *akçe* a year. The Jews now stated specifically that if one of the lessees died, the community could transfer his share to another Jew.[34] It is unclear whether the plots leased in Dayr abu Thawr were used to bury all Jews or Karaites only.

At the end of 1564 the Karaite Jews of Jerusalem leased a plot of land belonging to Dayr abu Thawr explicitly intended for "planting, building, and the burial of dead Karaite Jews." The plot was leased for thirty years and then for another six, until the middle of June 1601, when it was leased again for another thirty years in return for 14 Egyptian *qiṭ'a*. Permission was expressly granted to the Karaite Jews to bury their dead there.[35] Until the beginning of the sixties the Karaites had buried their dead on the Mount of Olives with the rest of the Jews. There is no way of knowing whether the Rabbinical Jews forced the Karaites to cease burying their dead among them. It is certain, however, that the Karaites' search for a new cemetery did not occur until after the dispute over the cemetery on the Mount of Olives had been settled. The area within the Ben-Hinnom valley became the main burial ground for the Karaite Jews of Jerusalem. The cemetery on the Mount of Olives was nevertheless the main cemetery for all the Jews of Jerusalem. It continued to be used while arguments with the local authorities continued. The intensity and frequency with which the subject of this cemetery was heard in the Shari'i court and was debated by the heads of the Jewish community and the leaders of the local Muslim public bear witness to the important place this institution held in the life of Jerusalem's Jews at that time and in the years ahead.[36]

## *Pilgrimage*

In addition to worship in the synagogue and burial of the dead, pilgrimage to significant holy places was also a part of Jewish religious observance in sixteenth-century Palestine. Three of those holy places were nabī Samū'īl, a village near Jerusalem, and the cities of Jerusalem and Hebron.

### NABĪ SAMŪ'ĪL

Northwest of Jerusalem lies the village of Nabī Samū'īl (or Shamū'īl, and in full Nabī-Allāh Samū'īl, meaning "Samuel, prophet of God"), a sacred place (*maqām*) to which Jews from overseas as well as from Jerusalem went on pilgrimage. According to tradition, the prophet Samuel is buried there. The Jews called the place Rama (hence the grave of Shamā'īl Ramātī, that is, "Samuel of Rama"), not to be confused with the village of Rām, then as now northeast of Jerusalem.[1]

Those who made the pilgrimage to the grave had to pay a special *khafar* tax, over and above the tax they paid at the entrance to Jerusalem. Jerusalem residents who went to Nabī Samū'īl on pilgrimage (*ziyāra*) also had to pay the tax, although it was a small sum, as apparent from the fact that in 1555 three Muslims leased the right to collect all tax revenues for a year for two and one-half gold coins. With the large increase in the Jewish population of Jerusalem during the 1550s, the number of pilgrims grew considerably. The tax collectors could therefore anticipate a higher income, and more money could be offered for the right to lease the concession from the treasury. Two other Muslims offered the kadi three times the going rate for the concession for the *khafar* tax. Their request was granted, and they immediately deposited the amount in the Jerusalem Citadel until the arrival of the man in charge of collecting the land taxes. He, of course, ordinarily leased the concession to the highest bidder.[2]

Pilgrimage to Nabī Samū'īl was not restricted to a particular time of year; we learn from the kadi's ruling in the autumn of 1554 that the Jews were permitted to go "any time they wished."[3] Another ruling, however, provides conclusive evidence that spring was the main season for the pilgrimage—during Passover and the seven weeks that follow (referred to as the counting of the 'Omer). Although the tax concession was leased on an annual basis, collection was actually concentrated "in the period of the *ziyāra* of the Jews [which] is from the beginning of the month of Jumādhā al-'ūlā [sic] of the year 961 to the end of Jumādhā al-thānī of the year 961"—in other words, during the months of April–May 1554.[4]

Because of the importance attributed to this pilgrimage, the prophet's grave was a source of conflict among the Jews themselves and between Jews and Muslims. The synagogue, called Sayyid Shmū'īl, had been erected on the site long before the Ottoman conquest and was an important part of the Karaite community's ties to Jerusalem.[5] Immediately after the Ottoman conquest, dissension broke out between the Karaites and the rest of the Jews; taking advantage of the disorder and confusion engendered by the change of regime, the Karaites prevented the other Jews from using the synagogue. The latter appealed to the government for help, and indeed one of the earliest decrees issued after the conquest—in 1517—instructed the kadi of Jerusalem to restore the status quo ante and again allow all Jews to come to Samuel's grave and pray at the synagogue there.[6]

This decree effectively put an end to the disturbances caused by the Karaites, although as a minority group the Karaites would soon have been overruled by the majority in any event. They did, however, maintain their special relationship to the village of Nabī Samū'īl. In 1565, for example, a Karaite jeweler from Jerusalem, *al-mu'allim* Ibrahīm ibn Faraj-Allāh ibn Ṣadaqa, bought half the ownership rights to a new oil press built by a Muslim resident of the village. Although the Karaites had given up their struggle for supremacy, they continued to acquire property in the village and to entrench themselves there.[7]

Jerusalem's Jews also had to contend with Muslim harassment. At the end of the 1530s, Muslims complained to the kadi that as the Jews approached Jerusalem on their way back from the prophet's grave, they would light candles and pray aloud in a manner offensive to Muslims. No action was taken in response to this complaint.[8] In July 1550 trouble broke out between Jews of Jerusalem and residents of nearby Bayt 'Iksā. One of the villagers from Bayt 'Iksā complained to the kadi that the Jews were not satisfied simply to visit the grave but that they went with pack animals, tools, and equipment, camping at the site for long periods and harming the local residents. The kadi ordered the heads of the Jewish community to keep close watch over their cattle and utensils to avoid damage to the land and property of the local residents.[9]

These attempts to limit the activities of Jews at the site in no way affected the pilgrimage itself. In mid-September 1554, however, the Muslims actually prevented them from visiting the grave. The Jews applied for and obtained a decree prohibiting further disruption of their ritual pilgrimage.[10] But this did not put an end to interference; in the following years there were repeated attempts to wrest the synagogue from the Jews. Less than a year after the last decree was issued, Muslims again took over the

Sayyid Samū'īl synagogue, introducing a niche (*miḥrab*) to mark the direction of prayer to Mecca, turning the building into a mosque, and forbidding the Jews to use it. Representatives of the Jerusalem community appealed to the Sublime Porte for permission to pray in the synagogue and to conduct their pilgrimage unmolested. At the end of 1555 an order was sent to the governor and the kadi of Jerusalem informing them that the Jews should be allowed to continue their traditional custom and enjoy the rights granted them by the Shari'a.[11] Evidence of their renewed hold on the site can be found in the description of a Portuguese traveler who visited there early in the 1560s: "this is the only place the Jews in the Holy Land maintain at their expense, and once every eight days several of them go there to look after the lamps."[12]

This did not mean an end to the trouble. Toward the end of the century there were further attempts to expropriate the synagogue, and Jews were forbidden by decree to go there on pilgrimage. The heads of the Jewish community sought the assistance of the Sublime Porte, and an order was issued (September 13–22, 1598) again instructing the governor and the kadi to ensure that the Jews could make their traditional pilgrimage. To give the ruling additional religious sanction, the Jews obtained a *fatwā* stating that although they had been temporarily prevented from using the synagogue, and the site was serving as a center for Muslim pilgrimages, Jews must be allowed to sanctify the synagogue and make it the focal point of their own *ziyāra* once more. Despite these official rulings the Jews apparently found it hard to regain all their former privileges at the site; in 1600 they were again forced to ask the kadi to register another ruling in their favor in the courthouse books.[13]

## JERUSALEM AND HEBRON

Historical sources offer little information about the extent of Jewish pilgrimage to Jerusalem either before or after the Ottoman conquest. It is well known, though, that such pilgrimages took place, and some of the Jewish travelers left records of the journeys overland or by sea to Palestine and Jerusalem. The deterioration of security in Palestine at the end of the Mamluk period probably reduced the number of merchants, visitors, and pilgrims willing to go to Jerusalem. But when the Ottoman conquest restored law and order and brought economic prosperity, the obstacles to pilgrimage were largely eliminated. Jewish pilgrims to Jerusalem, encouraged by the growing numbers of Jews in the city, even sought to stay on for a while.

Although there are no full statistics regarding the numbers of pilgrims, we do have information about several other aspects of overland pilgrimage. From the province of Damascus (*al-bilād al-shāmiyya*) in the north, there was brisk traffic of Jews on their way to Jerusalem. As each pilgrim passed through Nablus he had to pay a special tax (*khafar*, or *ghafar*) that varied slightly throughout the century. At first it was 48 *akçe* per person, 40 to be paid in the village of Funduqumiyya and eight in Nablus; in the mid-seventies an additional 8 *akçe* was collected on the way out of Nablus. Jerusalem residents were not required to pay. When pilgrims entered Jerusalem they would show the commander of the Citadel (*dizdar*) a receipt, and he would then let them into the city for no additional charge. In fact, the entire sum collected in Nablus was used for the upkeep of the garrison that manned the Citadel, and the money was sent from Nablus to the commander (*bölük bashi*) of the unit that was stationed in Jerusalem. For example, in 1538 the sum of 15,000 *akçe* was transferred to Jerusalem, representing the tax paid by some three hundred pilgrims to Jerusalem, "Jews, Christians, and others." It is not by chance that the pilgrims were listed in this order, for more than half of them were Jews. For security reasons, Jewish pilgrims usually came not as individuals but in groups. We know of three large groups that made their way to Jerusalem from the north. One consisted of 21 men and women, Musta'ribs, Arabic speaking—that is, Oriental (another possible reading: Mustaghribs—that is, from North Africa), and another 24 'Ifranji, or Europeans. Of 128 Jews in the second group, 28 were Jerusalemites and therefore exempt from the *ghafar*. The third group consisted of 37 Jews.[14] More than 180 Jewish pilgrims came from Damascus that year, or about 15 percent of the total number of Jews then living in Jerusalem. This is a very impressive figure, attesting to the extremely lively movement of pilgrims from Damascus to Jerusalem in the wake of the Ottoman conquest.

Although data for the following years is lacking, we assume

that the picture remained essentially unchanged. I did find two additional figures with respect to subsequent years: in 1547, 110 Jewish pilgrims arrived in Jerusalem from Damascus, a smaller figure than the previous one. However, the addition of 20 pilgrims from Gaza gives a total that justifies references to large-scale pilgrimage to Jerusalem.[15] In 1574, 191 Jewish pilgrims to Jerusalem from North Africa went through Nablus—only one, although certainly among the largest, of such groups of pilgrims that passed through the town that year.[16] The resident Jewish community in Jerusalem was developing as well, but groups of such magnitude still added significantly to the Jewish population of the city.

In economic terms, these pilgrims were welcome additions to the population of Jerusalem. These pilgrims, like tourists today, stimulated the city's economy. For this reason, the periodic influx of Jewish pilgrims was welcomed even by the Muslim residents. However, as the economy began to decline, the Muslims began to express resentment, particularly toward Jewish pilgrims from Egypt.

The mid-fifties brought official harassment of Jewish pilgrims. The functionary in charge of the survey of population and taxes from time to time registered Jewish pilgrims from elsewhere in the empire as permanent residents of the city, and he would illegally impose the *jizya* on them. The heads of the Jewish community submitted a complaint to Istanbul, and in May 1551 a decree was issued instructing the governor and the kadi of Jerusalem to forbid this practice, on the grounds that the pilgrims paid the *jizya* in their permanent places of residence.[17] At the same time, Istanbul received another complaint, this one from the Jews of Cairo, Damascus, and Safed, concerning another injustice they had suffered as pilgrims. Not only were they forced to pay the *ghafar* on their way into Jerusalem, but when they left the city, even to visit holy places in Hebron, other unlawful fees were again demanded of them. These mandatory sums were fixed by the *subashi* and *muḥtasib* officials, who would not permit them to visit Hebron and sometimes even prevented them from leaving Jerusalem, unless they paid. The Sublime Porte ordered the governor and the kadi of Jerusalem to end these practices (April 14–23, 1554).[18]

Two years later the Jews again appealed to the sultan. The *subashis* were imposing more hostile measures against Jewish pilgrims, not only extorting unnecessary payments but beating and imprisoning some Jews. Falsely claiming that the roads were unsafe, the officials would force Jewish pilgrims on their way to and from Hebron to hire escorts, which meant more money. To make sure that this ploy would be effective, the *subashi* would warn the village shaykhs not to allow the pilgrims to pass through without their consent. As justification for the fees levied on the Jewish pilgrims, the *subashi* would cite the potential harm these Jews caused the local economy: "you come from a place rife with plague," "you bring evil to the land."[19] The sultan ordered these practices ended.

During the sixties, and to an even greater extent during the seventies, these claims became a central motif governing the attitude of the Muslims toward Jewish pilgrims. While earlier references spoke in broad terms of people coming overland to Jerusalem from both the north and the south (Damascus, Safed, and Cairo), pilgrims were now referred to as having come only from Egypt. Several decrees issued in 1579 evoke a picture of tensions between the Jews from Egypt and Jerusalem's governmental personnel; with the Muslim residents of the city, their relations were even worse.[20] At the beginning of March 1579 'Aṭiyya ibn Shmū'īl ibn Shams Hacohen came from Cairo to Jerusalem at the head of a group of Jewish pilgrims. They were arrested at the gates of the city and forbidden to enter on the grounds that they were not coming as pilgrims but were fleeing the plague that had afflicted Cairo. 'Aṭiyya, who was prepared for this eventuality, displayed several documents attesting to their right to visit Jerusalem, including a decree from the sultan and letters from the rulers in Cairo to the governors of Jerusalem. The group was allowed to enter Jerusalem, staying longer than usual, and "caused an increase in the price of goods and foodstuffs sold to the Muslims." Soon after this, another large group of Jewish pilgrims from Egypt appeared at the gates of Jerusalem, this time led by 'Aṭiyya's father, Shmū'īl Hacohen. They too were denied admittance on similar grounds until they showed official documents. This group too stayed so long that they clashed with the people of Jerusalem. The tension grew so great that a large group of

Muslims, both laymen and religious personnel, demanded that the kadi banish the pilgrims from the city. A variety of grievances was brought to the attention of the court to justify the unusual request: "the Jews are stubborn"; both directly and indirectly they do Jerusalem and its residents great harm; "they ride horses, change their clothing [to resemble Muslims], follow in Muslims' footsteps, seize Muslim women and employ them as [their] servants, upset the local residents by causing prices to rise." Owing to the tremendous increase in the demand for food, "there is less food available, grain no longer reaches the Muslims," and "for a few days there was no bread or other produce" for the city's Muslim inhabitants. The most serious of these grievances was apparently that the Jews employed Muslim maidservants. The Muslims brought a specific example before the kadi: "in addition to the aforementioned Fāṭima, other Muslim servants (*marqūqāt*) are kept by [the Jews]." Finding that on the whole the charges were true, the kadi summoned ʿAṭiyya and some of his party and ordered them to leave Jerusalem within fifteen days. When the pilgrims did not return to Cairo, the Muslims repeated their charges, and the kadi again ordered them to depart. But it was not the weight of his arguments that decided the issue. When the plague broke out in Jerusalem in June 1579, the Jewish pilgrims hurried back to Egypt.

As can be seen from the dates cited, the whole affair went on for some three months, covering the period between the two Jewish holidays of Passover and Shavūʿōt. It may well be that these two groups stayed in Jerusalem longer than was usual for pilgrims, and it is also possible that the original fear of their bringing the plague from Egypt was genuine. Yet, it should be borne in mind that in those days plagues were endemic in big cities and that the same objection had been raised in previous years but had disappeared entirely when the pilgrims showed a decree from the sultan.[21] Moreover, the list of claims against ʿAṭiyya and his party included no mention of their bringing the plague to Jerusalem, even though it actually broke out during their stay and they had been suspected of carrying it upon their arrival. Although no limit was placed on the length of time pilgrims, Jewish or non-Jewish, could remain in Jerusalem, as a matter of course their stay was assumed to be temporary. In this case the Muslims knew that

Passover had ended and that the pilgrims ought to be returning home. Although the Jews had remained longer than usual (the counting of the ʿomer and then Shavūʿōt), this was not in itself a sufficient problem to require their expulsion from the city.

The unusual situation created can be explained primarily in economic terms. This was a year of scarcity. The large number of pilgrims staying for a prolonged period increased demand on the food supply and caused prices to rise. This was a more painful injury than the employment of Muslim women as maids. It is notable that even when public pressure mounted, force was never used to expel the Jewish pilgrims from Jerusalem. This indicates not only the degree of caution and prudence exercised by the kadi but also the perception of Jewish pilgrimage to Jerusalem as a pillar of the city's economic and religious life. The Muslims were careful not to upset it, even when the practice seemed to threaten law and order.

SIX

# *Social and Judicial Status*

TO WHAT extent did the legal rights of the Jews—men and women both—in sixteenth-century Jerusalem reflect their actual status in the eyes of their Muslim neighbors? The *sijill* volumes contain a wealth of information about the legal status of Jews, their treatment in the Muslim court, and the legal rights of women, in and outside of marriage. The picture these records give is quite different from what we have assumed to be the social position of the Jews in Jerusalem at that time.

## *Jews in the Muslim Court*

Jerusalem's Jewry had an independent legal system, headed by rabbis who functioned within the framework of the Jewish community and in accordance with traditional Jewish legal tenets. Nevertheless, there were times when the Jews had to appeal to the authority of the Muslim kadi and other officials. Jews appeared in Muslim courts as plaintiff, accused, and witnesses. In the course of the sixteenth century they made intensive use of the court for litigation covering a wide range of issues—private and public affairs, criminal and civil charges, contractual and business matters, marriage and divorce, inheritance, and guardianship among them. There was no apparent preference for kadis of any specific Sunni school, although more cases were referred by Jews to the Hanafi or the Shafi'i judges than to the Maliki or the Hanbali ones.

Although few trials in which Jews participated were held on the Jewish Sabbath, there is nevertheless no evidence that they refused to appear in court on this day or even that they protested the scheduling of hearings, although we may assume that they tried not to go to court on the Sabbath. In fact, there is no record of a trial being held on that day in which a Jew was the plaintiff, although records of Jews appearing as the accused on the Sabbath do exist. There were times when instead of the Jews coming to court, the kadi came to them. At the beginning of April 1599 the kadi of Jerusalem held an inquiry into the status of a new synagogue that the community had been using. To learn the facts, he came with some members of his court to the synagogue on a Sabbath morning. Upon entering, he found a group of Jews, men and women, praying and reading the Bible aloud; on the spot he clarified the matters of interest to him and issued an official document describing the situation.[1] At the end of August 1572 the *subashi* of Jerusalem heard that the shaykh al-yahūd was making wine from new grapes in his house without authorization. To clarify the facts he sent his representative to the shaykh's house on the Sabbath, and there he found a jug of new wine. That same day the shaykh, together with the incriminating evidence, was brought to the court and questioned by the kadi.[2]

In both of these cases the fact that the action took place on the Sabbath may have had to do with the process of obtaining evidence. Nevertheless, Jews were also summoned to court on the Sabbath when there was no urgency. In the middle of September 1594 court sessions were held on two different claims by Muslims who demanded payment of debts owed them by Jews. In both cases the hearings were held on the Sabbath. Early in April 1566 a Jewish physician, Yaḥyā, was summoned to court on the Sabbath to testify as to whether he had received the salary he was entitled to from the *muḥtasib;* this matter was obviously not urgent.[3] There is no way of knowing whether these Jews had asked for a postponement. However, if they had not wished to appear in court on the Sabbath, they could have given a Muslim power of attorney to represent them. The fact that they did not seems to indicate that they simply did not consider appearing in court on the Sabbath a serious problem.

## JEWISH CLAIMS AGAINST MUSLIMS

Jews brought Muslims to court when they felt that they had been wronged, or when they wished to ensure that Muslims, or Christians, would carry out commitments they had undertaken. There are numerous examples. On August 21, 1553, the Jew Yūsuf came to the court with his headdress (*'imāma*) torn to pieces. His story was that two Muslims had just assaulted him and dragged him to the *subashi*'s office. The accused were summoned to the kadi, in whose presence the *subashi* denied that he had issued instructions to bring the Jew to him by force. The two Muslims admitted having committed the act but claimed that they had done so to collect a debt the Jew owed them. This admission confirmed Yūsuf's story; his charge was accepted by the court.[4] In January 1539 another Jew, also called Yūsuf, from Malta, appeared at court with blood streaming from his face and complained that a Muslim had hit him. When the charge was proven true, the Muslim was convicted and sentenced to flogging (*ta'zīr*), the punishment to be carried out at once.[5] Less serious was the case tried on November 2, 1567. A Jerusalem Jew claimed that the Muslim Ma'ālī ibn Kharīṭūn from the village of Bayt Ta'mar near Bethlehem had stolen a sheep the Jew had left in the care of a shepherd. When the accused denied the charge, the Jew brought two Muslims who testified that they had heard him boasting of the act. As a result, Ma'ālī was convicted and sentenced to compensate the Jew for the full value of the sheep.[6]

Charges against Muslims did not always have such quick results. Sometimes force and even imprisonment were necessary to compel Muslims to redress wrongs done to Jews. In the middle of 1532 the Jew Sulaymān ibn Isra'īl complained that a large amount of gold and silver jewelry belonging to Zehava the beautician (*al-kaḥḥāla*, one who deals in antimony, *kuḥl*) had disappeared from his house. Sulaymān's Muslim neighbor Muḥammad al-Kārmī was accused of stealing the jewels and was put in jail to force him to return them. Only after he had spent a few weeks in jail was Muḥammad released, on the guarantee of two other Muslims who promised to bring him to court as required. Muḥammad al-Kārmī had certainly not been enthusiastic about spending time in prison, but when the Jew was unable to present incontestable evidence to support his charge, Muḥammad preferred to take a calculated risk and wait for further developments in jail. From the records, we learn that his patience was rewarded, and his Jewish neighbor eventually agreed to compromise with him.[7] In other cases the Muslims were not so amenable to compromise. At the end of 1546 the moneychanger Yahūdā ibn Mūsā charged a Jerusalem Muslim with not having paid full value for a flock of sheep Yahūdā had sold him. The accused admitted having bought the flock but claimed that he had paid the full price. The court accepted the Jew's sworn statement as to the outstanding debt and ordered the Muslim to pay. He refused to do so even if he had to spend a year in jail; threatening revenge, he swore, "If I pay this sum, may I turn into a Jew."[8] There were also claims off Jews against Christians. On October 1, 1553 Salamūn ibn Shullāl accused a Christian from Bayt Jala of failing to deliver a consignment of olive oil although it had been paid for. When the accused denied the charge, the Jew brought two Muslim witnesses to give evidence, and the Christian was convicted (*ta'dīb*).[9]

The legal redress granted Jews, and the Muslim court's readiness to hear their claims and even rule against Muslims, naturally encouraged the Jews to use the court extensively. They pressed charges not only against simple folk but against the powerful as well. In 1597 the Jew Yāsif ibn Sha'bān submitted a long list of monetary claims against a number of Muslim merchants in Jerusalem, including their leading figure the shaykh *al-tujjār*, Khawājā Muḥammad ibn Ibrahīm, who was charged with owing money for cloth.[10] At the beginning of 1574 a Jewish cloth merchant from Safed, Isḥāq ibn Lāwī, went to the Shafi'i kadi of Jerusalem with charges against the *mutawallī* of the al-Ḥaramayn al-Sharīfayn *waqf* (the *waqf* of the Temple Mount in Jerusalem and the Tomb of the Ancestors in Hebron) for a large sum owed him by the *mutawallī*'s predecessor in return for a loan. Since the sum was very large—200 *sultani*—and the accused was such an important figure, the Jew had to present conclusive evidence. He submitted the original loan agreement, brought two respectable Muslim witnesses, and was even requested to take an oath "in accordance with the practice of his religion." The kadi ruled in favor of Isḥāq and obligated the *waqf* to pay the debt.[11]

The Jews did not hesitate to press claims against men in influential political and administrative positions as well. At the beginning of 1562 the Jew Ibrahīm ibn Zakariyyā brought charges against 'Umar the *subashi* for a debt of 10 *sultani* for cloth the latter had bought from him. The accused denied the charges, and the Jew was asked to bring evidence to prove his claims.[12] At the end of January 1557 the kadi of Jerusalem tried the case of a Damascus Jewish merchant against the *subashi* 'Ashūr. The Jew claimed that 'Ashūr had illegally taken a large sum of money from his son Salamūn and from the beadles of the Jerusalem synagogue. The merchant complained to the *wali* of Damascus, who ordered the chief kadi of Jerusalem "to bring both sides before him and hear their claims; if the claims of Salamūn and the beadles turn out to be true, justice is to be done to them." The *subashi* brought in waivers the Jews had signed for the amounts in question, and the court accepted them as conclusive evidence. Even though the Jews had been compelled to sign these waivers, they nevertheless went to court to try to get what they claimed was due them.[13] Although they may seem to have been treated unjustly, the very act of pressing charges against a high official is proof of their trust in the court.

This trust was frequently rewarded. On April 15, 1589, several Jews came to the kadi to lodge a complaint against a Muslim soldier who was harassing them, extorting illegal payments, and informing on them to the *subashi.* One of them even described how he had been dragged to the Christian quarter and forced to pay this same Muslim a gold coin for his release. When the accused denied the charges against him, the kadi ordered that he be detained in the Citadel until the facts could be established. On the way there some of his fellow soldiers, forcibly freed the prisoner. On this occasion, although the Jews did not win their case, the kadi proved his readiness to adopt an unpopular stand in order to prevent similar harassment of the Jews in the future.[14]

There were times when secular officials also displayed a favorable attitude toward the Jews. On July 13, 1570, the kadi heard the complaint of the shaykh al-yahūd that Muslims were trying to interfere with three members of the Jewish community who had been producing and marketing cheese in the Jerusalem sub-district. The evidence brought by the Jews, and even a previous ruling in the matter issued by the sultan, did not satisfy the kadi, he tried to establish the truth with the aid of Muslim witnesses. Among the witnesses cited were a kadi, a commander of the Janissary unit, and a *sipahi.* With their support the Jews won their case. It was subsequently forbidden to disrupt their making and selling cheese in the city and its environs.[15]

A Jew would sometimes appear in court with a Muslim in order to offset possible future legal complications. For example, on May 17, 1542, a Jewish doctor and his Muslim patient came before the kadi. The Muslim declared that he had agreed to be treated by the Jewish physician and that he released the Jew from any criminal responsibility in the event of a mishap.[16]

It is clear from these many examples that when difficulties, real or potential, arose between Jew and Muslim, or when powerful Muslims attempted to provoke Jewish individuals or the Jewish community, the Jews did not hesitate to appeal to the courts.

## CIVIL SUITS OF JEW AGAINST JEW

When conflicts between Jews and non-Jews arose, the case was heard by the kadi, for Islamic law, the Shari'a, was the law of the land, and its judicial institution was the Muslim court. Claims of Jew against Jew could be heard by the dayyān, who tried cases in accordance with Jewish traditional law. Despite the value of this independent judicial mechanism within the Jewish community, and despite the great personal respect of the community for the dayyān, Jews nevertheless brought each other to the Muslim court on matters of private as well as public interest, over petty affairs and criminal charges, on claims dealing with movable property or with real estate. They evidently viewed the court as an important part of the fiber of personal and community life.

On October 10, 1547, Ḥayyim ibn Sulaymān sued Yahūdā ibn Menāḥīm of Damascus because he had not evacuated a house in Damascus. The plaintiff declared in the name of Najma bint Mūsā and her sons, for whom he held power of attorney, that the house had belonged to the dayyān of the Jewish community, Isḥāq ibn Ya'qūb, and that Najma was his divorced wife. This claim is instructive not only because it illustrates the use of the Muslim court to effect an agreement between Jews but also because it shows a case of the rabbi himself utilizing the Muslim court. The plaintiff stated that the rabbi had transferred to him the ownership of the house.[17] Despite the fact that all parties involved in this affair were Jews, and one of them was even a rabbi, the case was tried before the kadi. A similar suit was brought by Nassīm ibn Shū'a against another Jew at the beginning of May 1538. The plaintiff was the father of a Jewish woman, and the accused was her father-in-law. The latter had given his guarantee that his son, the woman's husband, would pay the remainder of the bride price, the woman's clothing, and other expenses, as originally provided for in the marriage contract "written in Jewish writing."[18] Here too, although all parties were Jews, and their rights and duties were expressly stated in a Hebrew document approved by a Jewish judicial authority, they nevertheless, appealed to the Muslim kadi to ensure implementation of their agreement. Another Jew received a court judgment against his rebellious son, ordering him to leave his father's house immediately.[19] In another case, in which the plaintiff was an ordinary man, Yahūdā ibn Isḥāq, and the accused was the shaykh al-yahūd of Jerusalem, the case was brought before the kadi, apparently to ensure greater objectivity than Yahūdā would have been likely to receive in a Jewish court.[20] For similar reasons, Jews visiting Jerusalem from other provinces preferred to bring their disagreements with local Jews before the kadi.[21]

Unlike both of these cases, in which the accused was a leader of the Jewish community, there are many instances of disputes between ordinary Jews being brought before the kadi. In a 1597 case the accused was in arrears in rent and admitted his guilt; in 1585 a Jewish landlord attempted to evict his Jewish tenant, although the latter had paid his rent in full; in 1565 a Jew claimed an outstanding debt owed him by his Jewish partner for a grain transaction; in another case, while a Jew had been absent from Jerusalem for many years, another had tried to take possession of his property, and a third claimed power of attorney (the suit was thrown out of court); in 1597 a Jew reneged on his agreement with a friend who had supported the man's wife during his absence in return for spices.[22] Regardless of outcome, the important point is that these cases all involved Jews only and all dealt with routine affairs of a local nature.

### CRIMINAL SUITS OF JEW AGAINST JEW

Criminal as well as civil cases were brought by Jew against Jew before the kadi. On April 2, 1582, one Jew sued another for informing on him to the *subashi*, who then fined him severely. The kadi ordered the informer never to do such a thing again. On November 15, 1583, Shmū'īl ibn Shiḥāda sued the Jewish woman Manūḥa bint Mūsā for having publicly cursed him; several times the previous day she had called him "son of a whore." When she denied the charges, Shmū'īl brought two Jewish witnesses to confirm his claim; their evidence was found impeccable, and the woman was convicted and sentenced to flogging, the sentence to be carried out at once. On October 3, 1534, another Jewish woman, Nūna bint Rūbīn, sued the Jew Nassīm ibn Mūsā, who had cursed her by calling her a whore. When she proved her claim, Nassīm was convicted.[23]

Punishment was meted out more severely in more serious cases than these. At the end of September 1550 a Jew was sentenced to flogging for having pulled out a nablus (*nābulsiyya*) knife on his comrade, who was saved by the intervention of other Jews.[24] In another incident 'Abd-Allāh ibn Isra'īl, the carpenter, brought a complaint to the kadi against his Jewish friend from Aleppo, whom he had received in his home and to whom he had given a daughter in marriage. When they quarreled, the ingrate stole cloth from the plaintiff's home.[25]

Most of the complaints involved crimes of violence. On April 4, 1585, the court tried the Karaite Sulaymān ibn 'Abd al-'Azīz, who, despite the sultan's explicit ruling forbidding Jews to wear the Muslim headdress, had done so several times at the synagogue. When he was forbidden by another Jew to do so, he grabbed the man by the nape of the neck and beat him.[26] Cases of assault inside the synagogue were not unusual. At the end of September 1559 two claims of assault were brought to court by Jews who charged that they had suffered beatings, beard pulling, and tearing off of their head covering in the synagogue. Since in both cases witnesses were brought, as required by law, the accused was found guilty and sentenced to flogging.[27] A year and a half earlier two cases involving beatings had been tried within a two-week period: one was the claim brought by the Jewish Zabīda bint Sulaymān, wife of Ibrahīm, against a Jew who broke into her house and beat her with his bare hands and with a rock; the other, heard by the Maliki kadi, was brought by a Jew against an influential man in the community, Shamīla ibn abu Jūkār, for striking him over the head with a club in the middle of the street. In both cases the plaintiffs brought Muslim witnesses to attest to their claim, and both won convictions.[28] There were also cases of recidivism: the Jew Mūsā ibn Isma'īl was accused in two different cases of beating and beard pulling and then of assault and causing the arrest and fining of an innocent person.[29] On November 16, 1559, a Jew was accused of beating his friend severely and tying him up, all for the purpose of collecting a debt. The Muslim witnesses not only confirmed the prosecution's version but further accused the assailant, "You fell upon him each time and beat him to within an inch of his life, harder than the blows of the administrator of justice (*ḥākim al-siyāsa*)."[30] In other cases of graphically described violence Jewish witnesses attested that one Jew had hit another and pulled his beard, and Muslim traders from the spice dealers' market confirmed that one Jew had struck another in the face until he bled.[31]

There was one other kind of criminal suit against Jews: that brought not by an individual but by the heads of the Jewish community for the good of the public. On March 12, 1541, the shaykh al-yahūd, the dayyān, and other notables came to the kadi complaining that a member of the community had gone mad, attacking people and losing control of his actions. They asked the kadi's permission to keep the Jew in detention "and take care of him until his reason returns to him." Their request was granted.[32] Fifty-two years later, on March 10, 1593, The heads of the Jewish community complained to the kadi about a Jew from Safed who had been in Jerusalem for some time. He had offered wine to Muslims and had attacked Jews "with his hand and his tongue." They requested that the kadi order him to return to Safed. He acquiesced, but permitted the man to remain in Jerusalem long enough to wind up his affairs.[33] About a year later, on July 29, 1594, some of the notables of the Jewish community complained to the kadi about a Jew who had converted to Islam but who continued to reside in the Jewish neighborhood, inciting the authorities against his neighbors. The kadi ordered him to leave; he leased his house to the heads of the Jewish community for three years and moved to another neighborhood.[34]

## JEWS BEAR WITNESS

As all these examples show, the *sijill* volumes record many instances of Jews giving evidence in the Muslim court, in contradiction of the accepted notion that testimony from Jews was not admissible. The dependability of the *sijill* is beyond doubt. It is clear that Jews did in fact appear as witnesses, and their testimony, called "testimony of *dhimmī* versus *dhimmī*" (*shahādat al-dhimmī 'alā al-dhimmī*) was accepted. The testimony of Jews was necessary to authenticate facts or identify people in cases involving Jewish matters. A factual declaration (*'iqrār*) made by a Jew in court, when confirmed and accepted by the kadi, became evidence (*'ishhād*). On August 20, 1546, for instance, the Hanafi kadi accepted the testimony of two Jewish witnesses concerning the granting of power of attorney to a Jew in the name of another Jew who had leased the concession for the income of the al-Ṭīra village. At the end of the judgment, where the names of Muslim witnesses (*shuhūd al-ḥāl*) always appear, only two witnesses, both Jewish, were listed: Ya'qūb ibn Mūsā, with "Jew" following his name, and Isḥāq ibn Hārūn, whose names confirm his Jewish identity.[35] There were other instances as well in which the testimony of Jews was accepted as confirming legal facts. Ya'qūb ibn Isḥāq appointed his brother as guardian for his seven small children and made their mother responsible for them in practice (*nāẓira*), authorizing them to use his legacy for this purpose. To avoid future doubt, in July 1561 two Jews gave testimony of *dhimmī* versus *dhimmī* regarding the arrangement.[36] The customary formulation in these cases was that the Jewish witnesses appearing before the kadi "were acceptable to him from the standpoint of the Shari'a" (*al maqbūlīn ladayhi shar'an*); only then did they testify on the issue itself.[37]

This formulation did not always apply to the admissibility of testimony in the Muslim court, even in regard to seemingly simple issues, if the evidence was prejudicial to the interests of the Muslim community. Thus, when Rabbi Menaḥim ibn Shamū'īl from Safed, called the *khākhām*, died in Hebron on September 18, 1573, two Jews testified before the Hanafi kadi of Jerusalem and that prior to his death he had appointed his nephew 'Azar ibn Sabatāy ibn Shmū'īl as his heir, in addition to his widow. The official in charge of the *bayt al-māl* in Jerusalem, who was one of the Janissary guard stationed at the Citadel in Jerusalem, had apparently tried to get control of the legacy. The Janissary was not attempting to nullify the content of the Jews' testimony but wished to contest the very right of Jews to testify in such a matter. 'Azar ibn Sabatāy submitted to the court a decree from the sultan dated April 1549 in which the mufti of Aleppo had been asked, "If a Jew dies and the official responsible for legacies without heirs (*amīn bayt al-māl*) wants to appropriate his legacy from his heirs, and [Jewish] witnesses [appear], is their testimony in this case admissible or not?" The mufti had answered, "Their testimony shall be heard." The sultan had decreed that the testimony of the Jews was to be accepted. Relying on this precedent, the Hanafi kadi of Jerusalem accepted the evidence, to the distress of the Muslim official at the *bayt al-māl*.[38]

The admissibility of factual evidence brought by a Jew must be viewed in the wider context of civil cases. At the end of September 1595 the Muslim court heard a financial dispute between two Jerusalem Jews. To prove his claim, the plaintiff asked the shaykh al-yahūd and his secretary to testify in his favor; "no fault or weak points were found in their testimony from the standpoint of the Shari'a, and the accused was obligated" to pay his debt.[39] More than thirty years before, a Jew's testimony had served to prove the innocence of an accused man in a dispute between two Jewish business partners. The accused brought two witnesses, a Muslim and a Jew, to testify before the kadi in his favor, and on the strength of their testimony he was absolved.[40] In criminal cases also, testimony from Jews was acceptable. On May 10, 1598, the Maghribi Jew Yūsuf ibn Shmū'īl sued a Jew who had converted to Islam for hitting him. The plaintiff brought two Jews to testify in his favor, and the kadi ruled against the convert. The importance of this ruling is that the testimony of the Jews was accepted as supporting evidence against a Muslim.[41] This was also so in cases involving Christians. On January 29, 1535, a Janissary soldier, a Muslim, sued a Christian whom he claimed had struck him. To prove his claim he brought two Jewish witnesses from Jerusalem to testify in his behalf, and the kadi found the Christian guilty.[42]

Greater weight was often attributed to the testimony of Jews than that of Muslims, not only in actions of Jew against Jew but also of Jew against Muslim or Muslim against Christian. (In the case of Christians, the rule of *dhimmī* versus *dhimmī* also applied.) The *sijill* reports many cases that broaden our understanding of the place of Jews as witnesses in Muslim affairs. At the end of July 1540 a Hebron Muslim was arrested for stealing lead plating from the roof of the al-Aqṣā mosque. His home was searched, and plates were found there, but the Muslim claimed that he had bought the plates from a Muslim merchant and lead ingots from a Jewish spice merchant in Jerusalem. When both merchants were brought before the kadi and testified to the truth of the defense, the accused was released. The testimony of the Jew, in addition to that of the Muslim, bore weight.[43] Nevertheless, in matters of great import and as sole evidence, the testimony of Jews was not sufficient. When, after a prolonged absence, Ḥasan ibn Sa'āda returned to Jerusalem and asked for the kadi's permission to serve as ritual slaughterer for the Jews, as he had done in the past, he was asked to produce evidence that he was a Jew. The kadi, not satisfied with the testimony of two Jewish leaders, requested conclusive evidence (*bayyina*) of the man's Jewishness. (It may reasonably be assumed that the kadi's attitude stemmed from pressure exerted by other Jewish and even Muslim butchers, competitors of the Jewish slaughterer.) Two Muslims, converts from Judaism who had known Ḥasan in the past, attested to his Jewishness and to his prior occupation as slaughterer; only then was he allowed to practice.[44]

The fundamental difference between the testimony of Jews, credible though it may have been, and that of Muslims becomes clearer in a case tried on October 2, 1586. A large group of Jews, men and women, complained in court against Aḥmad from Nablus, who was one of the Jerusalem *subashi*'s soldiers. They maintained that he had been extorting money and goods from them under false pretenses, and that he had harassed them at the entrance to the synagogue. Although many Jewish witnesses gave testimony, they were asked to provide more substantial evidence. Finally, they were forced to state "that they had no evidence from Muslim sources" (*lā bayyina lahum min al-muslimīn*). Aḥmad's oath as a Muslim was accepted as legal proof which the testimony of all the Jews could not outweigh, and he was acquitted. The judge had arrived at his decisions according to the accepted rules of evidence. He could not, however, shake off the impression that the Jews had told the truth. After acquitting Aḥmad, the judge warned him that he was "not to stand in front of [the] synagogue, was not to collect fines from [the Jews], was to take nothing from them, was not to inform on them to the authorities (*ḥākim al-siyāsa*), and was not to harass them in any way."[45]

In summary, the testimony of Jews in the Muslim court was acceptable evidence against Jews and Christians and served as supporting evidence to the testimony of Muslims. It was not, however, acceptable as exclusive evidence against Muslims, and in such cases sufficed only when accompanied by some further proof, either a document or the testimony of a Muslim witness.

## OATHS TAKEN BY JEWS

What happened when a Muslim plaintiff could not prove his charge against an accused Jew if the Jew was willing to testify under oath? Jews were often required to take such oaths in court. For example, on September 28, 1531, a Muslim villager from Jīb sued a Jerusalem Jew for a debt that the latter allegedly owed the Muslim's mother. The Jew denied the charge and was asked by the kadi to take an oath to that effect. He did so, and was acquitted.[46] A year later a Muslim from the village of Lidd sued a Jew for money he owed for silver jewelry. The Muslim could not bring supporting evidence; again the accused was required to swear under oath, did so, and was acquitted.[47] At the end of 1549 a similar dispute was brought to court. The plaintiff this time was a Janissary from the Citadel in Jerusalem, and the accused was the Jew Yūsuf ibn Shū'ā, a high official (*'āmil*). The plaintiff had no supporting evidence; the accused swore an oath and was acquitted.[48] Even when the Muslim plaintiff was more distinguished than a Janissary and the Jewish defendant less distinguished than the *'āmil* Shū'ā, the results were the same. On October 5, 1555, the officer in charge of registering the treasury's revenue from state property (*kātib al-khawāṣṣ al-sharīfa*) in Nablus sued a Jerusalem silversmith, the Jew Mas'ūd ibn Naftalī, who had underwritten another Jew's financial obligation. Since the plaintiff lacked evidence, the accused was required to take an oath, on the strength of which he was acquitted.[49]

The same rule also applied to criminal cases. About a year after this last case a Muslim sued a Jerusalem Jew for assault and for cursing him and his parents. The plaintiff could produce only partial and unsatisfactory evidence, and the accused Jew, after taking an oath, was acquitted. In a different case a Jew, accused of murdering another Jew, swore to his own innocence and was acquitted of all charges.[50] All these examples prove conclusively that an oath taken by a Jew at the Muslim court was not only acceptable but was considered sufficient proof of innocence, just as was an oath taken by a Muslim.

With respect to the wording of the oath, invoking the name of Moses, the Jews swore by God on the Bible. As the language used was Arabic, the Jewish oaths sounded similar to those of the Muslim, who swore by Allah on the Koran, invoking the name of the prophet Muḥammad. Some examples of oaths taken by Jews in court are quoted in judgments handed down in certain cases: "I swear by God, may He be exalted, on the Bible (*Tōrah*) in accordance with the version of my religion"; "I swear by the great God, may He be exalted, and He who handed down the law of Moses (*al-sayyid Mūsā al-kalīm*), may he rest in peace"; "I swear a Shari'i oath on this matter by the exalted God who handed down the Torah to Moses the prophet, [and] on the Book in the synagogue"; "there is no other god but God who knows the secret lore and the testimony (*al-shahāda*), who handed down the Law to Musa ibn 'Amrān."[51] Since the oath of a Jew was considered evidence, if a Jew tried to avoid taking an oath, it was held against him. In a dispute brought before the kadi in the spring of 1585, when the Jewish plaintiff was unable to bring proof, the Jew against whom he was pressing charges was asked to take an oath. "Three times it was suggested to him that he take an oath and he declined." The kadi therefore concluded that he was guilty and convicted him.[52]

ADMISSIBILITY OF HEBREW DOCUMENTS

Jewish documents, as well as Jewish plaintiffs and witnesses, were accepted in the Muslim court. Community documents written in Hebrew were sometimes brought into court and described by the kadi as "written in the writing of the Jews" or "written in Hebrew" (*muktatab bi-khaṭṭ al-yahūd, al-muktatab bi'l 'ibrānī*). Marital affairs fell within this category: a Jewish woman would submit her marriage contract to the court to claim the rest of the bride price (*al-ḥaqq al-mu'akhkhar, al-muhr al-mu'akhkhar*) promised by her husband when they were married.[53] Documents in Hebrew were also submitted in cases of financial disputes between Jews, usually promissory notes or statements of indebtedness. On May 14, 1532, the Jewish guardian of the baby Ibrahīm ibn Isḥāq ibn Ibrahīm ibn Natān Shullāl declared that he had received from the Karaite Ṣadaqa ibn Mūsā the outstanding amount on a debt due the baby's father from the beginning of April 1524, and this was also stated in "a document in the writing of the Jews, according to their rules and methods."[54]

Documents in Hebrew were not only exchanged between Jews but also given as security by Jews to Muslims. In July 1536 a Muslim woman from Gaza submitted to the kadi of Jerusalem a bond "written in the writing of the Jews" that had been given to her by a Jewish debtor. On October 31, 1549, a Muslim made a declaration in court canceling all debts owed him for commercial deals with several Jews of Jerusalem, debts that had been recorded in two documents "written in the writing of the Jews, in Hebrew."[55] Since these documents were submitted to a court that conducted its sessions in Arabic, summaries had to be translated for the hearings. Sometimes even the appearance in court of a Jew necessitated translation, for the Jews did not always understand Arabic. On March 21, 1562, the *'ifranji* Jewish woman Bella-Rosa was appointed guardian of her eight children in place of their uncle, who had relinquished the role, in part as a result of his "lack of knowledge of the Arabic and Turkish languages." All his statements in court were translated by a Jewish translator.[56] It is not clear whether such a translator was always present; it seems more likely that the interested parties provided one when necessary. The Jewish translator, in any event, was not part of the regular courtroom staff.

## BLOOD LIBEL

Among the many and varied matters tried in the Muslim court were cases of attempts to implicate the Jews of Jerusalem in blood libels. One element of blood libel, and an allegation prevalent in European Christian records—the charge that Jews used Christian blood for ritual purposes—does not appear in the *sijill.* However, there are claims that Jews had murdered non-Jews in connection with their holy days. At the end of September 1546 a Portuguese priest named Fiumo, head of the Franciscan community, sued Yūmtūb ibn Isḥāq, a Jerusalem Jew, claiming that a few days previously Paulo, one of the Franciscan monks, had visited Yūmtūb at his home on the afternoon of the Sabbath and had not been seen since. The priest demanded that the Jew be held responsible. The accused confirmed that the monk had visited him but added that he had been taken away by the Maronite interpreter employed by the Franciscans. The interpreter denied that this was so, even denying that he knew Yūmtūb. Because of the gravity of the charge, the Jew was instructed to bring admissible evidence; he brought two Muslim witnesses who confirmed his version of the story and confirmed also that the monk had since disappeared. The kadi accepted their testimony and acquitted the Jew of all charges.[57]

Thirty-nine years later during the month of the Jewish high holidays a blood libel against Jews was again brought to court, but this time they were accused of having murdered one of their own brethren. Maḥūmd bey, the new governor of the district of Jerusalem, testified before the kadi that when he had come to Jerusalem on September 17, 1585, he had heard that a few days before his arrival his predecessor had found the murdered body of a Jerusalem Jew, which had been thrown into one of the cisterns on the Temple Mount. The body was discovered when it began to decompose. Muslim dignitaries were questioned, since Jews and Christians were forbidden to enter the grounds of the Temple Mount, but they disclaimed all knowledge. They did, however, repeat a rumor that the Jews had bribed the *subashi* of the former governor to kill the Jew. When called in for questioning, the heads of the Jewish community absolutely denied this story. On October 20, 1585, after holding several hearings, the judge ruled that the Muslims did not have enough evidence to prove that the Jews were guilty, and the heads of the community were cleared of all suspicion on this count.[58]

In both of these cases the allegations against the Jews were very grave, but the slanderers were unable to produce any substantial evidence. Despite the temptation to malign the Jews, the kadi did not lend his hand to the libel, and acquitted them.

## SUMMARY

On the subject of Jews in the Muslim courts, two major questions merit consideration: what weight did their word carry there, and why did the Jews turn to this institution?

The answer to the first question is that the Jew was perceived as holding an inferior position in court as in society. Although the testimony of Jews was accepted against other *ahl al-dhimma*, in charges against Muslims it was considered only supporting evidence. An oath of innocence sworn by a Jew, however, was accepted as conclusive evidence.

With respect to the second question, Jews appealed to the Muslim court because they knew they would receive support both in principle and in practice. The court was open to bribery, though we cannot tell to what extent. In some cases, for example those concerning the rent on the Mount of Olives cemetery, in which the court reversed its opinion several times in the course of the century, it may be assumed that Jews at times used bribes to influence the kadi. Nevertheless, on the whole the Muslim court respected the rights of the Jews and protected them from injustice without unnecessary recourse to bribery. This conforms with the letter and spirit of the Shari'a's basic attitude toward the *ahl al-dhimma*. However, since Muslim society in Jerusalem constantly stressed the inferiority of the Jews to the Muslims, practice was far from theory. The kadi attempted to set an example by showing concern for the Jews and trying to apply objective criteria when judging their cases. Thus, the blood libels against the Jews were checked, the oaths and testimonies of Jews were accepted in court, and Jews received substantive support.

Jewish legal bodies had no means of punishing or enforcing sentences beyond the moral authority of the Rabbinical court or the threat of excommunication and banning. Jews therefore applied to the Muslim court for the purpose of enforcing decisions previously handed down by the Rabbinical courts. The means of enforcement at the disposal of the Muslim courts, their willingness to apply them in cases involving only Jews, and the basically positive attitude of the court toward the Jews all combined to motivate the Jews to appeal frequently to the kadi for help.

## *Status of the Jewish Woman*

"Men are superior to women on account of the qualities with which God hath gifted the one above the other" is the explicit statement that appears in the Koran ("Women," verse 38), and this attitude was consistently applied in Muslim society. Like her Muslim sister, the Jewish woman was considered inferior in rank and status to the man. She was, like all Jews, called after her father: the formulation for referring to a Jewish woman was "So-and-so, daughter of So-and-so, the Jew." Thus, even the adjective describing her relationship to the community referred to her father. However, just as the Jewish man's inferiority to the Muslim did not prevent him from engaging in a variety of occupations, appearing in court, and assuming other normal roles in Jerusalem's society, so the Jewish woman's inferiority to the Jewish man was less restrictive in practice than in theory.

Jewish women could own property inherited from their fathers, husbands, and brothers: Rivqa bint Ya'qūb, for example, inherited a house form her father in 1551, and in 1548 the mother of a Damascus Jewish silversmith deposited a sizable sum of money she had inherited from her sister six years before.[1] They bought and sold property, dealt with guarantees and securities, even posted bonds for public institutions and private individuals, usually their husbands. In 1599 Simḥa bint Isḥāq was sued by a number of Muslim merchants for one of her husband's debts, which she had underwritten.[2] Some women even had independent occupations, such as the Maghribi Jewish woman who sold sour milk (*laban*) during 1535.[3] Jewish women were appointed by the court as guardians over their minor children and over property the children had inherited from their fathers, and they remained the guardians until the children reached maturity. In

1569 Ḥilwa bint Ibrahīm even managed, in the name of her children, to collect a debt that the scribe of the Jerusalem Citadel owed her late husband.[4] Women were brought to court or came there alone for hearings; they testified, were put on trial, and were even convicted. When a Jewish woman was sentenced to flogging, the punishment was carried out in public. Her very appearance at the court was a form of public exposure, for she had to be fully identified by two witnesses. When a transaction for the sale of a house was concluded between a Jew and two Muslim merchants in mid-1567, for example, the Jew's wife appeared to witness the sale. Two other witnesses identified her in court "with no barrier to impair the truth of the testimony . . . and after the veil had been lifted from her face and jewels."[5]

From courthouse records it emerges that many Jewish women were not satisfied to remain at home in the traditional woman's roles. They chose instead to appear in public, and from time to time this got them into trouble. On May 19, 1554, the *subashi*'s deputy brought seven Jewish women to court on the charge that they had climbed the roof of *al-madrasa al-manjikiyya* so that they could see what was happening on the Temple Mount.[6] They admitted having done so and were punished, just as Jewish men were punished who had committed the same offense some time before. Women also appeared in court as victims of crime. A Jewish woman from Jerusalem who had left the city to do her laundry at the pool (*sabīl*) of Sultan Sulaymān near the city was accosted on her way back by a Muslim from the village of Bayt Ghawr, who asked, "Are you Jewish?" When she answered in the affirmative, he threw a stone at her head and injured a Christian passer-by who tried to protect her.[7] The case was brought before the kadi on July 28, 1538, and the Muslim admitted his guilt. This was not so, however, in another incident that occurred in mid-April 1585. A Karaite Jewish woman returning home from the baths was raped by a Muslim and his friend. The Muslim denied the woman's charges, so the kadi asked her to provide evidence in addition to her own testimony. "Had there been anybody else there, he would have saved me from those two," replied the woman. Unable to pass conclusive judgment, the court recorded the complaint, and the kadi promised to investigate the matter further. The investigation brought no results, and no one was punished for the incident.[8]

Violence was also perpetrated against Jewish women by other Jews. In the middle of September 1567 Stīr bint 'Abd-Allāh, daughter of the Jewish carpenter, complained that on two consecutive days two women, Mīra bint Manṣūr and Gālia bint Isḥāq, had attacked her, beaten her severely, and caused her to abort a baby boy. She even brought the corpus delicti with her to show the court.[9] At the beginning of May 1570 a Jerusalem Jew complained that another Jew had assaulted him and his wife so fiercely that his wife, who was pregnant, had started to hemorrhage. When the accused denied the charges, the kadi sent his deputy to the plaintiff's house to cross-examine the woman. She confessed that the accused had not hit her, but that hearing the fight that had broken out between the accused and her husband, she had become frightened and had started to bleed. The accused was acquitted.[10] In another case, when the *subashi* brought two Jewish women to the kadi, and they confessed to having quarreled, cursed, and beaten each other in public, they were both found guilty and punished on the spot.[11] On May 10, 1557, the government official in charge of the night guards (*'ases bashi*) brought a Jew to the kadi claiming that the man had beaten his own wife, Maryam bint Mūsā, and broken her hand. The wife did not dare incriminate her husband publicly. When summoned to testify she declared that she had fallen off an animal she was riding and had broken her hand that way.[12] These various incidents show that testimony brought by Jewish women was accepted in court in accordance with the rules of evidence that pertained to all Jewish witnesses.

A mature Jewish woman was considered responsible for her actions. If she decided to convert to Islam, her declaration was accepted, and she became a Muslim, although, owing to the delicacy of this matter, the kadi would have his ruling signed not only by the usual witnesses but by five other kadis as well.[13] Conversion was no guarantee of official leniency. At the end of March 1560 some Jerusalem residents complained about the immoral behavior of several women, including the convert Sulṭāna, daughter of Rūbīn the Jew. The kadi banished the women from Jerusalem, but Sulṭāna remained in the Jewish neighborhood and went on misbehaving. Again the Muslims complained about her, and the kadi banished her permanently.[14]

Despite the greater public significance of criminal cases, most trials involving Jewish women were civil cases and revolved around issues of personal status. At times the heads of the Jewish community would come to the defense of a Jewish woman whose reputation had been unjustly sullied. In the mid-1550s four notables of the Jewish community testified before the kadi in the presence of the *subashi* that Qamar bint Ya'qūb was "a respectable woman (*mastūra*), has committed no reprehensible act, behaves altogether commendably, and her honor is totally unblemished by any of the failings [some people] tried to impute to her."[15] Generally, the Jews brought cases before the kadi so that he might ratify agreements already arrived at. In recognition of their religious autonomy, the Muslim court tended to adopt norms acceptable to the Jews even if these broke Muslim law. On July 15, 1535, Lāwī ibn Ya'qūb, the Jewish dayyān, requested the kadi's opinion in the case of Yūsuf ibn Sa'īd, who had been married for some time to his own niece, 'Azīza bint Shiḥāta. The dayyān wanted to know if the marriage was valid under the laws of Islam. The kadi referred to the ruling of Abu Hanifa, which provided that among non-Muslims, marriage to very close relatives was acceptable to the extent that it was acceptable within the couple's community. Moreover, even if the marriage was invalid under Muslim law, if the wife requested financial support (*nafaqa*), she was entitled to it if the marraige were considered valid among the Jews. The kadi therefore ratified the marriage contract between the Jew and his niece, even though Islamic law would have forbidden their marriage.[16]

The Muslim court's support of the Jewish dayyān in such matters served not only to affirm the religious autonomy granted the *ahl al-dhimma* but also to prevent confusion and deceit. Jews who sought the kadi's support as a means of circumventing the internal authority of the Jewish community encountered certain deterrents. On December 3, 1550, a Jerusalem Jew asked the kadi's permission to marry Marḥaba, a Jewish widow. The kadi summoned the dayyān, who testified that he had given the woman in marriage just three weeks before to another Jew, "according to the practice of their religion." The husband had paid the bride price and marriage license tax (*rasm al-nikāḥ*). The petitioner's request was, of course, refused.[17] On January 7, 1579, a similar case was heard by the kadi. Ya'qūb ibn Yūsuf of Jerusalem, who had divorced his wife, a Jewish woman from Safed, came to court asking for help in marrying another woman, also from Safed. He claimed that the father of the girl, whose name was Mazel-tov (Mazalṭōf), had given her to him in marriage, even collecting a sizable bride price, but had not delivered her. The father, whose daughter was still a minor, maintained that nothing of the kind had taken place, and proved this by submitting an official document in which Ya'qūb ibn Yūsuf had declared eight months previously that the girl was not married to him. In the absence of any other evidence Ya'qūb's claim was rejected out of hand.[18]

Marriages were conducted entirely within the framework of the Jewish community. This was not true of divorces; in many such cases Jews had recourse to the Muslim court and Muslim practices. Particularly widespread was the practice of the husband unilaterally declaring in the Muslim fashion that he was divorcing his wife. On July 2, 1556, every butcher in Jerusalem promised to supply meat regularly to the residents during Ramadan and not to leave the city. Should they break this promise, they declared, they would divorce their wives outright; among them was the Jewish butcher, Shmū'īl ibn abu Jūkār.[19] Of course it might be claimed that in this case the Jew had to follow the lead of the other butchers; but there were other cases in which Jews quite independently took the initiative. On June 23, 1594, a Jewish merchant declared that if within six months he had not paid his debt to another Jew who had converted to Islam, he would divorce his wife.[20] Ya'qūb ibn Yūsuf divorced his wife, Sāra, and declared before the court that he had "driven her out three times" (*ṭalāqan thalāthan*), in the traditional Muslim fashion. The wife confirmed this, and the court then ruled that she was forbidden to her husband unless she married somebody else, a ruling that complied with Muslim law and terminology. Both parties declared before the court that they owed one another nothing and claimed nothing. Sāra added the explicit declaration that she had received her jewels and all her other possessions from her former husband.[21]

Although it was usually the husband who initiated the divorce proceedings, in isolated cases the wife took the initiative. On April 19, 1558, Zanna bint Rūbī approached the Maliki kadi and requested the annulment of her marriage to the cantor of the Jews. She apparently had weighty reasons for this request, because the kadi granted the divorce, and both parties renounced all further claims.[22] Twenty-five years later, another Jewish woman who attemped to obtain a divorce was less successful. In 1582 Sulṭāna bint Ibrahīm fell out with her husband because he had taken a second wife. She accused him of having unnatural sexual relations with her, which entitled her to a divorce. However, as she could bring no proof of her claim, and her husband swore that she was lying, he was declared innocent of this charge.[23]

On occasion the kadi would try to reconcile a couple. In May 1573 the kadi ordered the Jew Mūsā ibn Sūfān to return to his wife, Jawhara (Pearl), who had cursed and beaten him. The kadi warned her to cease such behavior, to return to her husband's home, and fulfill her wifely duties. The husband was obligated to bring her back to his house and provide for all her needs.[24]

As long as a marriage continued the husband was responsible for feeding and clothing (*nafaqatuhā wa-kiswatuhā*) his wife and for paying off the bride price specified in the marriage contract. In this matter too the Jews sometimes sought the confirmation of the kadi. In his presence both parties declared their obligations as well as the specific amount of the bride price stipulated in the marriage contract.[25] If the husband left Jerusalem for an extended period, he was required to provide for his wife in his absence, empowering another Jew to see to all her needs and promising to repay him upon his return. At the end of 1566 Qamar bint Sulaymān demanded the money her husband had left with another Jew to cover her needs. When the man paid her only part of the amount, she appealed to the kadi, who intervened in her favor.[26]

Husbands did not always fulfill their elementary duty of taking care of their wives. Early in February 1584, at the request of Dursā bint Isḥāq, the kadi ruled that her husband, Ya'qūb ibn Yūsuf, must pay her 3 *akçe* every day to cover her expenses for "food, drink and other needs." The husband may have refused to pay altogether, or may have paid only small amounts, for the woman subsequently appealed to the Muslim court for financial assistance. In a similar case in which the husband had been absent from Jerusalem for a long time, the kadi ruled that the man's wife had the right to take one Egyptian *qiṭ'a* every day from their common property even if no liquid assets were available and it would mean she had to borrow money.[27]

Islamic laws pertaining to inheritance were also accepted by the Jews. Family property belonged to the husband; the Jewish wife was entitled to own, bequeath, or inherit property only with her husband's consent. When a man died leaving a will, the inheritance was distributed according to his stated wishes. In all other cases the wife was entitled to one-eighth of her husband's legacy; the rest was divided among his sons, whether they were minors or adults. When the Jew Faraj-Allāh ibn Khalīfa died in 1547, his total wealth was estimated as 5010 *akçe.* One-eighth—630 *akçe*—went to his widow, and the rest was divided equally between his two sons.[28] This was an example of *qisma shar'iyya*—that is, allocation in accordance with the Shari'a. At the beginning of May 1554 the legacy of the Jew Salamūn ibn Isḥāq was apportioned, the widow receiving one-eighth and the rest being distributed among the other heirs, with the daughter receiving half of what was given to the son, exactly as stipulated by the Shari'a.[29] If a husband died without heirs, according to the Shari'a, his wife was entitled to one-quarter of his wealth, with all the rest going to the public. That was the arrangement that was made when the Jew Yūsuf ibn Da'ūd from Malta died at the end of September 1559, leaving only his wife, Rifqa bint 'Izar. Since there were no children to inherit his big house in the al-Rīsha neighborhood, the kadi ordered that one-quarter be given to the widow and the rest be transferred to the *bayt al-māl.* Although both his widow and the Jewish community had lost an important asset, this disposition was entirely in accordance with Muslim law, and no protest was made.[30]

The only way to circumvent this law was for a man or woman to stipulate who would receive his or her possessions after his or her death. At the end of 1531 the Jewish woman Ḍarīfa bint Mūsā declared that she was bequeathing her property, a vineyard and a grove of fig trees left to her by her husband, to her two married daughters, one of whom lived in Jerusalem and the other in Hebron.[31] She declared her intention before the kadi, ensuring that the *bayt al-māl* would be unable to appropriate her most important possessions.

The formal education of Jewish sons was under the exclusive authority of the father; the mother had no say in it at all. On May 14, 1578, Ya'qūb ibn Yāsif, who claimed that he had reached adulthood, appeared before the court and declared: "from this day on he will not disobey his father in whatever he tells him to do or not to do, will learn to read and write, and will not depart from his father's ways." The father confirmed the statement and reiterated a previous promise to give his son in marriage to a Jewish girl from Safed.[32] From this statement a picture emerges of a father's dominance over his son's personal life. The authorities made no attempt to interfere in private matters, all of which were to be settled within the Jewish community. Recourse to the Muslim court was reserved for formal confirmation of agreements already completed.

There were times, however, when the kadi was requested not only to give formal approval but to solve problems that seemed to be of a private nature. On March 12, 1563, two notables of the Jewish community, Salamūn ibn Mūsā Shullāl and 'Azar ibn Ibrahīm, appeared before the kadi at the trial of a woman who had been considered Jewish but now claimed that she was not. The woman, Ilaykār bint Shmū'īl, widow of the Jew Lyūn ibn Bandī, testified that she was a native of Ferrara, Italy, and had been born into a Catholic family (*naṣrāniyya 'ifranjiyya*). After their marriage she and her husband moved to Jerusalem, where they continued to practice separate religions. After her husband died, she planned to move to the "neighborhood of her Christian community." The notables of the Jewish community doubted her story, and she was requested to provide proof of her religion. When she brought two Catholic monks from the Dayr al-'Amūd monastery who testified that she was telling the truth, the kadi ruled in the woman's favor.[33] This incident suggests that a Jewish husband, though the dominant partner in marriage, did not force his religion on a non-Jewish wife, as long as her choice of religion did not mar the public image of the family. It is hard to resist pointing out the similarity between this situation and the relationships that prevailed in the society as a whole: as long as the Jewish community recognized the dominance of the Muslim majority, it was free to manage its religious affairs as it saw fit.

One more aspect of the status of women and the family is

worth mentioning: polygamy. Formally, there was nothing remarkable in this practice, although marriage to two women obviously required a certain economic standard. The husband had to pay two bride prices and provide for both the women and their children. Records dividing a man's property after his death provide several examples of Jews who left two living wives, including rabbis and dayyāns.[34]

Women were recognized as legal entities. They could borrow money with their husbands and were therefore jointly responsible for repayment. Jawhara bint 'Abd-Allāh, known as al-Ḥabashiyya (that is, the Ethiopian, who was nevertheless the "first lady"), and Salamūna bint Isḥāq were the wives of the Jew Nassīm ibn Yūsuf. In 1561 the kadi ruled that all three owed a considerable sum to a Muslim merchant of Jerusalem. Two years previously Nassīm had bought cloth and hides from the merchant, and his wives had appeared in court as their husband's underwriters. Their security would not have been accepted had the women not had property of their own, as proven by the fact that one of the women left goods and silk with the Muslim as security.[35] When difficulties arose over repayment of the loan, the two women were retroactively held to be borrowers.

This case may well give the impression that idyllic relationships prevailed between the two women married to the same husband. However, reality was much harsher. Both in Hebrew and in Arabic a second wife was called *Ṣarra* (mishap, calamity). Although in Arabic the word does not have the connotations of the Hebrew equivalent, it suggests the conflicts and tensions that were part of the relationship. On July 23, 1559, Ḥannā bint Ya'qūb sued her husband's second wife, Sulṭāniya bint 'Uwaynāt, claiming that Sulṭāniya and her two sisters had severely beaten her. The accused denied the charge and, as there was no evidence, she was acquitted. The outcome here is of less significance than the strained relationship the incident reflects. On July 22, 1582, a case of a similar nature was tried. The Jew Shūba ibn Da'ūd asked the court to help him bring his rebellious wife, Sulṭāna bint Ibrahīm, back to his home. The woman admitted that she had moved to her brother's house because her husband had married another woman. She even declared in court that she was cognizant of the fact that as long as she denied herself to her husband she was not entitled to his support, or any other wifely prerogatives.[36]

In his thorough research on the status of women in Kayseri society in the first quarter of the seventeenth century R. C. Jennings deals mainly with the Muslim woman; his occasional examples of the *dhimmī* usually refer to Christian rather than Jewish women.[37] His study of the Kayseri *sijill* of those years, supplemented by information from other cities in Anatolia, brought to light many incidents of women involved in court cases of various kinds. The main aspects of his findings are as follows. The Muslim woman owned property, which she inherited and bequeathed, endowed and sold, and she maintained and guarded her rights to her assets against all contenders, male or female. She even engaged in trade and usury, though the examples of this are few. She routinely appeared in court, where in almost all cases she enjoyed the same rights as a man and was even granted the court's support in certain family quarrels. Jennings summarizes, "The position of women in the social and economic order of early seventeenth century Kayseri may not be typical of the whole Ottoman Empire, but it is altogether clear that this case provides a challenge to popular Western notions of the debased position of Islamic women."[38]

A comparison between Jennings's conclusions and my own reveals many similarities. The Jewish woman of Jerusalem, far from Kayseri in place and so much earlier in time, practically speaking enjoyed rights similar to those of her Muslim sisters. Within her local society she inherited and bequeathed, sold and mortgaged, and endowed her property when she so desired. As a property owner she was the underwriter for others, including her husband, and at times was called to account for her actions in court. Jewish women appeared in some occupations as mediators (public crier, trader) and as professionals (specialist in treating eyes—*kaḥḥāla*—seamstress). All of this involved some measure of exposure to the public. These occupations brought women to the Muslim court, where they appeared in civil and criminal suits as plaintiffs and defendants and as factual witnesses, though not as expert witnesses (*shuhūd al-ḥāl*).

Men held the dominant position in the Jewish family, and in certain cases (polygamy, divorce) the adoption of Muslim practices further diminished the status of the Jewish wife. The Jewish woman, like her Muslim counterpart, accepted her inferiority to men in many respects. However, she also had many social, economic, and legal rights and knew how to insist upon them, and to this end she enjoyed the support of the Muslim juridical authorities. The challenge to prevalent concepts about Muslim women pointed out by Jennings can be expanded and applied to the Jewish woman of the sixteenth century. Active and intensely involved in the society around her, she was, for better and for worse, on an equal footing with her Muslim sister.

## *Social Status: The Extent of Inequality*

For the Jews living in Jerusalem, as for those in other parts of the Ottoman state, the concept of *ahl al-dhimma* embraced elements of both protection and humiliation. However, the concept itself tells little about the practical implications of being an outsider in Muslim society. Were Jews actually oppressed? How did they perceive their own status? And if they were oppressed, in what manner did this oppression express itself?

Jews were an integral part of the local economy. Even the taxes that seem to epitomize anti-Jewish discrimination—the *jizya* and *khafar*—in fact were not burdensome for either the community or the individual. The courts accepted testimony, documents, suits, and charges brought by Jews; and even at the Sublime Porte or in Damascus the Jews had advocates who were ready to give their problems a favorable hearing. Does this, then, imply that discrimination against the Jews was purely theoretical? Absolutely not. When a Jew was found guilty on charges brought by another Jew, he was punished. But a Jew who, for example, sold defective goods to a Muslim was charged not merely with cheating but "cheating the Muslims." *Jew* was a term of opprobrium, and when a Muslim wanted to swear by something of the gravest import he would declare, "If I am lying, may I turn into a Jew."[1]

In the middle of 1556 the sultan issued an order to the kadis and governor of the Damascus province that was also sent to Jerusalem. From the text it can be deduced that there had been attacks on Jews based on a variety of pretexts. Some people had accused them of cursing the Islamic religion; others claimed that the Jews should be forbidden to influence or educate their children who had allegedly converted to Islam. Some people had appropriated Jewish homes, illegally housing soldiers in them; others employed Jews as forced labor during Jewish holidays or on weekdays. Money was extorted from Jews, and entirely unjustified fines were levied on them.[2] The fact that the decree was sent to Jerusalem proves that such incidents took place there. (A decree of the same kind that had been sent only to Jerusalem two years before makes it clear that most of the charges listed above refer to specific incidents that took place there.[3]) Shortly after the 1556 decree was issued, another one was sent to the rulers of Jerusalem mentioning attempts by Muslim officials in charge of apportioning legacies (*qassām*) to force Jews to allocate bequests in accordance with the Shari'a. Compelling a Jew to behave against the tenets of his religion was explicitly referred to as contravening Islamic tradition and procedures.[4]

The most routine forms of oppression were part of daily life, and they concerned apparel and the use of the bathhouse. The restrictions applying to the covenant of 'Umar applied to the Jews, as we have seen, in the requirement that they wear a specific kind of headgear and certain colors. The *subashi* and the *muḥtasib* fined Jews whom they saw wearing a headdress made of the white cloth, which only Muslims were permitted to wear.[5] As we have also seen, a Jew entering the bathhouse had to wear a small bell around his neck to alert the Muslims to his presence.[6]

The bathhouse (*ḥammām*) was shared by all residents of the city, so it is not surprising that the true attitude toward the Jews manifested itself there. On January 6, 1547, the operator of one of the bathhouses (*ḥammām al-baṭraq*) was accused of giving the clients old, worn-out towels. The accused denied the charge in court, saying that he had given those towels only to "fellahin, to Jews, and to Christians." The kadi ignored this defense and ordered him to begin using "new, clean towels" and to distinguish clearly between those for Muslims and those for peasants and *ahl al-dhimma*. The operators of other bathhouses in Jerusalem were required to do the same.[7] Two years later the *muḥtasib* made a round of the bathhouses to ascertain that separate towels were indeed being given to Muslims and to *ahl al-dhimma*, and in the early 1550s other *muḥtasibs* did likewise.[8]

This distinction, in no sense the caprice of a single ruler but an enduring and systematic practice, was social rather than religious. Urban Muslim society, itself quite heterogeneous, looked with disdain upon two groups that it considered of particularly low status—peasants and *ahl al-dhimma*—with the latter the more despised. On the whole the townsmen looked upon the fellahin as miserable human beings, dirty, poor, and uncouth. The Jews could not be disdained for being primitive but were looked down upon for the very fact of their being Jewish. A Jew in Jerusalem was considered more worthy of respect than a slave but socially on a par with the common fellah. Therein lay the essence of his Muslim neighbor's contempt for him.

SEVEN

# Economic Activity

JEWS in Jerusalem made their living as artisans and in commerce, finance, and even agriculture, thus fully involving themselves in the local economy. They were considerably less involved in government and administration, which was largely the province of Ottoman functionaries and Muslim religious figures. However, some Jews did hold administrative posts in Palestine, and in Jerusalem in particular, even in relatively high positions.

## *Jews in the Bureaucracy*

The presence of Jews in official posts varied throughout the century and throughout the government. I did find records of Jews in responsible positions during the two decades from 1538–1557, with the second half of the 1540s the period of their greatest activity. After 1557 Jews do not seem to have held high-level posts, with two exceptions in relatively minor jobs: in 1559 Ibrahīm ibn Zakariyya leased the concession for the tax revenue of two *mazra'as* (cultivated land on the outskirts of a village on which no settlers lived permanently); and in 1574 the man responsible for supplies (*jebeji*) for the Jerusalem Citadel sold this job to the Jew Ya'qūb ibn Ibrahīm of Jerusalem.[1] During the years 1538–1557 a few Jews held the leases for the taxes of the *khāṣṣ* villages, and bore the titles of *multazim*, *'āmil*, or *kātib* for the revenues of those villages and *mazra'as*.

The income from taxes levied on various economic activities in the Jerusalem province, in other Palestinian provinces, and in the Ottoman empire as a whole fell into a number of categories. Some were allocated in advance to the governor of the province (*khāṣṣ-i mīr-i livā'*) or to the *sipahis* (*zi'amet, timar*); some were earmarked for the maintenance of the *waqf;* another allocation was for the state treasury (*khāṣṣ-i shāhī*). With respect to the first categories, the people involved lived in Palestine, and were bound to do their utmost to ensure efficient tax collection. This did not pertain to the last category, which involved revenue meant for Istanbul.

## THE 'ĀMIL

To make sure that the money designated for the state treasury, the Imperial Khass, would reach its destination, a high official was appointed to be responsible for its collection. The official, *al-amīn 'alā al-khāṣṣ al-sharīf*, was not part of the regular provincial administration, although he was sometimes responsible for collecting taxes in several districts of Palestine. Being a high-ranking functionary, occasionally bearing the title of *bey*, this official did not do the job personally but appointed others to act in his name.

The *amīn* (literally "reliable" or "responsible" collector) was assisted by the *'āmil*, or commissioner, who was actually his subordinate. There were a number of variations to the commissioner's full title,[2] but of all these titles *'āmil* was the most commonly used. It implied responsibility for an area that was frequently larger than the Jerusalem district. There were times when three different people bore this title simultaneously, for in order to ensure efficient collection from a relatively extensive area, sometimes several Jews were appointed to parallel or supplementary jobs. From 1538–1540, for example, the three were Shamīla ibn Sa'īd, Yūsuf ibn Shū'ā, and *al-mu'allim* Ya'īsh ibn Farḥān, the last two from Jerusalem. Shamīla was responsible for all the *ghafar* taxes of people going back and forth (*al-musāfirūn*) between Jerusalem, Gaza, and Ramla. He leased this revenue, which in the past had been collected by the 'Arab Sawālima Bedouin tribe, for a year and a third (1538–39) and even appointed two sublessors, one a Muslim from Gaza and the other Ya'qūb Fallāq from Jerusalem, eventually the shaykh al-yahūd, who promised to collect all the *ghafar* payments due the city of Jerusalem.[3] Shamīla is not mentioned after 1540, nor is Fallaq's role as collector of the *ghafar* referred to again. Their functions were thus relatively limited in scope and even more limited in duration.

The second man, Yūsuf ibn Shū'ā, is mentioned for the first time at the beginning of 1539 as holding the lease for the taxes collected in the Jerusalem and Gaza districts, and we are given a detailed outline of his functions: "he underwrote the obligation [to the treasury] with his person, his money and his responsibility" for all the income accruing from the "*khāṣṣ* of the villages, the *mazra'as*, the yield of the *muqāṭa'as* [taxation regions],[4] plots of land, protection money (*māl ḥimāya*), taxes that are not recorded in the registry (*taḥrīr*), the irregular taxes (*bād-i havā*)[5], and the rest of the *muqāṭa'as* belonging to the exalted *khāṣṣ* and those that are in the hands of the *sipahis*; excepted from this is everything held by the *sanjaq* [bey], the *timar* of the *zu'amā'*, the villages of Bethlehem and Bayt Jala, and the Bedouin tribes Bani Jamīl, Bani 'Aṭiyya, Jurm, Dughaym, Marāzīq, and Haytham." The obligation was for three years and a total of 1.1 million *akçe*. Because of the large sum of money, Yūsuf had to bring guarantors: his brother, three Jews from Gaza, and four from Jerusalem. The *defterdar* of Damascus, who officially confirmed Yūsuf's responsibilities, also gave him explicit permission to live in Safed, although Safed did not fall within his sphere of responsibility—which may have been exactly why he was given permission to reside there.[6]

The actual collecting, of course, was done by the government. But as a financial and fiscal expert, Yūsuf was responsible for checking all income, comparing it with the official lists, and even subletting contracts. It is not clear how long he stayed in Safed, or whether this was only his second home, but he continued to reside in Jerusalem, managing his affairs from there. When the three-year lease was up, he was no longer in a position of authority, being referred to by the end of 1541 as a "former *'āmil*." Nevertheless, although he no longer functioned as a high administrative official, his knowledge and contacts were still of such value that an important Muslim merchant in Jerusalem hired him.

While Yūsuf was managing the merchant's financial affairs, with the title of *'āmil*, his brother Bayram ibn Shū'ā was representing one of the Janissaries stationed in the Jerusalem Citadel, who had leased villages and *mazra'as* in the vicinity.

Yūsuf had been in his new job for less than a year when he was again officially appointed *'āmil.* From April 1542 until the end of 1550 Yūsuf ibn Shū'ā and his brother, Bayram, alternately held this central position in the districts of Jerusalem and Gaza. Even after leaving the job, Yūsuf was associated with the *khāṣṣ* tax collection: in the spring of 1552 he offered his person and his money as security for Yūsuf ibn Ibrahīm, known as Tarānā (or Turānā), the Jewish secretary (*kātib*) to the commissioner then in office. Thus, for some fifteen years Yūsuf ibn Shū'ā, a Jew from Jerusalem, held the difficult and responsible position of head of the internal revenue apparatus of the Ottoman treasury. This long tenure in a highly important position gives us a picture of a very influential and successful man.[7]

Ya'īsh ibn Farḥān was the third Jew who served as commissioner in Jerusalem during those years. He appears as the lessor of the *khāṣṣ* revenues from 1539–1546. In this capacity he sublet the contract for the *khafar* taxes on all goods, with the exception of grain, coming into and going out of Jerusalem, and the *khafar* tax levied on all Jews and Christians entering and leaving the city. He gave the contract for one year to a Muslim in return for 8000 *akçe.*[8] It may reasonably be assumed that he did so immediately after the Jew Shmīla ibn Sa'īd gave up the lease for the *khafar.* With respect to the relationship between Ya'īsh and Yūsuf ibn Shū'ā, it is clear that for one year at least they were both doing the same job: in 1545 a certain Muslim presented the kadi with a financial document (*ḥawwāla*) undertaking to pay the treasury taxes on certain areas for the year 1538–39. The obligation was confirmed by Yūsuf and Ya'īsh, identified as "the two Jews who hold the lease (*multazims*)," and the Muslim was given receipts (*raj'a*) from both Jews confirming that he had paid his debt.[9] Undoubtedly the two men found a way of dividing the responsibilities as well as the benefits between them.

These two were not the only Jews who held the post of commissioner. From 1545–1547 the commissioner was Shemtūf ibn Ya'qūb, who delegated his powers to Yūsuf ibn Shū'ā; in 1547

Sulaymān ibn Isḥāq and in 1557 Yūsuf ibn Mūsā held the post. As right-hand man of the official responsible for the imperial *khāṣṣ*, the commissioner had to rent out for a given year the taxation units (*muqāṭa'as*) of the villages and the various *mazra'as*, either as units or subplots. In addition he collected the *jizya* taxes of Jews and Christians and the *khafar* taxes for persons and merchandise. He also usually bought the Dead Sea bitumen (called *al-kafr al-yahūdī*, or "the Jewish bitumen," in addition to the usual name, *khummar*). The Bedouin of the Bani Haytham tribe, who gathered the bitumen deposits, would bring the mineral to the village of Taqqū' near Bethlehem, where the commissioner would buy it from them.[10]

The commissioner guaranteed the *amīn* or the *defterdar* all the income collected within the confines of the *muqāṭa'as* for which he held the lease. The commissioner also sublet the *muqāṭa'as* to others and collected what they owed. He was the one who checked the payments on account of taxes and compared all the data with the lists in the *taḥrīr* registries. He did not do all of this himself, however; the responsibility was his, but the jobs of recording, comparing, and issuing confirmations, documents, and so forth were done by the commissioner's secretary, the *kātib*. The latter was sometimes a Muslim, but Jews were also employed for this work. Yūsuf ibn Ibrahīm was the secretary of the *khāṣṣ* in Jerusalem in 1552, and his father had been secretary of the *khāṣṣ* revenues in the Gaza district before that. Although in the main the secretary's work was of a clerical nature, he would also go into the villages to supervise the collection of taxes levied in accordance with the agricultural yield. He was usually accompanied by the *'ulūfeji*, the person in charge of supplies, who had to be an expert in produce as well as in assessing the quantity and value of the yield.[11]

For many years during the sixteenth century, Jews of Jerusalem served as high officials in the tax-collection apparatus, although only a small part of their work involved their own community. Their major responsibility lay amongst the Muslim majority in both city and village—primarily its upper strata: tax farmers, high officials, influential merchants. Jewish officials collected their taxes and fees, ordinarily not a very popular position. However, these Jews were also the ones who rented out the job of tax collection to those Muslims. Even if these Jewish bureaucrats needed the approval of the *amīn* they nevertheless had a large measure of authority and broad scope for maneuvering, which gave them considerable status with the local Muslim population.

Not only were these Jews a significant part of the financial operation of the country, but they themselves were also able to acquire a great deal of property. Some affluent merchants found this a way of increasing their wealth further; the title *al-mu'allim* (expert) that was affixed to the names of three of the most important of these men attests to the respect they were paid and to their economic importance. One of them was even called *al-khawājā*, the title with which great merchants (Muslim and non-Muslim alike) were honored.[12] It may be assumed that large sums of money were paid for these jobs, as in the case of Yūsuf ibn Shū'ā, who declared himself in debt for 400 *sultani* to the *amīn al-khāṣṣ* in return for a "loan" the latter had given him the year before.[13] Great sums of money were also involved in the various lettings and leasings. If we take into consideration the fact that a significant number of Jews from Jerusalem, as well as other urban centers such as Nablus and Gaza, held key positions in the economic network for many years, we see a picture of significant Jewish involvement in the provincial system. Relatively speaking, they were no less important than the famous Jewish physicians and financial advisers of Istanbul.

It is interesting to note that the period in which Jews fulfilled central positions in the Jerusalem administration coincided with the period of the Jewish community's growth. After the end of the 1550s not a single Jew was appointed to a position comparable in importance to those of previous years, with the marginal exception in 1574 only proving the rule: The provincial administration no longer wanted the Jews of Jerusalem to be a central connecting link in the economic system of Palestine.

## MONEYCHANGERS

Moneylending on interest, financial transactions, and moneychanging all were practiced in the Jewish community in Jerusalem, but to a fairly limited extent. Although now and again Jews lent money to official personnel, they did not do so in a professional capacity. It is doubtful whether this was a means of earning a living beyond the extending of credit for items sold or a way for the strong and influential to collect fees and sundry illegal emoluments.

Nevertheless, there were some Jews who derived their income from such activities, and they were called *ṣarrāf* or *ṣayrafī* (moneychangers). I found some ten of these listed throughout the century, usually no more than one in any given year. Two of them were Karaites—Ṣadaqa and Ibrahīm ibn Shmū'īl in 1531–32. One, Yahūdā ibn Mūsā, is mentioned over the course of several years (1531–1549) as the moneychanger for the "two exalted *waqf*s", those of the Temple Mount in Jerusalem and the Tomb of the Ancestors in Hebron. In this capacity he assisted the superintendent of those *waqf*s, dealing in the main with collecting the very substantial sums of money due annually and paying money owed. This being an official position, he even received a regular monthly salary. There was nothing particularly unusual about this job. Jewish moneychangers were often responsible for the financial affairs of institutions and officeholders. For managing the *al-ribāṭ al-Manṣūrī waqf, al-mu'allim* Mūsā in 1541–42 was given a monthly wage. Ibrahīm ibn Faraj-Allāh, the dealer in precious metals, assisted the collector of the *jizya* in Jerusalem, *nāẓir al-jawālī,* in 1565–66. Isḥāq ibn Yūsuf during the second half of the 1540s, in the service of Sinan bey, attended to the financial affairs of the governor of Jerusalem.[14] Isḥāq ibn Yūsuf also helped the person in charge of the revenue of the sultan's treasury by collecting income in kind (wheat, barley) due from villagers in the Jerusalem district for the year 1544–45.[15]

Dealing with the man in charge of funds of a religious institution or with a high administrative functionary was not the only activity for the Jewish moneychanger in Jerusalem. There were moneychangers whose concern was the functioning of the local monetary system. A moneychanger of this type was appointed by the kadi to oversee the currency in circulation in Jerusalem, change denominations, change one currency into another, sell currency on demand, and detect counterfeit money or money that had been ordered out of circulation.[16] At least one moneychanger, Ibrahīm ibn Faraj-Allāh, was a dealer in precious metals, and indeed there is a natural link between the two professions. The shaykh of the guild of the dealers in precious metals had to give his approval to the appointment of the moneychanger, and the candidate had to express his willingness to accept the appointment, before the kadi could announce it officially. Apparently there had to be at least one formally appointed moneychanger in the city, because when Salamūn the Jewish moneychanger died, the kadi hurried to appoint Yūsuf ibn Ibrahām in his stead "because of [Salamūn's] death and because of the need the people have for him."[17]

In summary, considerable status accrued to Jews who served as moneychanger or as financial aide to a governor or an important *waqf*, for these positions carried influence and played a part in the lives and activities of many residents of the city. Moneychangers were also important figures within the Jewish community, both because of their administrative status and because of their economic situation. Sometimes their positions were enhanced by family connections that gave more property and power to those who were already wealthy: when, for example, Yahūdā ibn Mūsā married the daughter of the commissioner Yūsuf ibn Shū'ā, he was able to lease the rights to collect the tax revenues of the village of Ṭīra in 1546. He also traded in sesame on a very large scale in 1537–38 and owned a house that he rented to another Jew.[18] It is not surprising that on occasion the kadi would appoint the Jewish moneychanger to deal with special problems arising in the Jewish community, for example, the leasing of the cemetery in 1531–32.[19] Moreover, although the moneychanger held no official position in the community leadership, the kadi and even the district governor tended to look upon him as an unofficial but highly important figure through which to deal with the Jewish community.

## *Jewish Slaughterers and Butchers*

When Bernard Lewis first described the size of the Jewish communities of Palestine during the sixteenth-century he named three quarters in which most of the Jews in Jerusalem were concentrated: Sharaf, Rīsha, and Maslakh. It apparently seemed strange to him to find a Jewish quarter called "slaughterhouse," which is what Maslakh means, and he indicated his doubt by accompanying each mention of the neighborhood with a question mark.[1] Later descriptions no longer needed question marks, although there too the authors were evidently relieved when they could point out that the neighborhood was not always called "slaughterhouse" but was occasionally given the neutral name of "middle neighborhood."[2] Unlike the other two quarters, where Muslim and Christian residents lived as well as Jews, Maslakh is mentioned only in connection with Jewish residents and does not appear in any other context.

The neighborhood near the slaughterhouse, from which the area obviously took its name, was apparently a cheaper quarter where Muslims did not choose to live. Under the sanitary conditions that prevailed then, it must have been hard to escape the powerful odors permeating the establishment. But then, residence in this neighborhood might have arisen from the Jews' interest in butchering, which was a matter of utmost concern to them. Some of the residents were probably connected with the slaughterhouse, which was also called *maslakh al-sulṭān*, or the sultan's (or main) slaughterhouse. Others were much involved in matters connected with slaughtering as well as with various related professions. And for the community as a whole this was a matter of major religious importance.

## REGULATIONS AND RESTRICTIONS

The connection of the Jews with slaughtering stemmed primarily from their observance of Halakah, or Jewish traditional law, which was very strict in its regulation of these matters (*kashrūt*). Permission for the *ahl al-dhimma* to slaughter in accordance with the tenets of their religion had its source in the Muslim rule forbidding compulsion in matters of religion (*lā ikrāh fi'l-dīn*). Muslims were even permitted to eat meat slaughtered in the Jewish manner (*wa-ṭa'ām al-ladhīn 'uṭū al-kitāb ḥall lakum*).[3] The Ottoman rulers issued explicit directives forbidding interference, whether from other Jews or the local rulers.

The court archives offer much evidence concerning slaughtering done by Jews in Jerusalem. On the first pages of the 1530 protocol a Jewish slaughterer testifies that he ordinarily slaughtered sheep in the slaughterhouse on Mondays, Thursdays, and holidays.[4] Slaughtering on fixed days does not seem to have been a regular practice during those early years, but as of the end of May 1538 it was explicitly stated that the Jews could not "engage in slaughtering every [day of the] week, but [only] on two days, which are Thursday and Monday."[5] Permission to slaughter appears to have been an established fact from the very inception of ottoman rule; and in this the new rulers were only giving their official stamp to an existing situation. A *firman* written a few years after the conquest, at the end of April 1521, set down some of the rights of the Jews of Jerusalem, quoting testimony of the Jewish community to the effect that they generally slaughtered sheep and even stating specifically that "from olden days they used to slaughter sheep and no one prevented [them] from doing so."[6] The custom of two fixed slaughtering days eventually took hold and is mentioned as the ordinary routine throughout the century.[7] Nevertheless, there were many deviations. In 1552 the Muslims complained to the kadi that the Jews were slaughtering every day, contrary to accepted custom. When the Jewish slaughterer confirmed that he had slaughtered on a Wednesday, the kadi punished him and then asked the heads of the community to guarantee that in the future slaughtering would be done only on Monday and Thursday.[8]

Why was slaughtering restricted to specific days? Not for traditional Jewish considerations; the Jews were willing to slaughter every day, even if they had to use the same place regularly used by the Muslims. Segregation for religious reasons can be ruled out, and if the restriction had been motivated by the *muḥtasib* who had to inspect for purposes of taxation, he would have been more vociferous about violations. The only convincing explanation is fear of economic competition. Restricting the Jews to slaughtering on only two days a week was meant to benefit the Muslim butchers by reducing competition in the marketplace. Under the sanitary conditions then prevailing, meat was not easy to store; thus, the Muslim butchers, being able to slaughter every day, had a competitive edge over their Jewish colleagues. This situation was at the heart of the complaint of Muslim butchers about "the increase of [the Jewish] slaughtering in Jerusalem."[9] Jews would not under any circumstances have bought meat that was not slaughtered according to the Halakic rules, so there is no doubt that such a demand existed among Muslims for meat slaughtered by Jewish butchers that only the imposition of administrative restrictions could limit it.

Another regulation, mentioned in 1552, gives further indication of the attempt to lessen competition. The kadi of Jerusalem instructed the Jew to slaughter only two days a week "when there is not enough meat, and when it was available [in adequate quantities] they would slaughter every day."[10] On the surface this would appear to be a logical way of regulating meat rationing in general, but no such regulation applied to the guild of Muslim butchers; it was intended to give them an advantage over the Jews at times of increased demand and rising prices.[11] Relatively speaking, this seems to be a rather liberal provision, imposing restrictions only in times of general distress. However, in Jerusalem supplies of meat hardly ever satisfied demand. As usual, there were exceptions: on May 10, 1552, the kadi acceded to the request of the Jews, supported by the testimony of two of the *muḥtasib*s of Jerusalem, for permission to slaughter unlimited quantities on certain days.[12] (Less than two years later the Jews were again limited to two days a week.[13])

To what extent does this restriction reflect a broader control of economic activities? There was extensive government involvement in the city's economic life: prices were fixed and controlled; regulations governed trade, the location of markets, the quality of services, the source of supplies, and so on. The provision of meat, however, was considered a particularly sensitive area, and here the authorities were even more deeply involved. Since there was no regular supply of sheep and goats in Jerusalem itself, they had to be brought in from some distance.[14] Tradesmen dealing in meat, and nomadic tribes from outside the city, such as the Kurds, would bring flocks of sheep from afar to Jerusalem to sell to the city's butchers. Responsibility for these transactions rested with the butchers' guild, whose head was appointed by the regional governor. During the 1540s and 1550s a variety of mishaps affected the supply of meat. After influential people and ordinary residents had entered complaints, the governor himself intervened in the attempt to straighten matters out.[15]

On another occasion, when the residents again complained of

the lack of meat in the market, the butchers were summoned to the kadi. They were required, on pain of severe punishment, to supply the people of the city with a variety of meats. Each butcher swore that he would not leave the city or absent himself for any reason in the near future without a special permit. They additionally agreed to pay the governor a fine of 500 *akçe* if they failed. Quotas were fixed for the 11 butchers in the city to ensure a minimum weekly supply of meat to the shops. With the exception of the butcher of the *'imāret* (soup kitchen) of Khasseki Sultan, who had a particularly high quota (15 sheep and 15 goats), and of three other butchers who were given almost symbolically small quotas (one sheep and one goat), the majority of butchers were required to slaughter five to six sheep and goats each. Included in this category were the Christian butchers and the Jewish butcher Shmū'īl ibn abu Jūkār. Evidently the Jewish butchers were looked upon as part of the butchers' guild, and all arrangements for Jewish slaughtering were fully coordinated with the heads of the guild.[16]

Complaints that the Jews were slaughtering every day led to vigilant surveillance over the Jewish butchers,[17] which the Jewish community sought ways of circumventing. One way was to avail themselves of a Muslim butcher's assistance. The Jewish demand for meat was particularly great on Fridays, and in 1556, when meat was in short supply, the Muslim butcher Aḥmad ibn Zurayq agreed to "slaughter good meat for the Jewish community . . . on Friday, immediately after the prayer," for which he would be paid more than the price fixed by the kadi. From the wording in the court record it becomes clear that the man was accused of "slaughtering by the Jewish method" (*dhabaḥa bi'l yahūdī*), although it is clear that a Jew and not the Muslim did the actual slaughtering. He denied the charge, but it was confirmed by other Muslims. The description of the good meat sold to the Jews and the "stinking" meat sold to the Muslims conveys the fear of competition among the butchers. The proofs brought before the kadi were sufficient to persuade him to find Aḥmad guilty. The procedure that followed and the resulting punishment were unusually severe. The case was brought before the governor of Jerusalem, whose judgment was formulated in terms very rarely used in rulings that appear in the kadi's books.

The butcher was then taken around the town on a donkey, his head covered with a special hat with tinkling bells attached to it, for the purpose of deterring others from following his example.[18] There was evidently a need for deterrents, because Aḥmad's case was not exceptional: some five months before, another Muslim butcher had been accused of slaughtering for the Jews. The accused was from the al-Dahīna family, who had been butchers for many years. He had only been required to promise that he would not break the law again.[19] When the phenomenon became more widespread, however, the need arose for more severe punishment.

As it turns out, this form of deterrence did not suffice. At the beginning of September 1558, some two years after these incidents, the *muḥtasib* of Jerusalem again complained to the kadi about the lack of meat in Jerusalem "because of the slaughtering being done by the Jewish slaughterers every day." Again the Jews were restricted for the duration of the meat shortage.[20] But this did not discourage the Jewish community, who applied for and received official permission from Istanbul to slaughter every day of the week. At the end of July 1563 the heads of the Jewish community showed the kadi a *firman* allowing them to slaughter every day "to the extent of their ability" and prohibiting any restrictions on this practice. The kadi rescinded his order, but he interpreted "to the extent of their ability" in a very narrow sense: the Jews were authorized to slaughter as many goats as they wished, but with respect to sheep, which were in more limited supply, he fixed the relatively small quota of three head a week. He promised to ease this restriction when the supply of sheep returned to normal.[21]

In later periods of scarcity the Muslim butchers attempted to prevent the Jews from slaughtering altogether, so that the Jewish consumers would have to buy meat from them. In the spring of 1587, after the Jews showed the kadi the *firmans* giving them permission to slaughter, he again ruled that they were not to be prevented from slaughtering twice a week, whether meat was plentiful in the city or not.[22] In the final years of the century the community leaders had to appear before the kadi time and time again, for example in March 1591, displaying all the documents, rulings, and decrees they possessed, in order not to be prevented from slaughtering. At the end of April 1592 they even succeeded in acquiring permission from the new kadi to slaughter every day of the week ("whenever they want to").[23] Just a year later, at the end of May 1593, the kadi again restricted the Jewish slaughtering, following the request of the Shafi'i mufti, to two days a week during Ramadan. During Ramadan the Muslims fast by day, but at night, when eating is permitted, their meat consumption increases. Ramadan then fell during the spring, at which time many sheep were lambing, further reducing meat supplies. This time one of the two days was Friday.[24] The following year as well the kadi instructed the head of the Jewish community to see that their slaughterers worked only Mondays and Thursdays,[25] a situation that prevailed until the end of the century. In the middle of May 1601, when there were attempts to stop Jewish slaughtering altogether, the kadi confirmed the Jews' rights but limited them during periods of scarcity to Mondays and Thursdays only.[26]

## SELLING MEAT TO MUSLIMS

Another way to limit the demand for meat slaughtered by Jewish butchers was to fix a higher price for it. The Jewish community was not averse to this plan. In fact, the Jews themselves favored higher prices, for the additional income could serve public needs. But when official approval was given to a price 8 percent higher for mutton that had been slaughtered by the Jews, non-Jewish customers as well as Jews had to pay.[27] Another stratagem was to limit the sale of meat slaughtered by Jews to Jews only. Permits issued to Jewish butchers explicitly stated that they could slaughter to meet the needs of their community, and that the meat was to be sold only within the confines of their neighborhood. In reality, however, there was a large demand among the Muslims as a result of the widespread conviction that kosher meat was more sanitary. To facilitate inspection, the Jews were required to slaughter only in the slaughterhouse, and the *muḥtasib* usually saw to it that this provision was observed. Nevertheless, some butchers managed to do their slaughtering in other places, thereby circumventing supervision of both the amount and the frequency of slaughtering.[28] Ways were also found to sell meat outside the Jewish neighborhood. The kadi asked Muslim meat venders not to sell their Muslim customers meat from Jewish slaughterers, or even bring it into the market.[29] The Jews were instructed to keep their meat separate from that of the Muslims and to brand it so that it could be identified.[30]

Another way of trying to limit Jewish slaughtering was to levy additional fees, although this was illegal. The *muḥtasib* would collect a special fee called a butchers' brand tax (*resm-i damga-i qassabin*) from butchers who sold the meat. At the end of January 1569 Jews complained to the kadi that the *muḥtasib* had begun to collect an additional tax from the ritual slaughterer of the Jewish community who worked for the butchers, but separately. The kadi forbade the *muḥtasib* to continue levying the tax. However, the verdict adds, if a Jew slaughtered for his own use, whether he was a butcher or not, he would have to pay the tax as provided in the regulations of the *Qanun-Name.*[31]

The order to brand meat slaughtered by Jews indicates that despite all the prohibitions, such meat was likely to find its way into Muslim hands. Indeed, it was well known that the Jews ate only those parts of an animal that were considered *qūshīr* (or kosher, as it is pronounced in Ashkenazi Hebrew), and did not use the parts they call *'iṭrīf* (from the Hebrew *ṭaref*, nonkosher). These parts they were said to hang on a hook at the shop entrance and sell to the Muslims, either in the Jewish neighborhood or in the Sūq al-Sulṭān.[32] In the middle of 1578 and again at the beginning of 1580 two similar attempts were made to prevent meat supplied by Jewish slaughterers from reaching the Muslims, very likely at the initiative of the Muslim butchers. The pretext was on purely religious grounds. A group of Muslims from the Shafi'i school brought a doctrinal complaint with regard to the consumption of meat slaughtered by Jews. The Jewish slaughterer, they claimed, after killing and skinning the animal thrusts his hand inside and feels around in the entrails to find out if it is kosher. But this very act makes the meat undesirable for eating according to the Shafi'i school because there is no proof that the slaughterer is one of the "people of the book." The notables of the Jewish community claimed that this method of slaughtering had been used by Jews in Jerusalem for many generations without interference. At the kadi's request they submitted a legal ruling issued by Abu al-Su'ūd Efendi, the head mufti of the empire (*al-muftī al-a'ẓam bi'l-diyār al-islāmiyya*), to the effect that meat slaughtered by Jews was tolerable for Muslims (*ḥalāl*), even if the slaughterer feels around in the animal's innards—a thing considered objectionable by some Muslims. A *firman* was issued at the end of January 1568 explicitly stating that the provisions of this *fatwā* were to be followed. The Hanafi kadi, as well as the man who replaced him two years later, subsequently permitted the Jews to continue to slaughter in accordance with their custom.[33]

At the beginning of May 1592 a similar charge, although less detailed than the previous one, was brought in the name of a number of Shafi'i *'ulema*. But this time, despite their claim that Muslims were forbidden to eat meat slaughtered by Jews, the kadi rejected their case. He permitted the sale to Muslims of meat slaughtered by Jews, but on condition that the meat be marked with a brand and sold in the Jewish neighborhood from a separate shop.[34]

## THE RITUAL SLAUGHTERER

To this point I have referred inclusively to Jewish butchers. This general designation comprises several occupations that existed in both the Muslim and the Jewish communities: slaughterer (*dhabbāḥ*), butcher (*qaṣṣāb, laḥḥām*) and salesman-distributor (*bayyā'*). On occasion a single person fulfilled more than one of these functions, although on the whole different people functioned in each capacity.

Jews bought live animals, usually sheep, to be slaughtered by the ritual slaughterer (*dhabbāḥ*), who was appointed by the heads of the community or the dayyān. The dayyān himself was sometimes appointed as slaughterer, but the person was usually the community's candidate, who was then authorized and approved by the *muḥtasib*. Although the *muḥtasib* was not entitled to ask for recompense for the actual slaughtering, a number of references in the court books show that the slaughterer often agreed to pay the *muḥtasib* for his approval. At the beginning of May 1543, for example, Yūsuf, the dayyān of the community who had also been appointed slaughterer, agreed to pay the *muḥtasib* a quarter of his income in return for concessions, the most important of which was a considerable reduction in supervision, giving

Yūsuf the right to slaughter whenever and wherever he wished, as well as control over deciding which cuts and how much meat he would sell to non-Jews. The *muḥtasib* had to approve the implementation of each of these rights in advance. Should the slaughterer do anything to displease the *muḥtasib*, he had to pay a fine of 200 *akçe* to the Dome of the Rock.[35] This promise arose from the fact that the *dhabbāḥ* was responsible for fulfilling the regulations concerning the slaughtering of meat for the Jewish community. Hence, upon being appointed he customarily undertook to abide by all the restrictions concerning days for slaughtering, to refrain from selling unbranded meat in the market, and so forth. If he failed to do so, he had to pay a fine of 2000 *akçe* either to the Dome of the Rock or to the governor.[36] For this reason, when complaints were brought to the kadi concerning matters of slaughtering, it was the *dhabbāḥ* who was brought to court and instructed to enforce the regulations.[37]

When the dayyān did not double as the slaughterer, the heads of the community saw to it that at least one *dhabbāḥ* was appointed. At the end of 1550, for example, the heads of the Jewish community asked the kadi and the *muḥtasib* to appoint Yahūdā ibn ʿAwwad and Yaʿqūb ibn Mūsā al-Ḥāmī as slaughterers. The appointments were approved and duly recorded in the courthouse books.[38] There was no time limit for such an appointment; I found records of slaughterers, still fulfilling this function ten years later. But there were also times when the community would ask that such an appointment be rescinded. In the middle of May 1571 the heads of the community, including the dayyān, declared before the Hanafi kadi that ʿAmmān ibn Ḥasan, the community's slaughterer, was not doing his job properly, and they requested that he be forbidden to continue slaughtering. The charge was brought after a group of Shafiʿi Muslims had complained that the man was selling meat he had slaughtered to Muslims. The kadi assented to the request and forbade him to slaughter. At the request of the heads of the community two slaughterers were appointed to replace him: Da'ūd ibn Makhlūf and Salamūn ibn Ṣūfān. A week later the heads of the community, led by the dayyān, again appeared before the kadi requesting that the prohibition against ʿAmmān's slaughtering be lifted, and that the community be permitted to maintain all three authorized slaughterers. What took place during those seven days is not at all clear. Had the heads of the Jewish community found a different way of conciliating the Shafi'is, or had 'Ammān mended his ways after hearing the complaint that "he did not slaughter well in accordance with the rules of their religion"? It is more likely that external circumstances had changed, From that day on, with the kadi's approval, all three were authorized *dhabbāḥ*s.[39] This entire affair, which further portrays the pressure exerted by the Muslims to prevent the sale of meat slaughtered by Jews, is not a typical case. As a rule, there was only one slaughterer—in rare cases two—and the reference was always to "the *dhabbāḥ* of the Jewish community." He was rarely fired as a result of either internal or external pressure; but when he grew too old to work or died, a replacement was appointed.[40]

On one occasion the Muslims even complained on the grounds that the slaughterer was not "Isra'īlī," an adjective I have not found in any other context in reference to Jews of the time. (Although I did find a reference to *al-qaṣṣāb al-Isra'īlī*, the butcher, Yāsif ibn Yahūdā, was first and foremost a slaughterer.)[41] There is no indication at all of what quality this word describes or of the source of the appellation. It is certain, however, that this was considered an important characteristic without which a candidate for slaughterer would have been ineligible. In one case, in July 1599 when the slaughterer Ḥasan ibn Sa'āda, who had been away from Jerusalem for some time, asked the kadi to confirm his old appointment as *dhabbāḥ* for the Jewish community, the kadi asked him to show proof that he was an Isra'īlī and that he had been a slaughterer in the past. His word alone was not sufficient, so he brought two Muslims who had converted to Judaism to testify that he was telling the truth.[42] The fact that a slaughterer was an Israeli was sometimes appended to his name as a descriptive title, as if describing some particular characteristic; at other times it was explicitly stated that if "the *dhabbāḥ* is not proven to be an Isra'īlī, why, he is forbidden, from the standpoint of the Shari'a."[43] The term appears to have had nothing to do with a person's place of origin, nor does it indicate that he was a member of the traditional Jewish community rather than a Karaite. Apparently all it does mean is that the man was a Jew. In fact, the term seems to have been a euphemism, for there was a derogatory element in the term Yahūdī.[44] Proof of this can be found in the fact that in early 1580 a number of Shafi'i notables questioned the right of the Jews to slaughter at all, even asking the kadi to forbid the *dhabbāḥ* to slaughter in the meantime, "as long as it had not been proven that he was a *kitābī*"—that is, one of *ahl al-kitāb*.[45] With this the circle is closed: *kitābī*, or *dhimmī*, is one of the descriptive adjectives for "people of the book," including the Jews. If *Isra'īlī* is equivalent to *kitābī*, then surely *Isra'īlī* means "Jew."

## THE BUTCHER

The slaughterer was an important figure, especially from the ritual standpoint, but the contact of the people was largely with the butcher. The butcher would buy meat from the slaughterer, who was not supposed to sell to anyone but butchers. Sometimes the butcher slaughtered as well, although this was considered exceptional. (A clear distinction was drawn between the butcher and the *dhabbāḥ*, whose status was greater.) In addition to occasionally slaughtering, the butcher would also skin the animals, purify the meat, and sell it to his coreligionists. He too was appointed to his job by the kadi, at the recommendation of the heads of the community. The appointment was considered an official one (*waẓīfat qaṣṣābat ṭā'ifatihi*). When the butcher accepted it in the presence of the kadi and the *muḥtasib*, he would undertake not to sell the meat outside his shop or to Muslims.[46] Just as the appointment was based on the community's recommendation, so was its revocation. The butcher might voluntarily relinquish his job in court, as did Mūsā ibn abi Jūkār in 1558, but the Jewish community also had the power to remove him from his job. Yūmtūf ibn Mas'ūd, after serving a few years as one of two butchers for the community, was removed from his job at the beginning of 1560 after the Jews had complained that he was selling nonkosher meat and charging exorbitant prices, and that when slaughtering and purifying he did not observe all the religious tenets. The Hanafi kadi made him swear that he would cease slaughtering, purifying, and selling meat to the Jews; should he continue, he would be punished (*ta'dīb*) according to the laws of the Shari'a. It is hard to know, of course, whether the man misbehaved out of greed or was the victim of envy on the part of other butchers. In any event, after the kadi issued his judgment, he no longer worked as a butcher.[47] There were usually no more than one or two butchers among the Jews. When there were two, they took it upon themselves not to interfere with one another and to divide the available meat equally, each of them selling half.[48]

Among the Muslims there were certain families, such as the al-Dahīna family, whose members served as butchers for many years. It is difficult to tell if this was the case among the Jews, for their butchers are referred to only by first name and father's first name. In at least one case, however, we can be certain that the profession was handed down from father to son. Shmū'īl abi Jūkār, referred to as the most important butcher in the Jewish community at the end of 1556, bequeathed his work to his son, Mūsā; some thirty years later, at the beginning of 1583, the son was referred to as a butcher. The kadi forbade him to continue slaughtering sheep after a complaint had been lodged by the shaykh al-yahūd. The background of the incident is not at all clear. Although the man was forbidden to slaughter, he was not forbidden to continue selling or purifying meat, which were among the butcher's tasks.[49] Among the *dhabbāḥ*s too it is reasonable to assume that there was some measure of professional continuity. During the last decade of the century we find a reference to Sa'ada ibn Isḥāq followed by the name of Ḥasan ibn Sa'āda, who could have been the former's son. It is clear, in any case, that Sa'āda ibn Isḥāq was continuing his father's profession, as he declared explicitly that "he and his father before him worked at slaughtering sheep for the Jews."[50]

## MEAT VENDER

The lowest level of professional training and skill was required from the venders of meat, who were both Jews and Muslims. When meat slaughtered by Jews was distributed among Muslims, it was generally done from Muslim meat venders' shops (*ba'i'īn al-laḥm*) in the market.[51] Jewish meat venders were perceived as entirely different from butchers and were called *bayyā'*.[52]

Meat was usually sold by butchers in their shops. Such sales were subject to a price list fixed once every four months by the *muḥtasib*, and whenever extreme fluctuations in supply and demand took place. Following accepted custom with respect to the sale of other products, the *muḥtasib* collected a daily fee from each butcher as part of his compensation for controlling prices and inspecting their scales. When transgressors were found—Jews as well as Muslims—they were tried and punished,[53] although punishment was not automatic. In 1557, for example, the *muḥtasib* leveled charges against the butcher Shmū'īl ibn abi Jūkār for being five months in arrears in payment for his shop and also for using a defective scale for weighing meat. The Jew denied the charges; when the *muḥtasib* could not bring proof, Shmu'il was cleared.[54]

### SUMMARY

In principle, the rulers took a liberal stand toward the institution of Jewish slaughtering. The Jews were given the "right to slaughter in accordance with the conception of [every] school of thought (*madhhab*) of those Muslim religious scholars who approve of it."[55] Such tolerance was rooted in the overall official outlook that permitted a large measure of autonomy in Jewish religious life. However, it also stemmed from official awareness of the demand, among the Muslims as well as the Jews, for meat slaughtered in the Jewish tradition. Although Jewish slaughtering was permitted, attempts were also made to safeguard the rights of Muslim butchers.

The Jews were expected to be loyal to the spirit of the privilege granted them and not sell their meat outside their neighborhood. Additional steps were taken to implement this restriction. Jews were permitted to slaughter only two days a week, a highly discriminatory measure that was not imposed on other members of the butchers' guild. Thus, we find another expression of the quality of life of the Jews in Jerusalem: autonomy in the internal management of community affairs overshadowed by inferiority with regard to the majority and in the eyes of the rulers.

## *Shoemakers and Processors of Hides*

I found records of two callings followed by Jews who bought and treated hides: there were tanners (*dabbāgh*), whose main work was to clean, dry, and treat the skins, preparing them for use; and there were the *adamī*, a term still used in Arabic today, who bought not only the hide of the animal (*adīm*) but the fat as well. From this fat, primarily of sheep, they produced *samne*, one of the basic staples of the Middle Eastern kitchen. These Jews all lived in Jerusalem, but since the city could not supply enough hides, they would make the rounds of the villages throughout the district to find the necessary supplies.[1]

From tanning and related processes to shoemaking is a short step. In 1550 the Jew Yūsuf ibn ʿAbd al-Karīm was found guilty of making an inferior product when the stitches of a shoe he had sold to a Muslim ripped apart.[2] By his own testimony Yūsuf had previously been an *adamī*—a fine example of economic mobility. Shoemaking was a profession of some consequence; a man was held responsible for his product, and a shoemakers' guild existed to ensure high professional standards. Jewish shoemakers (*'iskāfī*) had an organization recognized by the kadi, who, at their recommendation, even appointed one of their number to preside over the rest as shaykh. In 1586 there were eleven Jewish shoemakers in Jerusalem, some of them apparently members of the same family, and at their request Sāfī ibn Shūʿā was appointed their shaykh.[3] It seems likely that the Jews did not have their own guild but rather made up a special section of the Jerusalem shoemaker's guild, much like the situation of the butchers.

At the end of the 1540s there were four Jewish shoemakers in Jerusalem. They swore before the kadi, in the presence of the *muḥtasib*, that they would scrupulously endeavor to maintain a high professional level and would use suitable raw materials—never hides taken from dead animals (*faṭā'is*)—to produce the best possible shoes.[4] From time to time until the end of the century, mention is made of Jewish shoemakers who purchased hides from butchers and sold leather or made shoes from it. They did business with Muslims as well as Jews: one Jew hired a Muslim shoemaker to work for him; another bought a large quantity of shoes at once—260 pairs made of water buffalo hide—from a Muslim.[5]

There were also harness makers and saddle makers (*barādiʿī*, *sarrāj*) who worked in leather. Jews from Jerusalem who worked in this field are mentioned several times during the last third of the century. Harness and saddle making seem to have been profitable occupations, for some of these artisans bought gold, silver, and real estate. On occasion this craft seems to have carried a certain social status. One such craftsman, Ibrahīm ibn Mūsā al-barādi'ī, was the shaykh of the Jerusalem Jewish community in 1600, and even earlier than that some of his professional colleagues seem to have been among the leading Jews of the city.[6]

## *Dealers and Workers in Precious Metals*

As an urban center Jerusalem could offer the outlying villages a variety of services—municipal, administrative, and economic. Among the craftsmen who supplied the needs of Jerusalem's rural hinterland no less than those of its own inhabitants were the dealers and workers in precious metals. Jerusalem's many churches and synagogues attracted a lively influx of pilgrims who enlarged the numbers of those engaged in the trade. It is therefore no coincidence that the city's trade in artifacts of precious metals was intensely active throughout the sixteenth century, especially among Jews and Christians.

Though all the workers and dealers in precious metals (for reasons of brevity I shall refer to them as jewelers) were organized in a single guild, it was divided into two secondary groups, or *ṭā'ifa* (a word also meaning "guild"), Christian and Jewish. Of course, there were Muslim jewlers too, and occasionally a Muslim would head the guild (shaykh *al-ṣuyyāgh*, shaykh *al-ṣayyāghīn*). But the relative importance, and possibly skill as well, of members of the other communities is indicated by the fact that one of their number would sometimes be elected to serve as shaykh of the whole guild. On March 4, 1592, a group of noted Christian and Jewish jewelers complained to the kadi about the Muslim shaykh of their guild, the 'Ustā Shams ibn 'Alī ibn Khālid. Though he denied the charges against him and no other proof was produced, their pressure forced him to resign. The jewelers asked the kadi to nominate a new head in his place; Arsalān ibn Shū'ā the Jew was at once appointed shaykh, and the members of the guild agreed to obey him in everything.[1] All this occurred some three months after the jewelers had gained the kadi's approval for the appointment of Shams as their head. When they found him unsuited to the post which they themselves had offered him, the jewelers of Jerusalem acted to replace him with a Jew. This was not unusual. In August 1559 the Jew Mūsā ibn Hārūn served as shaykh of the jewelers' guild and represented its Christian members before the kadi just as he did the Jews.[2]

The head of the guild was the supreme authority on all matters concerned with the craft (*yakūn shaykh . . . fī ṣināʿatihim wamā yataʿallaq bihā*). All purchases of raw materials—silver and gold—were to be made through him, or at least with his knowledge; the delivery of finished work to clients required his approval; he had to set the price of every product; he arbitrated all disputes between guild members; and in all matters relating to their craft, his decision was binding.[3] It is reasonable to suppose that the jewelers would not have proposed a candidate for so powerful a position without being convinced of his professional ability. The appointment of Jews to this post reflects the respect and appreciation their colleagues felt toward them; it was a significant tribute to their high professional standards.

In recompense for his various services the head of the guild would collect payments from the jewelers, at times even demanding large sums. For example, the jewelers complained to the kadi about Shams ibn ʿAlī ibn Khālid: "he constantly causes them damage and losses, whenever one of them does any work he takes one half the fee, and whosoever gives him nothing, he beats him with his hands and acts to cause him losses."[4] The head of the guild also served as the link between the government and his colleagues. He had to make sure that each jeweler had a guarantor to underwrite him in the event of his being required to pay damages for faulty work. Similar arrangements may have existed in other guilds, but for the jewelers, this was a matter of great importance because of the high cost of the materials. The guarantor would be proposed to the shaykh of the guild; if accepted, the proposal would be brought before the kadi, who would add his formal approval.[5]

Because of the value of the materials, particular importance was attached to determining costs and controlling prices. The jewelers of Jerusalem were forbidden to purchase gold or silver outside the jewelers' market (*sūq al ṣuyyāgh*); they were required to buy materials exclusively through the auctioneer (*dallāl*) who announced the deal, and with the approval of the head of the guild.[6] At the end of the century this procedure was described as a custom preserved from the past. In the early 1580s the jewelers' market was one of the most important in Jerusalem, but this had not been so at the beginning of the century. As far back as 1530, although the jewelers' market was mentioned as the place where silver could be bought in Jerusalem, many of the jewelers did not operate there; in fact, the term *jewelers' market*[7] was not at all prevalent. At the beginning of the 1540s the city's jewelers assured the kadi on oath that they would concentrate all their sales and purchases, as well as the production of silver jewelery, in one place: the sultan's market (*sūq al sulṭān*). A few years passed before this agreement developed into a binding custom. In 1549 a Jewish jeweler repeated his oath to work exclusively in the market, by this time already being referred to by two names: "the sultan's market, known as the jewelers' [market]."[8] The latter name was taking root but was still far from being generally accepted. In 1557 a large group of jewelers came to the kadi to notify him that they had decided to concentrate all their operations in one market. Some of the jewelers still occupied shops they had rented in other parts of the city (in the wickerwork market—*sūq al qushshāsh*—or in the *ḥārat al-yahūd*) and the kadi gave them permission to continue their occupation until the leases expired. But all the others were required to move to the jewelers' market, which was specified as a cluster of shops within the bounds of the merchants' market (*sūq al-tujjār*).[9] One of the Jewish jewelers preferred to work in the Jewish quarter in a shop he had leased from the Muslim religious endowment. Even after the lease expired in 1557 he refused to move to the jewelers' market as requested. He pleaded that "the jewelers' market inside the merchants' market is dark" and that, consequently, he could not work there. When this was found to be true, the weak-sighted craftsman was permitted to go on working in his old shop.[10] The trend toward centralization took shape slowly, but once the custom became general and binding, it served to prevent, or at least to reduce, unfair competition among the jewelers, as well as to strengthen the guild itself.

A primary goal of the guild was to fix prices. To this end the jewelers agreed to manufacture their jewelry from a uniform grade of silver of uniform quality and price.[11] It is reasonable to assume that they used pure silver (*khāliṣ*), the decision to do so being designed to prevent faking or price gouging. However, this regulation proved unenforceable and was apparently revoked some time later. Around 1590 a similar regulation was again published, and the jewelers responded by complaining to the kadi that the prohibition on using low-grade silver (*mu'āmala*) was costing them money. They therefore requested a return to the previous custom of employing both grades of silver. Accordingly, the prohibition was revoked in October 1592. Some six months later manufacture of jewelry from both grades was resumed, and different prices were fixed according to the grade and the quality of the workmanship. The jewelers' guild established two principal categories of silver jewelry: one was manufactured out of pure silver from ingots (*fiḍḍa ḥajar khāliṣ*), whose price was to be 3 *qiṭ'a* per *dirham*, and another *akçe* for the labor; the other employed 14 karat silver (*fiḍḍa mu'āmala al-latī sitta min al 'ashara*), and its price was to be no more than 2 *qiṭ'a* per *dirham*. The first category was for the more expensive jewelry: necklaces (*baghma, janāzir*), bracelets (*'injāṣ*), earrings (*balkhat al-khalk*), and cast pendants (*hayākil*). The second category was for cheaper ornaments: the so-called farmers' jewelry, bracelet rings for the arms, the neck, and the legs (*aswirat al fallāḥīn wa-aṭwāquhum wa-khalākhīluhum*).[12]

Normally, the jewelers' operations were concentrated in the *sūq al-ṣuyyāgh*, where townspeople and neighboring villagers came to buy and sell. There were, however, two exceptions to this rule. One was work carried out in the home of the client, on which there was no restriction whatsoever as to time or place. Attempts appear to have been made by the authorities to eradicate this old custom, but at the request of the jewelers in June 1587 the kadi gave his permission to continue as before.[13] The second exception related to those jewelers who toured the villages, purchasing jewelry from the fellahin, offering their own wares, and fashioning and repairing ornaments to order. This custom had been in existence since the beginning of the century, and no objections had been raised. Most of these tours were confined to the villages in the vicinity of Jerusalem, but they also went farther afield. In 1555, for example, the jeweler Mas'ūd ibn Naftalī went to Nablus on business, continuing to Qabāṭiyya, which was even further; two years earlier, he had sold a gold artifact to one of the high officials in Nablus. Another jeweler, Ya'qūb ibn Yūsuf, had business connections with Sinān, the governor of that town, at the beginning of the 1550s.[14] A number of cases are known of close connections between jewelers and holders of high office, particularly *sipahis* and Janissaries in Jerusalem and Hebron, while there are numerous examples, throughout the course of the century, of the purchase of ornaments from the villagers around Jerusalem and of sales to them.[15]

For obvious reasons, it was difficult to supervise the activities of itinerant jewelers or to control their prices, and the guild attempted to prevent them from working outside the city. In June 1592 two jewelers, Jirjī ibn Yānī the Christian and 'Abd al-Raḥīm the Jew, told the kadi that the shaykh of the jewelers' guild had tried to prevent them from working in their customary way and had even demanded payments from them. Having investigated the matter, the kadi ordered that the two jewelers be permitted to conduct business outside Jerusalem.[16] The volume of trade conducted in the villages seems to have been quite small, and was not enough to exert significant influence on prices in the city or on the quantities of merchandise changing hands there.

Inside the city the authorities exerted supervision with the aid of the *muḥtasib*. Evidence exists, for the first half of the century at least, that he maintained contact with the jewelers directly, without recourse to their shaykh. It is far from clear whether this was the case in the second half of the century, or whether supervision was then enforced with the partial assistance of the shaykh. In any case, by the second half of the 1530s the *muḥtasib* was collecting payments from the jewelers and controlling their prices, as he did in other sectors of the market. Tāj al-Dīn al-Sukkarī, the *muḥtasib* of Jerusalem, declared before the kadi that he was in the habit of collecting a special levy from the jewelers "in season" (*al-mawsim*), the overall sum being divided in a fixed ratio: he took two-thirds of the levy from the Jewish jewelers and one-third from the Christians. Probably the season was the period of pilgrimages—spring, with its festivals of Passover and Easter—especially since the same order mentions Christian and

Jewish pilgrims. That time of year probably witnessed an increased demand for jewelry, mementos, religious requisites for the fulfillment of vows, and gifts, and the *muḥtasib* was in the habit of collecting his share. Evidently the Jews saw nothing wrong with this arrangement, so it is clear that the Jews did better business than their Christian colleagues. There is no reason to suppose that Jews bought most of their ornaments from Christian jewelers, but Jewish jewelers sold at least part of their merchandise to Christian pilgrims, thus increasing the turnover of their business. The Jews were therefore required to pay more.[17]

By mid-1538 the *muḥtasib* was collecting a fixed annual tax from the jewelers known as the Thursday tax (*ʿādat al-khamīs*), and in that year its collection was to be completed by the beginning of March. The timing of the collection suggests that this development arose out of the earlier levy. This tax was collected at the rate of 600 *akçe* annually "when Thursday came around" (*ʿinda awān al-khamīs*) or "whenever it occurred," terms that point to some specific public event, most probably a Christian feast day falling on a Thursday, when the jewelers—Jews as well as Christians—gained increased income from sales to pilgrims and perhaps to residents too.[18] The jewelers paid this tax for several years but regarded it as an unjust burden. When Jaʿfar Bey, charged with registration and examination of incomes in the district (*kātib al-wilāya al-sharīfa*), visited Jerusalem, the jewelers complained about it. The official found their claim justified: even the new tax registers contained nothing to sanction the collection of this tax by the *muḥtasib*. In September 1541 Jaʿfar decreed that it was forbidden to collect any tax of this kind, since it was contrary to the Shariʿa and the *Qanun*.[19]

From that year onward such illegal levies were no longer imposed upon the jewelers, but the *muḥtasib*s did not relinquish their attempts to obtain supplementary revenue. At the beginning of July 1555 the Jerusalem jewelers complained to the kadi about the two *muḥtasibs* then officiating in the city on the grounds that these men harassed the jewelers by imposing payments on the pretext that their weights were faulty. The jewelers claimed that these accusations were false, and moreover that the testing of their weights was in contravention of past custom and of the laws of the Ottoman *Qanun*. The jewelers submitted documents to the kadi proving that this function required the appointment of a Jerusalem kadi, whose commission was to come from the capital. Mawlā Tamīmī Çelebi was brought before the city's Hanafi kadi, to whom he presented a valid letter of appointment that entrusted him with responsibility for the scales, weights, and other instruments employed by the city's jewelers. The *muḥtasibs* were then forbidden to test the jewelers' weights or to employ such a pretext to disrupt their work or make demands for unsanctioned payments.[20] This decision is of interest beyond the narrow context of the relationship between the guild and the *muḥtasib*. There was apparently nothing illegal in the demand of the *muḥtasibs*, who were, after all, responsible for testing the weights and measures in use in the city, a task they discharged by virtue of the *Qanun-Name*, and which was one of their principal functions in all other economic sectors. But in view of the high costs of the materials used by the jewelers, it was of great importance to maintain strict control over their instruments and weights, for which purpose a separate functionary was appointed—a kadi who displayed a high level of religious learning and enjoyed an equally high level of public confidence. It is not clear whether this exceptional arrangement was upheld for any length of time. It seems probable that the *muḥtasibs* succeeded in the course of the century in bringing this task back under their supervision. In any case, this episode is further proof of the great economic value of the jewelry trade, its special status among the crafts, and the unusual sensitivity the authorities displayed toward the members of this profession. It is not at all clear whether the appointment of the kadi also arose out of a desire to maintain close control of the guild, most of whose members were Jews and Christians. The presence of a large number of protected persons (*ahl al-dhimma*) among the jewelers, probably played its part in establishing an arrangement whereby a person of religious authority and exceptional public and moral standing was put in charge of a vital feature of their operation.

Jerusalem also had its Muslim jewelers, some richer and more important than their non-Muslim colleages, who even numbered Jews among their clientele.[21] And jewelers belonging to the minority communities naturally had numerous dealings with Muslims, whether high officials, city residents or villagers from the vicinity. Thus, there was considerable professional integration among members of the various communities, even if, as seems likely, the purchaser's religious and family ties were often instrumental in the selection of a jeweler. One of the unusual features of this craft was that the number of Jews and Christians engaged in it far exceeded their relative ratio in the population of Jerusalem. Consequently, many of the regulations and complaints concerning jewelers originated with, and related to, members of the minority communities. Hardly a year went by without mention of dealings or litigation involving a Jewish jeweler. Since the jeweler was often referred to by his first name alone, it is impossible to establish identity. Still, it is possible to draw a number of clear conclusions. Five Jewish jewelers referred to by name are mentioned several times, particularly during the latter half of the century. In the early 1590s as many as ten Jewish jewelers are mentioned. These numbers represent a very large concentration of Jews, exceeding anything encountered in other trades. No doubt the impression created among the public and the ruling circles was of a presence that exceeded their actual numbers. Several of the jewelers are mentioned repeatedly over a long period: 'Azar ibn Hārūn (1530–1536), Isḥāq ibn Sabtōn (1531–1550), Ibrahīm ibn Isḥāq (1550–1558), Da'ūd ibn 'Amrān (1554–1562), Sulaymān ibn Sulaymān (1591–1597). Two others were active over a particularly extended period: Mas'ūd ibn Naftalī (1552–1567) and Ibrahīm ibn Faraj-Allāh (1541–1567). It may be assumed that these persons operated over an even longer period, but since they did not appear before the Shari'a court, no evidence has been preserved.

There are indications that, in at least some instances, the trade was passed on from father to son, or among several members of a single family, such as Isḥāq ibn Sabtōn (1531–1550) and Nissīm ibn Sabtōn (1530–1542); 'Abd al-Raḥīm the Karaite, the son of Ibrahīm, a Jerusalem jeweler from 1584 till at least 1592, was almost certainly the son of the Karaite Ibrahīm ibn Faraj-Allāh; Ibrahīm ibn Mas'ūd (1581–1587 at least) was probably the son of Mas'ūd ibn Naftalī ibn Ibrahīm.

The nicknames of some of the Jewish jewelers seem to show that they originated in various parts of the empire. Several were tagged *al-Maghribī* (from North Africa); there were also *al-Shāmī* (from Damascus), *al-Rūmī* (from Anatolia or Rumeli),[22] *al-Miṣrī* (from Cairo), and others. Of particular interest is the status of the Karaite jewelers, who were active throughout the century; moreover, they achieved a degree of skill and importance surpassing that of their colleagues. Ibrahīm ibn Faraj-Allāh the Karaite was known throughout his long years of activity as *al-mu'allim*, meaning that he had reached the highest grade in the guild's hierarchy.[23] Moreover, Ibrahīm also functioned as a moneychanger (*ṣayrafī*) in the service of a high official, Muṣṭafā Çelebi, charged with collecting the *jizya* in Palestine in 1565–66. He even conducted various deals with the head of the Jerusalem administration, such as the *sanjaq bey*, his lieutenant (*ketkhuda*), and the *subashi* of the city.

This same Ibrahīm, the son of Ṣadaqa, who had been the lessee of the mint in Damascus (*mu'allim dār al-ḍarb*), in addition to inheriting his father's interest and expertise in money matters probably also inherited more substantial assets. In any event, there is evidence in various forms that he owned considerable property in Jerusalem.[24] Another jeweler, Mas'ūd ibn Naftalī, also attained a position of importance: at the beginning of 1562 he was even appointed shaykh and mutakallim of Jerusalem's Jewish community, a capacity in which he dealt with a very wide range of matters of common interest to the community.[25] As we have seen, persons appointed to the latter post were characterized by their solid financial standing, and it is no surprise that Mas'ūd the jeweler was a man of means. There is no way to obtain a quantitative assessment of the wealth of the Jewish jewelers, but one figure might serve as some indication: A Muslim jeweler who died in Jerusalem in 1572, left property that amounted to the almost legendary sum of a quarter of a million *para*.[26] Even if he was exceptionally wealthy, it is reasonable to assume that his colleagues also earned impressive incomes. This unusual level of comfort was especially true of the Jews and Christians, who were, after all, members of an underprivileged minority that, according to the conventional stereotype, suffered great poverty and misery.

## *Spice Merchants*

Despite the discovery of the route around the Cape of Good Hope at the end of the fifteenth century, the spice traffic continued to pass through the Middle East on its way to Europe from the Orient. It was believed for many years that the discovery of the sea lane around Africa had diverted this trade from its traditional routes. But the studies of F. Braudel and others in European sources, as well as those of H. Inalcık showed that this was not true. For many years to come, and through the first half of the sixteenth century, the spice trade continued to flow briskly from the Far East to Europe through Egypt and the Mediterranean Sea.[1] A study of the protocols of the Shari'a court shows that Inalcık's conclusion can be extended to include the second half of the sixteenth century as well, and that some of this commerce reached as far as Jerusalem. Coffee, obviously an imported product, appeared in Jerusalem at that time in even larger quantities than before, and in the early 1560s five new coffee houses opened in the city.[2] Evidence that the spice trade was flourishing in Jerusalem at that time is much broader and more far reaching. The spice merchants' market was renovated, along with other markets in the city, as a means of stimulating commerce. But in the spice market, unlike in the others, not only were the existing shops repaired but new ones were built and surrounded by protective walls to separate them from the old market. In January of 1565 people in the city were already differentiating between the new spice merchants' market (*sūq al-'aṭṭārīn al-jadīd*) and the old one (*sūq al-'aṭṭārīn al-qadīm*).[3]

The distinction between the two centers did not last long. Since they were adjacent to one another, and the nature of the business transacted in them was very similar, people were soon referring to the spice merchants' market without differentiating between new and old. Jews played various roles in this market, and their presence was quite conspicuous. Precise quantitative conclusions are hard to establish, for the statistics available are incomplete, but certain data allow us to grasp the importance of the Jews in the development of Jerusalem's spice trade. In 1587 the spice merchants' market, which belonged to the *waqf* of the Dome of the Rock, had 17 shops, all rented for the extended period of nine years, rather than the usual one to three years. Such long-term leases were intended as a further spur to trade, for they introduced an element of stability, encouraging the lessees to invest in renovations and maintenance and to intensify their overall activity. One shop was rented to a Christian, five to Muslims, and 11, or two-thirds of the shops, to Jews. No attempt was made to impose equal quotas on these three groups, such as was made in Jerusalem's *sūq al-qaṭṭānīn*, and the Jews were clearly the dominant element.[4] This does not mean that the Jews accounted for two-thirds of all the spice dealers. It may be assumed that some Muslims and Christians involved in spice trading subleased or owned the shops in which they conducted their business. Nevertheless, other documents do indicate that there was an active Jewish element in this trade, and relatively few Muslims and even fewer Christians. The shops run by the members of the three religious groups existed side by side, and good neighborly relations prevailed despite natural competition.[5]

At least one of the Jews, Murdakhay al-Qarrā, was a Karaite, but the majority were not. There were some for whom selling spices in the market was only one way of making a living; among those who had other callings were Yahūdā the locksmith (*al-ḥaddād*), Yūsuf the slaughterer (*al-dhabbāḥ*), and ʻAbd al-Karīm, a doctor who had a shop in the spice dealers' market which he probably rented.[6] There were some Jewish families in which this trade was the hereditary occupation. For example, Yūsuf ibn ʻAbd al-Karīm and his son Yaʻqūb were both spice dealers, and Yūsuf's wife, was the daughter of another spice merchant, Ibrahīm ibn Hilāl.[7]

Some of the spice merchants were among the heads of the Jewish community: Saʻīd *al ʻaṭṭār* at the close of the 1550s; Salamūn ibn Shullāl and Ibrahīm ibn Hilāl at the beginning of the 1560s; and Yūsuf ibn ʻAbd al-Karīm at the beginning of the 1590s, who was even appointed the spokesman of the community.[8] This indicates a certain economic as well as social status; indeed, there were dealers in spices in Jerusalem who owned real estate in Cairo, and others among them bought fruit orchards not far from the city, in one case in the village of Bayt Mazmīl.[9]

The wares sold by these merchants usually came from Cairo, which may explain their purchase of real estate there. But some of them imported their merchandise from Damascus. Thus, spices and flavorings from the distant Orient reached Jerusalem's merchants over the Red Sea or by the traditional *Ḥajj* route. Ordinarily these merchants disposed of their wares inside the city, but on occasion they sold to other parts of Palestine as well. For example, indigo was marketed in Safed. As their name indicates, most of their trade was in Oriental spices and condiments: indigo, coffee, sugar, pepper, cloves, cinnamon. They sometimes sold soap, and one Jewish spice merchant's shop also carried lengths of cloth, a bow, and a sword.[10]

While this last was rather an unusual inventory, it nevertheless indicates another commercial realm in which the spice merchants engaged to an ever-greater extent: the buying and selling of metals. At the beginning of the 1540s a Jewish spice merchant's sale of lead sheeting to a Muslim buyer, although exceptional, was a manifestation of the gradual development of trade in iron. In 1590 the leaders of the Muslim, Jewish, and Christian spice merchants complained to the kadi that the locksmiths (*ḥaddādīn*) were provoking them with their attempts to prevent them from buying iron and their threats to confiscate it. As a result of this dispute, in the presence of the head of the locksmiths' guild (shaykh *al-ḥaddādīn*) and the head of the veterinarians (shaykh *al-bayāṭira*), the heads of the spice merchants declared that they would not buy or sell any more iron, for which promise the kadi gave assurance that they would not be molested further.[11] The spice merchants were so powerful that in the long run the metalworkers were unable to keep them from selling iron in the city. At the beginning of February 1592 representatives of the veterinarians and the locksmiths again came to the kadi, accompanied by a group of spice merchants—only Jews this time. They declared that they had reached agreement among themselves to share equally in the purchase of iron, as well as in selling it to customers in Jerusalem and elsewhere. By the end of the century the Jewish spice merchants, to a greater extent than the non-Jewish ones, were dealing in iron, with the approval of the kadi and the grudging support of the iron merchants.[12]

It may be that the Jews were granted this prerogative because of their contacts with suppliers from abroad; or it may have been a result of their presence in great numbers in this trade. The Jews, however, were not isolated. The spice merchants' guild included members of all the religious groups. In February 1565 the guild members were procrastinating over the choice of their leaders, so the kadi summoned some of their influential members and instructed them in clear, even threatening terms to "appoint a shaykh and crier (*dallāl*) in order to deal with the sale of merchandise [in their possession] in accordance with past custom."[13] The structure and systems that governed this trade were essentially like those of other groups. The Jews, although conspicuous in their strength and status within the trade, were nonetheless considered part of the guild as a whole.

When the spice merchants felt that they were being harassed and turned to the kadi for assistance, Jews were again conspicuous among their representatives. At the beginning of October 1538 Mūsā Ibn Faraj-Allāh the Jew[14] submitted to the kadi a document in the name of the *defterdar* 'Alī bey, which explicitly forbade the *muḥtasib* of Jerusalem to enter the spice dealers' market for the purpose of confiscating their wares and obligating the venders to purchase soap at an exorbitant price. In short, it forbade the *muḥtasib* from harassing them in any way at all. This document had been written at the end of March 1534. The fact that five years later it was submitted by the Jewish spice merchants and adopted by the kadi indicates that the harassment had not ceased even after the original *muḥtasib* had been replaced.

In the middle of June 1552 a delegation of three Jewish and three Muslim spice merchants again lodged complaints with the kadi against the two *muḥtasib*s of the city, who were compelling them to buy goods at unreasonably high prices (*ṭarḥ*). Although the men denied the accusation, the kadi read them the *firman* cited in the 1534 document and explicitly prohibited further harassment.[15] For a few years the spicedealers seem to have been relieved of pressure from the *muḥtasib*s, although at the beginning of June 1563 the issue arose again. This time the spice merchants of Jerusalem were represented by a Muslim, a Christian, and Salamūn ibn Mūsā, a Jew. They told the kadi that at the end of 1562 they had sent a representative to Istanbul to complain about the "*muḥtasib*'s henchmen" who interefered with them, mainly in the sale of seasonings (*bahar*), and the Sublime Porte had issued instructions that the subject was to be studied and the facts clarified; if the claim was found correct, a recurrence was to be prevented. The public importance of the issue can be gathered from the fact that in addition to the two incumbent *muḥtasib*s, the city's *subashi* was also present at the hearing, having been sent to represent the governor. The kadi compared the complaint with the document issued in 1538 and with the text as formulated in the *Qanun-Name* of Jerusalem. He determined that the *muḥtasib* had no right to levy charges on the spice merchants' market and thus forbade the *muḥtasib* to enter the markct, to disturb the venders, and to oblige them to purchase wares at exorbitant prices. A year later the judgment had apparently not been implemented, for again representatives of the Muslims, Christians, and Jews (Salamūn ibn Shullāl and Ibrahīm ibn Hilāl) had to complain to the kadi.[16]

There is only one logical explanation for the recurrent attempts to prevent the *muḥtasib*s from interfering with the spice merchants: In this case the interests of the merchants coincided with those of the empire's economic policy makers. Of course, the *muḥtasib*s kept trying to corner a portion of these merchants' profits, and their obstinate endeavors to do so despite prohibition after prohibition is a good indication of the profitability of the spice trade in Jerusalem and the envy in which those who plied it were held.

The Jews, an important element among the spicedealers, were frequently the spokesmen for the entire guild, and were always well represented in the delegations to the authorities, either in Jerusalem or in the capital. It should, however, be stressed, that they never petitioned the authorities about difficulties they experienced as Jews but spoke in the name of their trade. From this standpoint, they were an integral and important part of Jerusalem's society and economy.

## *Jewish Physicians*

During the sixteenth century Jews served as high-ranking physicians in Istanbul.[1] There were also quite a few Jewish doctors in Jerusalem; I found records of at least ten (the first in 1531, the last in 1587), and there were very likely more. Three of these men were mentioned over a long period of time: 'Abd al-Karīm ibn Mūsā (1532–1552), 'Abd al-Karīm ibn 'Abd al-Laṭīf (1550–1561), and Yūsuf ibn Ibrahīm (1552–1578). The others were mentioned specifically in the *sijill* only at certain times, but it may be assumed that many of them also were professionally active for a number of years. The relatively high proportion of Karaites among the doctors is conspicuous: ʿAbd al-Karīm ibn Mūsā, ʿAbd al-Karīm ibn ʿAbd al-Laṭīf, and Shams al-Dīn (1587) were all Karaites. The first two were leaders of the sect, managed its property and trust funds, and looked after its members' affairs. One of the other doctors, Yūsuf ibn Ibrahīm, was originally from Alexandria.

There was a variety of names for these Jewish doctors—*ṭabīb, ḥakīm, muṭabbib*—sometimes used interchangeably, indicating that there was no real difference. There were also Jews in Jerusalem known as *jarrāḥ*, or "he who heals wounds," "surgeon." These have always been regarded as less important than the physicians and less reliable professionally, but in order to become qualified they had to undergo special training. In 1577, for example, the Muslim head of the *jarrāḥ*s in Jerusalem announced that he was warning the Jew Shiḥāda ibn Ibrahīm not to offer himself yet as qualified to undertake the duties of this profession; until completing his *jirāḥa* studies, he was strictly forbidden to undertake any independent medical tasks such as amputating limbs.[2] There were Jewish women known as *kaḥḥāla*, a title specific to eye doctors. They probably dealt in cosmetics and prepared the special materials used for antimony (*kuḥl*), as a result of which they also acquired skill in dealing with eye maladies.[3]

The Jewish physicians in Jerusalem doctored all the residents of the city. There was, however, a special delicacy in their treating a Muslim: any mishap or calamity, which in the case of a Muslim doctor would not elicit extraordinary reactions, could well call forth individual or group revenge. Thus, there were times, probably in connection with a severe or complicated illness, when a Muslim would declare before the kadi that he had agreed to be treated by the doctor and would not hold him responsible for his failure.[4]

The Jewish physician was considered by his patients and his colleagues to be on a par with the Muslim physicians. In 1547 the Muslim head doctor (*ra'īs al-aṭṭibā'*) had to leave Jerusalem to stay in Istanbul for a few months. Having to appoint replacements for himself in the hospital (*fi khidmat al-bimāristān*), he appointed a Christian and a Jew, ʿAbd al-Karīm ibn Mūsā.[5] The latter, as we have seen, took an active part in public affairs and also attained a high professional status: he was called *al-ra'īs* or *al-rayyis,* that is "head and first," although formally he was no longer the head of the physicians' guild. Another Jewish physician, Kamāl ibn Mūsā, was also given this title, and he actually did hold the position of head of Jerusalem's doctors. In July 1571 Kamāl (referred to not only by his official title, but also with a description of his great skill, *al-ṭabīb al-ḥadīq,* "skilled doctor") had to leave for a three-month stay in Cairo. As a substitute for himself he chose a Muslim doctor, who also bore the honorable title generally reserved for judges or high religious personnel—*mawlānā, "our master."* The kadi formally granted Kamāl's leave and approved his replacement.[6]

The temporary substitute for a head doctor received not only the responsibilities but also the salary (*waẓīfa*) of the man he replaced. The other doctors also received regular salaries, no doubt graduated in accordance with their professional status. The Jewish doctor Yūsuf ibn Salamūn was court physician to the sultan (*tabib-i khassa*) in the Galata Saray hospital in Istanbul. His request to be transferred to Jerusalem was approved with the added provision that because of his outstanding skill in medical science (*tibabet*) and in the field then known as intuitive physiognomy (*firaset*), he would be given a 50 percent raise in salary. The increase in salary may also have been intended as compensation for moving from the capital of the empire to the relatively isolated city of Jerusalem. He was appointed for six months as of the middle of October 1564, during which period he received his salary at the new rate from Damascus. After that, beginning April 2, 1565, his Jerusalem appointment was renewed for a year at the same salary. During that year, as stated in the *berat,* his official appointment, he would be paid from the state treasury 15 *akçe* a day, which is a total salary of 67½ *sultani* per year. The *muḥtasib* of Jerusalem was responsible for making the payments that were to be transmitted to Yūsuf ibn Salamūn in several installments in the course of the year. A study of the expenditures made by the *muḥtasib* shows that he actually paid the total sum due to the Jewish doctor.[7]

Although physicians sometimes came to Jerusalem from as far away as Istanbul or Alexandria, they were considered part of the local community, and an important part for that matter. Just as the Karaite physicians played a central role in the conduct of the affairs of their congregation, the other Jewish doctors were in an even more prominent position, for they influenced the management of affairs affecting all the Jews. An important aspect of their involvement in the community was their readiness to act as guarantors for Jews who needed security. The Karaite doctors, quite naturally, tended to underwrite loans for the Karaites in Jerusalem as early as 1532. There were some outstanding Jewish personalities for whom only doctors, because of the social and economic status, were in a position to stand security. The physician Yūsuf ibn Ibrahīm, for example, in 1552 put up a guarantee for another Jew, secretary of the *khāṣṣ* revenues. When the secretary did not appear in court after being summoned, the guarantor was arrested. Rifqa, wife of the physician, then undertook to bring the secretary to court, promising that otherwise she herself would pay his debt. However, as the matter was apparently a most serious one, the doctor's wife had to bring somebody to put up security for her. She brought Yūsuf ibn Shū'ā, the commissioner of the *khāṣṣ* revenues. In another case, in 1575, when the wealthy cloth merchant Ma'īr ibn Ibrahīm needed a guarantor, another doctor, *al-rayyis* Yūsuf ibn Isḥāq, was his underwriter.[8]

It is not surprising that Jewish physicians were accepted as guarantors, since they were considered men of great means. An example is the Jewish doctor Yūsuf ibn Ibrahīm, who owned a house in Jerusalem and in 1578 bought himself another one. By virtue of their wealth and status they served the public in a variety of ways. Salamūn the Jewish doctor, who appeared before the kadi several times as one of the leaders of the community when important public issues were debated, is one example. Another is the Karaite physician 'Abd al-Karīm ibn 'Abd al-Laṭīf, who appeared several times in the role of public figure. Such personal standing and profound involvement were undoubtedly among the factors that motivated the Jewish community to recommend that the kadi appoint the doctor Kamāl ibn Mūsā as their dayyān and leader in 1570–71.[9]

Some of these doctors worked in the hospital in the city, while others, like their non-Jewish colleagues, maintained clinics in which they treated patients. They were not concentrated in one area of the city, although shops were rented for this purpose in the spice dealers' market, and these merchants very likely supplied the doctors with some of the ingredients they used for medicines. The Jewish doctor could feel quite at home there, although Muslim doctors used the same shops. In 1570–71, for example, the Jewish doctor Kamāl ibn Mūsā paid 5 *para* a month rent for a shop in the market that had previously been used as a clinic by a Muslim doctor. Another Jewish physician maintained his rights to a shop and even kept many bottles of medicine there, although he was absent from Jerusalem for two years.[10]

Jewish physicians also lived in the Jewish neighborhood. This was not an obligation imposed upon them by others; they chose to live there for the same reasons all the other Jews did. The regulations that applied to all other Jews applied to him as well. At the beginning of December 1564 a group of some five Jewish men came to the kadi. They were heads of the community, artisans and businessmen—a jeweler, a tanner, a spicedealer, and so on. They complained that the doctor Sulaymān ibn 'Alī, who had been living in their neighborhood in Jerusalem for a long time, had become an undesirable element in the community, acting in an antisocial fashion. Since public pressure was not making him change his ways, they wanted him removed from their midst. They apparently brought quite convincing evidence to the kadi, for he ruled that Sulaymān must leave the Jewish neighborhood.[11]

## *Locksmiths*

In the course of the sixteenth century it was possible to find more than 20 Jews in Jerusalem who were called locksmiths (*ḥaddād*) or were described as working in the metal crafts. In any year there were usually one or two, although in 1556 five Jews were named among "the Jewish group of locksmiths" (*ṭā'ifat al-yahūd al-ḥaddādīn*). The year 1565 was altogether unusual in that nine Jews appeared before the Hanafi kadi and declared that they belonged to the locksmiths of the Jerusalem district.[1] At least two of them seem to have come from other professions: one had coated household utensils with zinc (Shmū'īl *al-mubayyiḍ*), and the other was the son of a carpenter (Ibrahīm ibn *al-najjār*). But at that time there appears to have been a great demand for locksmiths, and many more new people than usual were attracted to the craft. The 1560s were years of economic development in Jerusalem in general, but between 1563 and 1566 the gates and doors of several markets and many shops in the city were either being repaired or were made anew.[2] This was certainly a factor in the increased demand for locksmiths.

In 1544 the *subashi* of Jerusalem learned that the key to one of the city's gates had fallen into the hands of thieves. This endangered the safety of the city's inhabitants and property, since no guards were stationed at the gates that were locked every night. By order of the governor all the locksmiths of Jerusalem were brought to be interrogated, two Jews among them—Ḥabīb ibn Shmū'īl and Sāsī ibn Ibrahīm.[3]

These men were considered locksmiths of the district, and not only the city of Jerusalem; they were thus expected to do work in the nearby villages. It was quite usual for some of them—Jews and non-Jews—to make the rounds of the district's rural communities, doing the necessary jobs. Those who worked outside the city (*fi'l-barr*, or "in the field") had to get explicit approval to do so from the head of their guild. Anyone who went out to the villages without such approval was heavily fined (2000 *akçe*), and it was even said hyperbolically that "his blood [was] on his head" (*yakūn damuhu hadr*).[4] These men were not satisfied to work at their own craft only, and as they made the rounds from village to village, they tried their hand at commerce as well. During harvest time they would buy fruit from the peasants and bring it back to sell in Jerusalem. Thus, the *muḥtasib* accused the Jewish locksmith Yahūdā ibn Mūsā, who at the beginning of June 1560 sold apples from his home, of two transgressions: not only was he using defective weights and scales, but he was selling produce, albeit to Jews, before it had been brought to the market as required, and before his weights and scales had been tested.[5]

The Jewish locksmiths were part of the general locksmiths' guild, which was headed by the shaykh *al-ḥaddādīn*, sometimes also called *mutakallim* or *rayyis*.[6] From the few examples available, it appears that a Christian sometimes held this position (for instance in 1591) and sometimes a former military man (*timar* holder, 1536–37, *jawīsh*, 1549), but I found no case of a Jew being at the head of the locksmiths. However, Jewish locksmiths were included among the heads of the Jewish community. In 1538–39, when the *subashi* of Jerusalem chose ten Jews whom he would accept as guarantors for their brethren, one of them was Mūsā the locksmith. In the second half of the 1570s Yahūda ibn Mūsā the locksmith was among those who came to complain or to make demands in matters of public concern such as attacks on the synagogues or the reporting of the Jewish community's *jizya* taxes. In the 1580s Mūsā ibn Yahūdā the locksmith—called in one place "son of a locksmith," possibly the son of the abovementioned Mūsā—was also one of the Jewish notables who underwrote a large debt that the community owed the *waqf*.[7] It may be that there was some confusion in the listing of the name, and that rather than being the son of Mūsā it was Mūsā himself. To further confound the issue, in that same year, 1585, Yahūdā ibn Mūsā the locksmith is again mentioned as a wealthy man who in addition to working in his craft dealt in the purchase of silver and gold.[8] The exact identity of the man or men is not clear, but the available information is sufficient to enable us to reach certain conclusions. First, it is probable that this is an example of father and son following the same profession, a situation found in other callings and with respect to Jews as well as non-Jews. Second, a high social status, at least in some cases, accompanied the locksmith's craft. Third, this social status went hand in hand with economic status, and perhaps even stemmed from it. The locksmith traded in precious metals, which required a large capital investment. Further proof of his solid economic situation was his willingness to offer his property and capital as security, in the case of Mūsā for a debt of 400 *qurūsh*.[9]

The locksmiths too were organized in a guild headed by a shaykh. The guild dealt with the organization of professional activities and also with the centralized purchase of iron and its allocation among the various locksmiths. Nails and steel were bought separately on an individual basis. The guild as an entity also paid certain fees that the members then repaid. The larger the number paying, the smaller the amount each had to pay, so the members sometimes tried to shunt part of the burden onto people who were not in the profession. At the end of March 1601 the Jewish shoemaker Nāṣir ibn Sa'āda complained to the kadi that the title locksmith had been forced on him. According to him the shaykh of the Jewish community was in collusion with those who were molesting him and had testified that he had to pay the same fees as the locksmiths. Only after Nāṣir had brought two Jews to testify to the truth of his claim before the judge was the shaykh al-yahūd ordered to stop harassing him in this way.[10] It is interesting to note that no mention is made of the shaykh of the guild in this case. The power of the locksmiths' guild was obviously limited, at least at the end of the century, and the role of its shaykh even more so. Determining whether a person belonged to the guild was surely one of his basic functions, but in this case the shaykh of the Jews had assumed the right to make such a decision. It seems clear that although the guild functioned normally in some spheres, its structure was relatively loose as compared with that of other such organizations, at least at the end of the century, and various matters that concerned the locksmiths, Jews as well as non-Jews, were arranged directly with the authorities.

## *Cloth Merchants*

Jews in Jerusalem dealt in cloth as both manufacturers and traders. The various stages of production were not as well developed in sixteenth-century Jerusalem as they were in Safed and even in Nablus, for Jerusalem lacked the resource of nearby flowing water that was vital for this industry. Jews who were professional clothmakers would not have settled in Jerusalem.[1] Nevertheless, at the end of the century there is reference to a shop in the Jewish neighborhood "that is intended for beating cloth"[2] as part of the dyeing process; there is also a single reference, in 1558, to a Jewish weaver (*ḥayyāk*).[3] But these may be looked upon as exceptional cases. In this craft the Jew was mainly involved in the final process: tailoring. Jews in Jerusalem worked in this profession (*khayyāṭ*) throughout the century. They sewed to order, working with whatever fabric either Jews or Muslims, more frequently the latter, gave them. The professional level of these tailors was apparently considered high; this may be assumed from the title *al-mu'allim* affixed to the name of a Jewish tailor, as well as from the fact that the governor, who surely sought the best craftsmen in the city, used the services of a Jewish tailor. There were also Jewesses who worked as independent seamstresses (*khayyāṭa*) for many years, sewing for men as well as women; Klārā bint Shmū'īl the seamstress is mentioned in 1558–59, and again in 1565, and Stiya the seamstress in 1577.[4]

Jews, however, were best known as cloth merchants (*jawkhī*). Sometimes, of course, the tailor also bought and sold cloth, whereupon he was known by the double appellation *al-khayyāṭ al-jawkhī*,[5] but more usually buying and selling cloth was a separate calling. Since there was a developed textile industry in Palestine, it is not surprising to find Jewish merchants who dealt in fabrics. The rapid development, particularly in Safed, of textile manufacturing in the course of the century undoubtedly influenced the growth of markets both abroad and within the country, while increasing the volume of business carried by the merchants of Jerusalem.

Jerusalem's Jewish cloth merchants imported from Muslim merchants in Damascus various kinds of cloth, some of it produced in Syria and some brought from afar with the *ḥajj* caravans. The Jewish merchants also had commercial contacts with cloth merchants in Istanbul. Maintaining close relations with the Christian monasteries in Jerusalem, they were able not only to sell to pilgrims but to buy from them as well. Knowing foreign languages was of great help to the Jews in creating and maintaining these commercial contacts. The notables of Jerusalem itself, both the supreme kadi (*qadi al-qudat*) and the governor, were also good customers for their wares, and sometimes were even a source of supply.

Despite their expert knowledge, these cloth merchants were not above trying their hand at buying and selling other products. In the early 1560s, when the governor chose to pay in kind for a debt he owed the Jewish cloth merchant 'Iliās ibn Ibrahīm, the Jew agreed. He received a consignment of olive oil and another of alkali, which the governor had illicitly collected from the city's soap manufacturers. As part of their trade with Damascus these Jews imported, in addition to cloth, various spices from the Far East. Painters (*ṣabbāgh*) bought a large quantity of indigo for their paint from the Jew Ma'īr ibn Ibrahīm al-Jawkhī, and on another occasion this same Ma'īr bought a large consignment of wheat from the former governor.[6]

Some of the outside occupations in which the cloth merchants engaged deviated quite sharply from their usual calling. The best example of this is Yāsif ibn Sha'bān, a respected cloth dealer who at the end of the century was appointed moneychanger in the public soup kitchen (*'imaret*) of Khasseki Sultan, for which he received the usual salary of one *akçe* per day.[7] Another cloth dealer doubled as interpreter for pilgrims from Europe.

Over and above their network of contacts and the constant development of textile manufacturing in Palestine, and beyond their diligence and varied occupations, there is another reason for the success of the cloth merchants. In Jerusalem at that time cloth was considered not only as the raw material for clothing but as a means of payment and a form of savings. People paid cash debts in cloth, while in legacies of both Jews and non-Jews various kinds of fabrics were an important component of a person's property.[8] Jews also used cloth to pay taxes and various other fees. In the middle of 1535, for example, the *subashi* of Hebron accompanied a group of Jewish pilgrims from Jerusalem to hebron and back. They paid him for his services and also paid the khafar tax on the way with six *dhirā'* (that is, arm lengths) of cloth for the *subashi*, and five *dhirā'* for the tax.[9] There was certainly a measure of economic logic in this approach to cloth as legal tender, the best proof of which seems to be the continued use of the system. The very concept of cloth as a credible means of payment certainly advanced its sale, and obviously the Jewish cloth merchants were not the only ones who benefited.

The Jewish cloth merchants conducted an extensive and varied trade with a widely assorted clientele and apparently made a fine profit. For example, the Jew Yūsuf ibn Isḥāq al-*'Ifranjī*, a cloth merchant from Jerusalem, in 1547 was owed large sums of money by the kadi of Nablus, the *ketkhuda* of the Jerusalem Citadel, and others. At the end of March 1566 another Jewish cloth merchant, 'Ilyās ibn Ibrahīm, collected 500 *sultani* from the governor of Jerusalem. In September 1594 *khawājā* Ma'īr ibn Ibrahām, the Jewish cloth merchant, owed the head of the merchants in Jerusalem, the shaykh *al-tujjār*, a large debt for great quantities of fabric. The title *khōjā* (sometimes *khawājā*), which was ordinarily applied to wealthy Muslim merchants, was used alongside the names of some of the Jewish cloth merchants as well. In 1546 Aslān ibn Ibrahīm was so called, as were Ma'īr ibn Ibrahām (or Ibrahīm) and Yāsif ibn Sha'bān, in the last decade of the century. The last two were among the leading members of the Jewish community for many years and as such not only represented the rest of the Jews in matters of public interest but even, in the presence of the kadi, underwrote the community's debts, sometimes in conjunction with other Jews.[10]

The great wealth of Ma'īr and Yāsif and their intense involvement in public affairs and commerce with other parts of the empire are underscored by the fact that on August 16, 1594 these two Jewish merchants appeared before the kadi and showed him a document according to which the kadi of al-Madina owed a Jewish merchant from Istanbul, whose name was Karsūn, 20,000 *akçe* for cloth and for a loan. This Karsūn had transferred his right to collect the debt to Ma'īr and Yasif in Jerusalem, and they had collected the entire amount from the kadi of al-Madina. Appearing now before the kadi of Jerusalem, they reported the entire affair and declared its successful conclusion. Surely the reason for this arrangement was that the Jewish merchants from Jerusalem had ways of forcing the kadi to pay that Karsūn in the distant capital did not have, for example, by subtracting the amount of the loan from payments to which he was entitled in Jerusalem. Although the two Jewish *jawkhīs* presumably exercised their personal influence, they themselves gained no profit from their successful action. Karsūn had authorized them not only to collect the debt but to distribute the entire sum among the poor Jews of Jerusalem. They did so, and confirmed their actions before the kadi.[11]

Evidently the Jewish cloth merchants were a powerful and wealthy group within the Jewish community and in Jerusalem as a whole. 'Azar ibn Ibrahīm, a Jewish cloth merchant, is mentioned in April 1556 as the interpreter for a group of Catholic pilgrims during the Easter season.[12] He needed great courage, or boundless self-confidence, to dare enter the Church of the Holy Sepulchre with them, for the governor had explicitly forbidden Jews to approach or enter the church at any time, above all on or near Christian holidays. When 'Azar was brought before the kadi he made no attempt to deny that he had entered the church, claiming that he knew nothing about the prohibition or the fine of 100 *sultani* that was automatically imposed on anyone who transgressed this order. In his defense he brought the Jannissary who guarded the church entrance, as well as many other Muslims who testified in his favor, and he was declared innocent. In addition to the light this incident throws on the relationships that prevailed among the different groups in Jerusalem, it further confirms the impression that the city's Jewish cloth merchants generally enjoyed a secure status, possibly by virtue of their affluence.

## *Dealers in Grapes and Wine*

Jewish men and women were often brought to trial for having purchased grapes from Muslims. The quantities referred to were always large, several *qanṭār* in each case,[1] and seem rather exaggerated in terms of the consumption of a normal household. However, in light of the Halakic prohibition against drinking wine made by non-Jews, the desire of Jews to produce their own seems reasonable.

Of course, Muslim society absolutely forbids the drinking of wine, a prohibition strictly enforced in Jerusalem during the sixteenth century. The Jews and Christians, however, were permitted to carry out the rites and rituals of their religions, which included imbibing wine. This situation, in which a minority was allowed a concession forbidden to the majority contained the potential for transgression, and indeed there were apparently Muslims who were tempted to violate the prohibition. The Jews and Christians were warned not to produce wine freely, but only when given permission by the kadi, while the *subashi* of Jerusalem declared explicitly that they were not to sell wine to Muslims.[2]

A permit to produce wine was not issue generally, but was given specifically to those Jews and Christians who requested it. No specially trained people dealt in wine making, although many Jews bought and sold grapes, for which they did not need a permit. Various Jews, the butcher Shmū'īl ibn Jūkār among them, would buy grapes directly from the vineyards in order to make wine. When attempts were made to prevent them from doing so on the pretext that the wine would eventually reach the Muslims, the Jews sought the kadi's protection. In the middle of September 1557 the kadi ruled that they could continue to make wine on condition that they again promise, on pain of severe punishment, not to sell or give any of it to Muslims in Jerusalem. Since the entire issue had religious connotations, in the records of this case the city was called Bayt al-Maqdis rather than the usual al-Quds al-Sharīf.[3]

The Jews made every effort not to give their ill-wishers any excuse to interfere with their purchase of grapes and making of wine. The heads of the Jewish community considered themselves responsible for seeing to it that Jews did not drink wine in public or distribute it to the city's Muslims. At the beginning of March 1576 a group of influential Jews appeared before the Hanafi kadi to bring charges against one of their number, Yūsuf ibn Shmū'īl. They claimed that not only had he been drunk in public, disgracing himself and the rest of the Jews, but that he had even bought wine from Christians and sold it to Muslims. Such conduct deviated from accepted behavior, they maintained, and hurt the community as a whole. Their influence on Yūsuf was apparently limited, since they were asking the kadi to intervene. He forbade the man to drink wine in public and to sell it to Muslims. If he violated this prohibition, he was to pay the governor a fine of 1000 *akçe*.[4] As a result of this policing by the community leaders, the community as a whole was permitted to continue producing and consuming wine.

## *Cheese Makers*

The combination of climate and sanitary conditions in sixteenth-century Palestine made it impossible to keep milk fresh even in cool, hilly Jerusalem, and it had to be used up quickly. Anyone wishing to keep dairy products for a longer period—a need felt more urgently in the city than in the village, of course—made a thick sour milk (*laban*) for a relatively short period of storage and cheese for longer periods. There were Jews who bought *laban* from the Muslims in the villages around Jerusalem, such as Bayt Ṣafāfā, and then sold it to both Jewish and non-Jewish customers in the city. Jewish women too dealth in this trade; in 1534–35 a North African Jewish woman swore before the kadi that she would not sell Jews anything but good, undiluted *laban* at the fixed price of 2 *dirham* per *raṭl* (approximately 2½ kilograms).[1]

On the whole, the Jews specialized in cheese, which they both produced and sold, an occupation arising from the prohibition on eating cheese produced by non-Jews (and therefore presumably not kosher). Jews of Jerusalem went out regularly to the villages around the city and with their apprentices made cheese on the spot, later selling it to their fellow Jews in the city. Although this was an old and accepted custom, a special permit was required. In 1557, for example, Ibrahīm ibn ʿAbd Allāh and Mūsā ibn ʿAyyād, both Jews from Jerusalem, asked the kadi to issue a permit for them and their apprentices.[2] More than ten years later the shaykh al-yahūd asked the kadi to facilitate the perpetuation of this custom, which was based on an official document the Jews had received from the Sublime Porte. Yāsif, Ibrahīm, and 'Isāq, the shaykh explained, were all Jews from Jerusalem who customarily made cheese in the subdistrict of Jerusalem and then sold it in the city, where certain people were trying to stop them. To add force to his claim that this custom had prevailed for many years, he brought as witnesses high military personnel from Jerusalem, a *sipahi* and the commander of the Jannissary unit in the Citadel. In the middle of June 1570 the kadi ruled that the Jews were to be permitted to continue making and selling cheese.[3]

The *muḥtasib* supervised the making, selling, and pricing of the cheese, and saw to it that all Jews producing cheese (*jabbān*) did so in the same way. When it became apparent that one of them was attempting to deviate from the norm, the kadi would warn him. The unlimited sale of cheese was permitted inside Jerusalem to local Jews and to pilgrims, but Jewish cheese venders who went to sell their wares outside the city needed a special permit. At the end of April 1556 the kadi heard the case of a Jew who had been forbidden to sell cheese outside of Jerusalem: Shmū'īl ibn abi Jūkār, the butcher. It is clear that he had been following these two pursuits simultaneously.[4] Shmū'īl did not produce cheese but rather sold it, like many Jews who sold a variety of products. This combination, however, is especially intriguing: a butcher, of all people, selling cheese in Jerusalem. Perhaps Shmū'īl bought cheese when he went into the villages to buy sheep. Or perhaps, since for both meat and cheese the Jewish community levied an internal assessment, it might have been convenient to centralize the collection of the fee in the hands of a single individual—in this case the butcher.

The Jewish community collected a special tax for cheese produced in Jerusalem. The price of the cheese, like that of other products, was fixed in advance by the *muḥtasib*, and the venders were forbidden to raise it. Cheese made by Jews had two fixed prices, for Muslims 18 *ḥalabiyya* per *raṭl* and for Jews 20 *ḥalabiyya* per *raṭl*. This price difference was officially fixed and publicized and on occasion reached even 20 percent.[5] It was forbidden to sell cheese to Muslims at the higher price, although the attempt was sometimes made.[6] Of course, the cheese was made by the identical process. The difference in price was probably meant to serve as a kind of internal tax, to help the Jewish community cover its many expenses.

## *Millers and Bakers*

For many years the Jews were active in milling and baking. In August 1531 a Muslim sold a Jew most of the equipment he needed to operate a flour mill.[1] There were probably Jewish millers and bakers before that too, but the court archives do not contain such records for earlier years. At the beginning of August 1537 two other Jews and a Muslim were jointly operating a flour mill, called *ṭāḥūnat ibn nā'ib al-qal'a*, in the Jewish neighborhood. Sulaymān ibn Ya'qūb ibn Da'ūd, one of the Jews, was responsible for acquiring the wheat and barley and for the mare that turned the millstones; the Muslim was responsible for operating the mill and sifting the flour; the job of the other Jewish partner, Sha'shū'a ibn 'Ayzar, was to bake ten *raṭls* of unleavened bread every day out of white flour.[2]

Jerusalem, like every metropolis, depended upon wheat supplies that had to be brought in from outside the city. Regulations stipulated that grain had to be sold at a central outdoor grain marketplace (*'urṣat al-ghilāl*), where quality and prices could be controlled. The product was brought there by the grain merchants (*ḥaddār*)[3] or by the growers themselves, who transported it directly from the fields, and there it was weighed and sold. Since their produce was vital to the city's population, the *ḥaddārs* were granted exemption from the *ghafar* tax that was collected from all others who brought grain to Jerusalem. There were no Jews among the peasants in the villages around the city, but some of the grain merchants who transported wheat from those areas (*al-yahūd al-ḥaddārīn*) were Jews, and they too were exempt from all duty on the grain.

From the inception of Ottoman rule in Palestine, Jews functioned in this capacity, as mentioned at the beginning of July 1535.[4] They were still active twenty years later, and there are even indications that toward the middle of the century their involvement had intensified. In the first half of 1555 some of those *ḥaddārs* sent a delegation to the Sublime Porte to complain that illegal fees were being extorted from them. The *subashi*, the night watchmen, and other officials would waylay them on their way back to town, alleging that they were making commercial contacts with the rebellious Bedouin. The Jews were being made to pay fines of a tenth of all the grain that they were bringing into the city. Early in June of the same year the Sublime Porte issued an order forbidding further harassment of the Jews in this manner, although despite the order the harassment continued. In January 1557 several Jewish *ḥaddārs*—among them Mūsā ibn al-ḥaddād, Ḥanān ibn Ibrahīm, and Da'ūd ibn Ḥayyim—came to the kadi, requesting that the *subashi* send a representative also, and they asked that the *firman* of the Sublime Porte be recorded in the court records. The kadi so decreed, instructing all parties to conform with the order.[5]

These were not the only complaints, nor were the Jews the only ones who sought the kadi's aid. Two Muslim merchants who held the lease for the outdoor grain marketplace wanted to ensure that grain would be sold only from there. Their appeal was only partially effective, for in September 1550 they brought the Jew Isḥāq ibn Menāḥīm before the kadi, where he swore that he would never again sell wheat anyplace else under penalty of a fine of 500 *akçe* toward the upkeep of the Dome of the Rock mosque. However, supervision was relatively lax, and the Jews as well as others continued to sell grain outside the official market, sometimes even at higher prices; for example, the Jewish grain merchant Da'ūd ibn Ḥayyim did so in 1552. In 1580 Jews were brought to trial for having bought grain outside the controlled market. This time it was not a Jewish merchant who had brought the grain to Jerusalem but a Muslim supplier (*jallāba*).[6] It seems likely that throughout much of the century Jews had a hand in purchasing grain outside the market, although this practice became less prevalent—or the authorities knew less about it.

After 1537 the names of Jews also appear as millers (*ṭaḥḥān*). In 1540 three of Jerusalem's millers were Muslims and two, Shmū'īl and abu Dānī, were Jews. Five years later al-Zahabānī the Jewish miller, was convicted of having asked an exorbitant price for grinding a sack of flour. By the end of the 1550s not a single Jew was included in the list of Jerusalem's millers, and even the flour mill in the Jewish neighborhood had been leased to Muslims. But in 1566 the Hanafi kadi once again rented the flour mill near the Citadel, east of Dayr al-Sulṭān, to a Jew, Mūsā ibn Isḥāq, for one year.[7]

Jews were involved in baking as well as milling. There was an oven in the Jewish neighborhood, and naturally some of the bakers were Jews. This bakery had been leased to a Jew at the end of the 1530s by the man in charge of the Muslim *waqf* of al-Ṭawāshī, which received the bakery's income, and Jews leased the oven for given periods thereafter; it was leased to a Jew for a year and a half, for example, starting in 1552. This does not mean that only Jews used the oven. In 1559 Salamūn ibn Mūsā and Isḥāq ibn Ibrahīm rented the same oven, located opposite the synagogue, and then sublet it at a profit to a Muslim.[8] Jewish bakers may have used more than one oven. At any rate, their active participation in baking is mentioned frequently. Zaqilman, Mas'ūd ibn Ma'īr, and Yahūdā the Ashkenazi (*'Iskanājī al-Yahūdā al-'ifranjī*) are referred to as bakers in the second half of the 1540s and the beginning of the 1550s. They were brought to trial for a variety of misdemeanors, such as selling bread or rolls that had not baked through or that were not up to standard weight or had an unpleasant odor.

The bakers, called *farrān* or *khabbāz*, were their own salesmen, although sometimes others sold their products. In 1545 the Jewish woman Anā bint Ya'qūb, daughter of the painter Ya'qūb (*al-dahhān*), was selling unleavened bread (*kmāj*) in Jerusalem. But by the end of the 1550s the number of Jewish bakers had declined to the point where only one appeared in a list of about fifty bakers in Jerusalem.[9] Finally, as the population and importance of the Jewish community declined in the last third of the century, the number of Jews who supplied grain and milled it as well as baked bread also declined.

## *Dealers in Olive Oil and Soap*

Jerusalem's Jews usually bought their supplies of olive oil from the villagers in the vicinity, primarily from the area north of the city. But these were not their only sources. They were also supplied by Jerusalem's Muslim oil merchants as well as some of the religious and secular functionaries (*nāẓir al-ḥaramayn*, *sipahis*) who were entitled to the oil—in the case of the *nāẓir* as the tithe he collected for the *waqf*, and in the case of the sipahi as his income from the villages. The Jews used some of the olive oil for their own needs and sold the surplus, some to the rural population, some to other urban consumers, and some to the soap industry.

Jews were involved in several stages of the soap-making process. A soap factory (*maṣbana*) in Jerusalem's Jewish neighborhood was rehabilitated a few years after the Ottoman conquest and operated throughout the sixteenth century. Available information indicates that the lessees and operators of the factory were Muslims.[1] The Jews had a hand in exporting the soap, possibly because they lived so near the factory, but more likely as a result of their widespread commercial contacts. The simplest and most usual form for such a transaction started with the Jewish merchant buying the soap, called Jerusalem soap, or *qudsī*, in the city. Jūkār and Mūsā in 1547, Khalīfa ibn 'Ayyād in 1548, and Ibrahīm ibn 'Azar and Isḥāq ibn Ibrahīm in 1549 were among these merchants.[2] From the quantities bought and the prices paid, it is obvious that these were commercial purchases and not for ordinary household use. Payment was usually in cash, but since the amounts of money involved were very great, the Jewish buyer sometimes paid part down and undertook to pay the rest at a later date. There were different ways of guaranteeing eventual payment, the usual one being to find someone to underwrite the debt; another way was for the Jewish merchants to promise not to leave Jerusalem until the debt was paid, even to "visit the places holy to them." Still another method was for the buyer to mortgage part of his property to the person who sold him the soap.[3]

Soap bought by Jewish merchants was resold to Muslim dealers in Jerusalem or marketed abroad, primarily in Egypt. Exporting soap to Egypt was one aspect of the continual commercial expansion of those years. By the last quarter of the century soap exporting had become a flourishing business that ensured a fine income to the merchants who dealt in it. The very large sums of money involved testify to the great volume of trade (900 *sultani* changed hands in one of the deals made by a Jewish merchant from Jerusalem, who continued, even after moving to Damascus in 1578, to buy large consignments of soap on a scale that reached some 15 tons) and the impressive quantities marketed (42 *qanṭār*, the equivalent of over ten tons, in another deal made at the end of the 1570s).[4] An important Muslim soap dealer negotiated the latter transaction, but the buyer in Egypt was a Jew.

Jerusalem soap was much in demand in those years. A Cairo merchant sent a very substantial sum of money, 800 *sultani*, to his colleague in Jerusalem not to pay for soap but to have it produced. According to the instructions accompanying the money, the Muslim was to buy olive oil and alkali, from which the soap would be manufactured in Jerusalem; when it was dry, he was to send the consignment to Egypt under escort by the safest route. There is a good deal of evidence that throughout the century Jewish soap merchants were also approached in similar fashion, although not always on so large a scale. For example, on June 13, 1579, an argument between two Jews was brought to the Hanafi kadi in Jerusalem: One of them was *al-mu'allim* Da'ūd ibn Ya'qūb, a high-ranking official in Cairo, and the other was Mūsā ibn abu Jūkār, a soap merchant in Jerusalem. "On the third day of [the] Passover holiday" (*'īd al-fṭīr*) Da'ūd paid Mūsā 200 *sultani* for the purchase of soap. However, Jūkār did not supply the goods and even tried to deny his responsibility. The testimony of two others Jews, Mūsā ibn ʿAzar and Ḥayyim ibn Yūsuf ibn Da'ūd Hacohen, verified the story and was instrumental in bringing about the soap merchant's conviction.[5]

By order of the sultan a special soap consignment tax (*rasm aḥmāl al-ṣābūn*) was collected when the goods left Jerusalem. Since in the early 1580s most of the export was to Egypt, it was customary to collect the tax when the consignments reached Cairo. This tax went to the state treasury, but the *waqf* also received an income from the export of soap. In the 1590s Yāsif ibn Shaʿbān, a wealthy Jewish cloth merchant, in partnership with a Muslim religious functionary (*khādim* of the al-Aqṣā mosque), leased all the annual revenues accruing from the sale of soap exported from Jerusalem for the al-Aqṣā *waqf* and the *waqf* of the Tomb of the Ancestors in Hebron.[6]

Jews had other connections with Jerusalem soap as well. On August 17, 1573, the representative of the *subashi* of Jerusalem appeared before the Shafiʿi kadi to complain that the Jewish community of Jerusalem was disposing of its garbage the same way that the soap factory was disposing of its waste: by piling it up alongside the south wall of the city, not far from what he called the "gate to the Jewish quarter" (*bāb ḥārat al-yahūd*), apparently Dung Gate. This gate had been referred to as such in Hebrew texts from the time of Nehemia, while in the tenth and fifteenth centuries al-Maqdisī and Mujīr al-Dīn mentioned that only foreigners continued to call it that. But in the sixteenth century it appears that the site actually was used as a garbage dump. The *subashi*'s representative reported that garbage and olive waste heaped against the wall, both inside and out, had reached such a height that it sealed the doors and windows of some of the houses adjacent to the wall. The kadi and the *subashi*'s representative found that there were indeed piles of garbage, including waste from the soap factory, "at the mound that was next to the gate of the Jewish quarter." The shaykh al-yahūd was summoned to clarify whether the Jews were throwing their garbage out there. He denied it, maintaining that every few days they removed their garbage from the city and deposited it at some distance from the wall. The kadi, however, did not believe him, especially after the chief builder of Jerusalem reported that the garbage and soap waste were damaging the wall.[7] In view of the increasing soap production in the following years, it seems unlikely that the kadi was able to put a stop to the practice.

Jews were also active in the trade of sesame oil (*sayraj*), used primarily for lighting. On the whole, the same people dealt in oil, soap, and sesame. Jūkār and his sons bought and sold olive oil, soap, sesame oil, and so forth. As merchants in this field, they were subject to the authority of the *muḥtasib*, who in 1554 tried to force them to buy soap and a variety of oils at exorbitant prices. They appealed to the kadi and received a favorable judgment forbidding the *muḥtasib* to impose illegal levies on them in the future. The appellation *sayrajānī*, meaning a dealer in sesame oil, occasionally appears alongside the name of a Jew. One of them, Shmīla ibn Yūsuf, held the distinguished position of shaykh of the Jerusalem Jewish community at the beginning of the 1580s, and in the middle of the 1570s Ibrahīm *al-sayrajānī* was one of the heads of the Jewish community.[8]

It is clear that the Jews of Jerusalem were deeply involved in the oil and soap trade, both within the country and for export. They had a network of connections with Muslim merchants, producers, experts, and suppliers, and of course with Jews in other countries, particularly Egypt.

## *Jews in Trade*

Jerusalem's Jews also dealt in such products as rice, most of which was imported from Egypt, kali bought from the Bedouin of the desert for the city's soap industry, and sweets such as date jam (*rubb*) and condiments such as salt, selling these products to the city's residents.[1] In more general terms it may be said that the Jews were involved in international trade, in commerce between the city and other parts of the country, and of course in local trade.

Jerusalem's trade with foreign markets consisted primarily of the export of soap to Egypt. The city's merchants traded elsewhere in Palestine mainly in connection with the buying of grain, fruits, and vegetables, and selling items such as jewelry in other urban centers and in rural villages. Examples of this trade abound. In 1576, for instance, two Jews from Jerusalem spent several days in the village of 'Ajlūl in the Banī Zayd subdistrict north of Jerusalem, where they bought a variety of farm produce; and in 1555 several Jews went as far as Qabāṭiyya, where they transacted business that kept them there for a few days. There were times when Jews were sent out of town by Muslims who were in debt to them: for example, in 1585 when the *mutawallī* of the Khasseki Sultan *waqf* signed over to a Jew the right to receive ten *qanṭār* of olive oil that the residents of the Ni'illīn village owed his *waqf*. For a number of years the Jew made futile attempts to collect this debt, and finally appealed in 1589 to the kadi to force the village shaykh and his people to make payment.[2]

Jerusalem's Jews did not limit their commerce outside the city to direct transactions with the villagers; they also did business with the nomad population, the Bedouin. As we have seen, one Jerusalem *subashi* and his minions tried to impose special fines on the Jews, alleging that they were trading with the Bedouin. At that time these fines were declared unlawful and were forbidden. Although that incident casts no light on the question of whether Jerusalem's Jews did or did not trade with the desert nomads, other descriptions give us a more complete picture. At the beginning of March 1571 in the village of Sārīs a court session was convened, headed by the Shafi'i kadi of Jerusalem. The *subashi* of the Banī Zayd subdistrict charged the Jewish merchant Ilārshū'a (or Ilār Mashū') ibn Ibrahīm of trading with the rebellious Bedouin tribe of Banī 'Aṭṭiyya. He was accused specifically of having bought what seems to have been the proceeds of robbery: 50 *raṭls* of pepper, 30 *raṭls* of indigo, 20 white silk scarves, and three guns. Confessing his guilt, and even displaying all the items before the judge, he was duly convicted.

It was in fact not unusual for a Jew to do business with the Bedouin. At the beginning of August 1570 the court, headed by the deputy of the Jerusalem Hanbali kadi, was convened in the village of al-Bīra, north of the city. There the Jew Aslān ibn 'Amrān al-ḥarīrī, originally from Damascus, was convicted of conducting business with the Bedouin. Some of the items he bought were silk head coverings, guns, pepper, silver-inlaid swords, and gunpowder.[3] The dimensions of such trade are not easy to determine, but it should be borne in mind that the villages along the length of the Jerusalem district bordered on the desert, and their inhabitants were in constant contact with the nearby Bedouin tribes. Jews making the rounds of the villages to ply their trade very likely had some relations with the Bedouin, whom they probably barely distinguished from the rest of the rural population. Moreover, certain advantages could be gained in doing business with them, since they were able to supply some of the goods, such as spices and kali, most needed by the Jewish tradesmen in Jerusalem. We can safely assume that trade between the fellahin and Bedouin of Palestine and the Jews of Jerusalem was a basic element of Jerusalem's economy.

Jews were also involved in a capacity related to trade: they functioned as public criers (*dallāl*). Not all trade was conducted from shops and marketplaces. Business was also conducted through public criers who announced what goods were being sold where. The Jewish criers were part of the guild, and the guild's shaykh organized their work just as he did that of the other criers. All had to bring before the kadi a witness who would guarantee their reliability. Jewish women also served as criers. There are records of a North African Jewish woman, A'īra bint 'Abd-Allāh, who was a crier in 1558; in 1595 Maryam bint Ya'qūb and Ḥannā bint Shūbā were criers, and later that year Kalālā bint Ibrahīm the Maghribi and Simḥa bint Yūsuf are also mentioned in the same context.[4]

Interesting as it is to note that Jews were widely accepted as town criers, the merchants, of course, were a more important factor in the city's commercial life. A long list was compiled in 1595 of shops maintained by Jewish merchants in the various markets. Although some of these shops were privately owned, most of them belonged to the *waqf*, which received the rent money. Most of the shops, obviously, were rented to Muslims, and Christians leased a few, but an impressively large number were rented to Jews. Two shops in the western merchants' market (*al-tujjār al-gharbī*) were leased to Jews; in the eastern spice venders' market (*al-'aṭṭārīn al-sharqī*) Jews rented four shops, and 11 in the western spice venders' market. There were 13 shops held by Jews in the moneychangers' and jewelers' market (*al-ṣarf*), about 45 percent of all shops located there. In the cloth market (*al-jawkh*) there were four, a quarter of the shops there. Thus, some 35 shops in the city's markets were in the hands of Jews. Both relatively and absolutely this is a large number, and it attests to their significant role in the commercial life of the city.[5] The picture that emerges here, however, is of Jewish concentration in specific commercial areas. For example, in the cotton spinning market (*al-qaṭṭānīn*) at around the same time, out of the 25 shops rented by the *waqf* not one was leased to a Jew. Even if their shops did not belong to them, some of the Jewish merchants had capital. On occasion, however, their businesses were financed by others. At the end of 1584 a Christian in Jerusalem gave Shmū'īl ibn Khalīfa a quantity of gold coin as an investment in the Jew's business.[6]

Commercial transactions were conducted either in cash or on credit extended for a specified term. The inflationary process that the entire Ottoman Empire was undergoing made its mark on Palestine as well. As the century was drawing to a close, there was a significant fall in the value of currency. In 1591, when the Jewish merchant Ibrahīm ibn Shmū'īl tried to exploit this inflation by paying a smaller sum to a Muslim who had sold him soap, the latter objected. He produced a *fatwā* explicitly stating that in the event of a change in the value of the currency, debts were to be calculated in accordance with the fixed rate of the gold coin. Hence, the Jew had to pay 6 percent more to compensate for the depreciation in the value of the Ottoman silver coin.[7]

In conclusion, Jerusalem's Jewish population dealt in trade on a large and diverse scale. As shopkeepers, their business inside the city was probably not on a very broad scope, but Jews conducted a heavy volume of trade with the rest of the country, with desert tribes, and in foreign countries. They were found in all economic sectors, were involved in commerce and in production, and also served as connecting links for handling goods. They were criers, intermediaries (*simsār*), and caravan guides, primarily inside Palestine. It is hard to determine the relative weight of trade and commerce as compared with other types of Jewish economic activity, but there is no doubt that Jews were involved in these callings to a significant extent.

## *Jews and Real Estate*

The property used by Jews in Jerusalem was either rented or owned by them, or it constituted part of a *waqf* endowment.

## RENT

Jews leased not only living quarters but also shops that usually belonged to a Muslim *waqf.* In the revenues listed for the *bimāristān* of Ṣalaḥ al-Dīn at the end of the 1550s, there is a record of several shops leased to different people, five Jews and one Jewess among them. Throughout the century Jews could be found as lessees of shops in the spice venders' market, in the grain market, near the *Bāb al-Silsila* (a Jewish doctor from Safed), in the large market (*al-sūq al-kabīr*), in the merchants' mart (*sūq al-tujjār*), and other places.[1] I found no instance of a Jew conducting his business from a shop he owned, but there were isolated cases of a Jew leasing a shop to a Muslim.[2]

When the lessor was the Muslim *waqf,* the deal was concluded through the *nāẓir* or *mutawallī* responsible for administering the *waqf.* The rental of shops and lodgings was consummated in the presence of the kadi, for deferred payments were frequently involved in renting property. Conducting the transaction before the kadi also helped avoid a situation in which the lessee might at some future time claim ownership of the property. In Jerusalem in the course of the sixteenth century, some forty different houses and rooms were rented by Muslims to Jews, transactions that were duly recorded in the courthouse records. In a few cases a Jew leased residential quarters from a private individual, although in three-quarters of the cases the lessors were members of the religious establishment, who were usually acting as the administrators of religious trusts. There were almost no cases of a Muslim renting rooms from a Jew, but in the few examples I did find, the lessor was almost always a Karaite who leased property belonging to his sect, for which he was the trustee.[3]

Houses or rooms were usually leased for periods of three to four years, though some were rented for eight to ten years. When the property belonged to a Muslim religious trust, there was little fear that a long lease would lead to a misunderstanding concerning the ownership of the house; some of the contracts leasing such property to Jews, therefore, were for ten, 15, 30, and even 100 years.[4] The Jewish lessees were usually men, although there were not a few instances in which the lease was in the name of a Jewish woman.[5] It would be misleading to attribute this to far-reaching independence on the part of Jewish women; more frequently, this was a way of dividing legal responsibility between husband and wife to enable the former to manage his estate with greater flexibility, or, on occasion, a means of guaranteeing an unmarried daughter or sister certain rights.

Some leases were renewed upon expiration; others explicitly stipulated that the Jew had a right to sublet. Rental, calculated on an annual basis, ranged from one to one-and-a-half *sultani* per year, but there were exceptions of rents as high as 10 *sultani* annually. Many contracts stated specifically that a large part of the rent money—sometimes all of it—would go toward paying for repair of the property. It appears that much of the property rented to Jews was in run-down condition and was leased as a way of preventing further deterioration. Sometimes buildings on the verge of collapse were rented as a first step toward their repair. In 1541 Ya'qūb Fallāq rented a complex of ruined buildings (*ḥawsh kharāb*) and one that was partly destroyed, and then set about making the necessary repairs. In 1538, when Ibrahīm Kastro leased a large plot of land near Zion Gate in the al-Rīsha neighborhood from the *'imāms* of the Dome of the Rock, the contract contained a clause explicitly stating that he had the right to build whatever he wished on it. That same year he also bought a large plot outside Jerusalem from three Muslims. A big, dilapidated building called *qaṣr al-bayṭār*[6] came with the site.

It is not by accident that in these cases of leasing property as a step toward its improvement the lessees were among the heads of the Jewish community. This action on their part should be viewed as an indication of the status of Jews in Jerusalem and their participation in the development and rehabilitation of the city as a whole. The fact that so many of the buildings rented by Jews were in poor shape should not be construed as a sign that they were impoverished. Some of them undoubtedly were, but among the other lessees were the shaykh al-yahūd, Ya'qūb Fallāq; Ya'qūb the tailor; Mūsā ibn Hārūn, teacher of Jewish children; Yahūdā ibn Ibrahīm ibn Rūz *al-'ifranjī*, who rented two houses in a single year; and Yāsif ibn Sha'bān, a wealthy cloth merchant.[7]

Evidence of Jews leasing property shows that the practice was prevalent from the beginning of the century up to the early 1540s, but in the final quarter of the century it tapered off until there were only a few isolated cases. Most of the rental transactions, however, involved Muslims leasing property to Jews during the relatively short span of the 1540s and 1550s. Thus, there is almost total correlation between these statistics and the demographic trends as evidenced by the *taḥrīr* surveys. As the community grew in the first half of the century and reached peak size in these two decades, there was a growing demand by Jews for rented living quarters. Since Jerusalem contained a great deal of publicly owned property and not a few neglected houses, the increased demand stimulated a response by Jews as well as Muslims to lease their property. During the last quarter of the century, as the size of the Jewish community steadily decreased, the demand for living quarters shrank to almost nothing.

## OWNERSHIP

Since some rental agreements authorized lessees to sublet, the fact that one Jew could rent property to another did not necessarily mean that Jews owned property. Nevertheless, the *sijill* archives clearly indicate that more Jews were property owners than were lessees.

The sale of property, like the signing of a lease, required public legal sanction; the parties were careful to have the transaction recorded in court and confirmed in a document issued by the kadi. This document was not a writ of ownership (*tamlīk*), and it is doubtful that these transactions were recorded in Istanbul. However, the terminology used—*mulk* (property)—and the kadi's confirmation of such transactions as purchasing, bequeathing, mortgaging, and endowing property, enable us to identify these transfers of ownership.

Most transactions involving Jewish buyers that were recorded in the Muslim court involve the transfer of ownership of houses from one Jew to another,[8] although about ten cases of Jews purchasing property from Muslims were recorded throughout the century.[9] Transactions in which Muslims purchased the property of Jews was far more common. Such sales occurred throughout the century, although more than half of them took place between 1555 and 1568. Some 20 percent of all the houses owned by Jews were sold to Muslims in this relatively short period. This reflects either unprecedented growth in demand on the part of the Muslims or unprecedented growth in supply offered by the Jews. We can hardly find a reason to justify an increased demand by the Muslims, since during those very years their numbers began to decline in Jerusalem.[10] But an increased willingness of the Jews to sell is altogether consistent with the decline in Jewish population associated with this period. It is therefore not suprising that a growing number of houses and rooms—some of which Jews had owned for many years[11]—were offered for sale. Although in absolute figures the Muslim population too was declining, it was still several times larger than the Jewish population. More and more Muslims, merchants and others, were interested in buying the property of Jews, and many took up residency in their newly purchased houses. This vastly diminished the sense of security that the Jews had felt in their neighborhoods until then.

How many houses were owned by Jews in sixteenth-century Jerusalem? From the standpoint of size and quality, houses was very different, a dwelling (*dār*) sometimes being nothing more than a number of separate rooms (*bayt*, unlike the more modern meaning of the term, "house") in a partially ruined building. The absence of accurate data concerning sites, as well as the use of buyers' and sellers' first names, with no other identification, hampers the attempt to differentiate between one house and another. For my calculations, I considered only those houses that could be positively identified as individual dwellings. My research indicates that in sixteenth-century Jerusalem at least 100 to 120 different houses were owned by Jews, and most of these did not change hands in the course of the century. Each of them was involved in one transaction or another, such as leasing or arranging repairs, and partial descriptions of them are extant. Another 20 to 30 houses of which no description exists were also owned by Jews. These are merely mentioned in the records as landmarks. We can assume that, beyond this group of 120 to 150 positively identified dwellings belonging to Jews, there were others as well. But even employing the smaller of the two figures, and subtracting from it the number of residences sold in the 1550s and 1560s, we find about 100 houses in Jerusalem that were owned by Jews even as the century was drawing to a close.

Some of the houses had two stories. Many had a nearby cistern (*ṣihrīj*), which of course raised the value, a kitchen, and a toilet. Some had adjoining courtyards with fruit trees and even a vegetable garden (*ḥākūra*). It was quite common for a woman to be listed as the homeowner: in different years more than 20 Jewish women were declared to be the owners of either part or all of a dwelling.[12] The women were not only the formal owners of the property but were involved in all actions pertaining to it. Simḥa bint Mūsā Shullāl, for example, in the course of renovating her home, "Palm Tree House," broke through walls to make doors and windows, added an upper floor and a staircase, and even "built a bathtub with a colored marble finish."[13]

We have already seen that Jewish lessees applied much of their rent money to repairs, but the house in those cases were owned by Muslims. Where property owned by Jews was involved, the situation was very different. Among the various prohibitions accepted for years in the Muslim state was one forbidding the building of new houses of prayer or making renovations that changed an existing structure. Some of the most rigid law-enforcement authorities even forbade the repair of a house of prayer that had been damaged; when repairs were absolutely necessary, the approval of the kadi was required. The prohibition referred specifically to houses of prayer, but since transforming a private house into a house of prayer did not entail many changes, to prevent circumvention of the regulations they were applied to private homes as well.

The city's houses had to withstand earthquakes, rain, and snow, in addition to poor maintenance year after year, all of which undermined walls, damaged ceilings, and ruined the fabric of the buildings. Like all property owners, the Jews were interested in keeping their homes in good repair, but they were forbidden to do so. The Jewish property owner who wanted to make repairs had to appeal to the kadi, citing "concern for passersby" should the building collapse. This was usually not convincing enough for the kadi, who would send investigators to verify the need for repairs. Even then he would give his permission to begin work only on condition that the owner not build any additions or change the purpose of the structure.[14]

Apparently not every property owner waited for permission.

At the end of February 1550 a Jew from Damascus who was serving as dayyān of the community was brought before the kadi and made to promise that "from this day on he and his people would not repair any existing building or construct any new one without the permission of the kadi," and that when they did so, the builder would be paid according to the usual rate. The woman previously mentioned as having installed a beautiful bathtub in her home was brought before the kadi in 1574. She had asked for and received his approval to make a number of repairs, but she was accused of exploiting the permit to "build on new additions." The kadi approved all the additions retroactively "because she did them on her own property" (*mulk*). This justification on the part of the kadi seems very unusual and leads one to suspect a bribe.[15]

Not all Jewish property owners fared as well. In February 1577 the Jews of Jerusalem sent a representative to the Sublime Porte to describe their distress: they "live in Jerusalem in partially ruined houses, but when they want to make repairs and build on, they are prevented from doing so," despite the *fatwā* forbidding Muslims to interfere. The envoy was granted a decree by the Ottoman authorities to the effect that no obstacles were to be put in their way, an order that was hard to implement. Two years later, in February 1579 both the decree and the *fatwā* were brought to the kadi of Jerusalem "who gave the Jewish community permission to build and repair their [existing] houses."[16] It is clear that this harassment had the support of the kadi; were this not so, the Jews would not have had to submit documents they had received from Istanbul two years previously, confirming rights they had hitherto enjoyed.

Until the end of the century, despite the favorable rulings the Jews had received, attempts were constantly made to prevent them from renovating their houses. At the end of July 1580 the heads of the Jewish community again complained to the Hanafi kadi of Jerusalem, Muḥi al-Dīn, describing their plight in the gloomiest terms: "some of the houses . . . in the Jewish neighborhood are a shambles, while the rest are on the verge of collapse." According to the Jews, this grave situation had been caused by rains and repeated floods and by the lack of proper maintenance. The kadi gave the Jews permission to undertake all necessary repairs on their houses, which "are their property (*mulk*), their possession, and their responsibility." The permit this time was not couched in general terms but described the main types of repairs the Jews were to make in walls and roof, inside the house and outside.[17]

In the middle of December 1590 the Jews again had to send a representative to Istanbul to petition the Sublime Porte for its assistance. The appeal this time was very much like the earlier ones, with an additional complaint concerning a fine being levied on Jews who wished to make house repairs. The fines were doubtless large, for otherwise the Jews would simply have paid and not bothered to complain to Istanbul. The identity of the *ahl al-'urf* ("people of legal practice") who demanded payment is not noted, but there is reason to believe that it was the kadi himself, along with members of his immediate circle. When the community again received a decree from the sultan forbidding the levying of such fines its most influential members brought it to the kadi in Jerusalem, asking that it be recorded in the court records. Not until the end of February 1592, a year and a half later, did the kadi have it recorded in the *sijill* of Jerusalem "that it might be kept safely and so that actions would be in accordance with it."[18] Probably after the decree had been brought to Jerusalem the harassment subsided for a while. But when it started up again a year and a half later, the Jews insisted that the *firman* be recorded in the kadi's books, thus giving it a formal local validity.

In summary, although there was no official prohibition against the Jews' maintaining their property, during the last twenty-five years of the century the local authorities nevertheless made it harder for them to do so. This can be viewed as another manifestation of the change for the worse that took place in the situation of Jerusalem's Jews during the latter part of the sixteenth century.

There is no uniform profile of Jews as property owners. Some houses were large and expensive; others were dilapidated structures in which only a room or two were habitable.[19] A property was not necessarily owned by a single person or even a single family: often one part of a house was sold to one person, another part to someone else. Jews usually sold to Jews, but occasionally the buyer was a Muslim, resulting in joint Jewish-Muslim ownership of a property.[20]

The authorities did nothing to prevent Jews from building on plots with abandoned ruins, as long as it could be proven that the new structure was being built on the site of an old one.[21] For example, in 1558 Jews were given permission to rebuild a disintegrating house in the Jewish neighborhood.[22] Non-Jewish owners also repaired dilapidated property in other parts of the city. This renovation was part of a general trend throughout the first half of the century: with the increase in population there was a demand for more housing, which led private owners to improve their property. At the same time, the authorities were initiating public works and development projects.

Aside from, construction, one important measure for assessing economic improvement and population growth, particularly in Palestine, was the state of the water system. Under Suleiman the Magnificent work was done to increase Jerusalem's supply of water.[23] This project affected Jerusalem's Jews specifically in that the growth of the city's Jewish population, and the growing number of Jews who owned or leased houses in a relatively concentrated area, were making increased demands on the water supply. A report dated 1554 informs us that the bathhouse in the Jewish neighborhood that had fallen into disuse and neglect many years before was once again in operation, having become *'āmir* ("a place full of people") rather than the *kharāb* ("ruin") it had been.[24] In 1560 an order came to Jerusalem from Istanbul asking the governor and kadi to ascertain whether the operation of the *ḥammām Da'ūd* in the Jewish neighborhood "would damage . . . the supply of drinking water for Muslims." After a thorough investigation a detailed answer was sent: the operation of the bathhouse would bring in revenues for the *waqf* of the Dome of the Rock; it would not limit the supply of water to Jerusalem in general and the Muslims in particular.[25] Indeed, two years after the bathhouse was put into operation, revenue from it was recorded.[26] Twenty years before in a count of bathhouses in Jerusalem this one had not been mentioned, and the first record of income is dated 1562–63. This new bathhouse is another proof of the improving standard of living of the period.

## THE JEWISH NEIGHBORHOOD

The Jews who owned property within the city took certain measures to protect it both by concentrating in the Jewish neighborhood and by hiring special guards. Although the term *Jewish neighborhood* does not define a specific area of Jerusalem, in descriptions of houses owned by Jews the phrases *maḥallat al-yahūd* and *ḥārat al-yahūd* nevertheless appear frequently. References in the *sijill* make it clear that the term refers to property in the al-Rīsha and, to a lesser extent the al-Sharaf quarters.[27] There were also Jewish houses near the Armenian monastery and Zion Gate, in what was called the Zion quarter (*ḥārat Ṣahyun*), a term also used as a synonym for al-Rīsha.[28] The Karaites had their houses in the so-called Karaite section (*maḥallat al-qarrā'īn*), which was simply part of the Jewish neighborhood, or more precisely a street or row of houses (*khaṭṭ*) of this neighborhood, which itself was part of al-Sharaf.[29] Houses belonging to Jews are also mentioned as being in *ḥārat al-Salāṭīn*, but they were not differentiated from the others; another name for this neighborhood was *Banī 'uwaynāt*, which, according to a judgment from the year 1578, is "today called al-Sharaf."[30]

The homes of Muslims neighbored on houses owned by Jews, and sometimes there was no real separation between them. Jewish children could easily enter a Muslim neighbor's house by mistake, and when this happened their parents took them home as quickly as they could.[31] As the century progressed, more and more Muslims made their homes among the Jews, although the fact that Jews lived close to one another and were clustered around such communal institutions as synagogues, free kitchens, the Jewish almshouse, the market, the bakery,[32] and so on endowed their residential quarter with a special character that led to its being called the Jewish neighborhood.

This was, as we have seen, an ambiguous designation. The Muslim population distinguished the Jewish neighborhood from al-Rīsha or al-Sharaf, a distinction that even found its way into texts: "the al-Sharaf quarter, which is close to the Jewish neighborhood," "the Jewish neighborhood that is part of the al-Rīsha quarter" (*maḥallat al-yahūd min maḥallat al-Rīsha*).[33] There were also physical landmarks attributed to the Jewish neighborhood: a gate next to the 'Umari mosque, near the gate to the "great market," and possibly even the "old gate to the Jewish section" (*bāb ḥārat al-yahūd al-qadīm*).[34] Moreover, there was a shaykh of the Jewish neighborhood, although in the two instances in which he is mentioned—in 1575–76 and 1591—he was a Muslim. In the second case his function was described explicitly: he would sleep in the Jewish neighborhood in order to guard its residents from thieves, burglars, and untrustworthy night watchmen.[35] The Jewish neighborhood shaykh must be looked upon as a special functionary, not bound by the same obligations as the shaykhs of other neighborhoods but primarily acting as a guard. It is not surprising that the only examples are from the last quarter of the century. The Jewish community then was in a decline, its numbers decreasing steadily and its people under pressure; they may well have needed extra protection. With the century drawing to a close, the Jewish neighborhood was losing its compactness and particularity; its residents were already being referred to as Muslims and Jews. Putting a man on guard there was a response to a newly dangerous situation.[36]

Calling the guard shaykh may imply a growth in the relative importance of his function. There had been guards in the Jewish neighborhood before. In 1556 the Jews hired a Muslim guard for one *sultani* for four months' work. In 1562 the shaykh al-yahūd hired two Muslim watchmen from the Silwān village for a monthly wage "as was usual with such people," for the period of a year. They were responsible for guarding at night only, summer and winter. In 1572 there was an armed guard, a representative of the *subashi.* The job seems to have entailed a certain amount of risk, because the watchmen were required to renounce all claims against the community should they be wounded or killed while on guard duty.[37] The head of the night watchmen received a special wage for duty at the jewelers' market, with its many Jewish shops, and another guard served the spice venders' market, where there were also many Jews. This guard, sometimes called *'ases bashi* and sometimes *wālī* of the city of Jerusalem, came on duty at sundown. Drumbeats would sound throughout the city (*daqq al-nawba*) to announce that from that moment "not a soul is permmitted to be in the streets and lanes," and anyone violating this order would be punished. This curfew was meant to make the work of the guards easier and keep thieves from preying on the city. Danger existed throughout Jerusalem, but was more severe in the Jewish neighborhoods.[38]

Muslim shaykhs exercised authority over the al-Rīsha and al-Sharaf neighborhoods. Their authority depended on the support and cooperation of the Jews. If they lost the trust of the Jews, their authority was lost as well. In mid-1556 the Jewish grain merchants complained that the shaykh of the al-Rīsha neighborhood was confiscating their beasts and making their lives miserable. The shaykh was punished by the kadi, relieved of his responsibility, and replaced by another Muslim.[39] During the second half of the century, when the Ottoman rulers had come to know Palestine, they no longer depended on the neighborhood shaykhs as they had in the past, and the institution may have been dropped altogether.[40] This hypothesis is confirmed toward the end of the century, at least with respect to al-Sharaf. Several of the residents of the neighborhood complained to the kadi in 1588 that the *subashi* was exerting pressure to force them to appoint a shaykh for the neighborhood. They refused, on the grounds that they had had no such functionary in their neighborhood for the past twenty years. The kadi agreed that they need not appoint a neighborhood shaykh.[41]

In summary, as long as the shaykh *al-ḥāra* was an active and recognized institution, the Jewish residents of the al-Rīsha and al-Sharaf neighborhoods were subject to his authority. As time passed, this institution lost its power and eventually ceased to exist in those sections of Jerusalem. This happened just as the position of the Jews was deteriorating, and they were more vulnerable than they had been before. A special shaykh was then appointed to provide physical protection for the community. The shaykh al-yahūd, however, continued to be looked upon as the Jews' representative vis-à-vis the authorities into the next century.

## AGRICULTURAL PROPERTY

Despite the fact that Jerusalem was a walled city, during the sixteenth century many plots inside the walls were farmed and produced fruits and vegetables. Vineyards and fruit trees were usually planted in yards around the houses, and the owner of the property owned the trees and vines as well as the house. Vegetable gardens (*ḥākūra*) were generally separate, self-contained plots, which Jews sometimes bought from Muslims and continued to cultivate.[42]

The largest part of Jerusalem's agricultural land, of course, was outside the wall, where land and water were more abundant. Jews, sometimes in partnership with Muslims, owned groves that produced figs, pears, almonds, pomegranates, and olives, as well as vineyards in rural areas outside the city. These groves existed in almost all the villages around Jerusalem, and they are mentioned time and again in the course of the century in connection with property transactions and litigation. Although it is hard to know exactly when Jews came to own these lands, there are nevertheless five cases in which this is explicitly stated; the orchards in question were purchased by Jews from Muslims almost immediately after the Ottoman conquest, between 1519 and 1537.[43] Evidently only a short time after the conquest the Jews of Jerusalem felt secure enough to invest money in real estate outside the city. The profitability of these early investments encouraged other Jews to invest too.

## *WAQF* ENDOWMENT

Property that was owned outright could be sold, bequeathed, or mortgaged. It could also be endowed—that is, put into a *waqf* or religious trust, a practice followed by Jews in the sixteenth century.

In the early 1530s three Jewish landowners, apparently in order to ensure uninterrupted ownership of their lands, put their agricultural property into trust funds. A Jewess who owned an orchard in the Bayt Iksā village, a Jew from Damascus who had moved to Jerusalem, and another Jewish woman who owned land in Bayt Ṣafāfā all took this step. All three specified that the endowment was for the Dome of the Rock mosque in Jerusalem, and that the administrator was to be the Muslim superintendent of the great al-Ḥaramayn al-Sharifayn endowment. Since there are no additional details in the *waqfiyya* document, it is impossible to know why in those particular years different Jews took the same action: pressure and compulsion might have played a part, or perhaps the *waqf* of the Dome of the Rock was only the final beneficiary and the property was actually intended to be held by members of the family until the lineage came to an end.[44]

Throughout the century the prime motive behind establishing an endowment was to secure all kinds of property against illegal confiscation, either by powerful individuals or representatives of the government or religious establishment. If these reasons caused Muslims to establish endowments, they were even more applicable to the Jews. Although it may be purely coincidental that most of the examples that have come down to us are of trusts formed by Jewish women, there is reason to believe that women were less personally secure than men. This step also helped ensure that a woman's property would remain within her own family.

On December 8, 1531, Rifqa (or Rīka) bint Sulaymān declared all the property in her possession: clothing and modest household furnishings, a fruit orchard in the Baq'a lands, and a house in the Jewish neighborhood. In the presence of the kadi she declared that her two-story house was to become an endowment. She herself would be the sole beneficiary as long as she lived; after her death her daughter and then her daughter's children would be the beneficiaries. If the family line came to an end at any point, all revenues from the property were to go to the poor people in the Jewish community (*ṣa'ālīk al-yahūd*).[45] This provision ensured that the beneficiaries would always be Jews. Hannā bint Hārūn established a similar endowment on August 29, 1532. The practice, in fact, had existed as much as a century earlier. In 1458 the Moroccan Jewish woman Bannīṭa bint Barakat had formed a trust that continued to function even after the Ottoman regime replaced the Mamluk. She had endowed her house, the beneficiary being her son and after him his children and their progeny. When the line ended, the beneficiaries would be the poor of the Jewish community. But "if it cannot be spent on them," she had stipulated, "the endowment will be used for the Dome of the Rock mosque."[46] In this case the ultimate beneficiary was a Muslim institution. This provision gave the endowment added strength, for damage to the property would automatically hurt the endowment eventually destined for the mosque.

Two other Jewish endowments also made Muslim religious institutions their ultimate beneficiaries, and very likely for a similar reason. On May 22, 1542, Mūsā ibn Da'ūd ibn Ya'qūb put his house in the al-Sharaf neighborhood in trust. He was the beneficiary during his lifetime, his sons and their offspring after him, and then his brother's children. If none of these remained, the beneficiaries would be the Dome of the Rock mosque in Jerusalem and the free kitchen of the Tomb of the Ancestors in Hebron. When and if the property was transferred to those institutions, it was to be divided equally between them. Mūsā appointed himself superintendent of the endowment; after his death his sons would fill the post. In return for the revenue, each superintendent was to pay a total of 50 *dirham* to the *waqf* of the Dome of the Rock and al-Aqṣā mosques in Jerusalem.[47]

Some six years later the *musta'rib* Jew Sulaymān ibn Da'ūd put four shops in trust for impoverished Jews who lived in Jerusalem or came there as pilgrims, to be followed by poor Jews from anyplace else, and then the poor Muslims of Jerusalem. Lacking these, the income was to go to the free kitchen of the Tomb of the Ancestors. In this case the income was intended for the Jewish public rather than the family itself.[48]

Six years later Esther bint Ibrahīm, wife of Hārūn the blind man, put two houses she owned in the Jewish neighborhood "next to the old city gate [wall]" in trust for her during her lifetime. After her death her son Ibrahīm, then his offspring, and finally, the poor Jews of Jerusalem would benefit from it. She also made herself and the beneficiaries who would come after her the administrators of the trust. If it eventually passed to the poor Jews, the "dayyān of the Jews" was to be its administrator.[49]

It is hard to draw unequivocal conclusions with respect to the absence of the Muslim link in certain Jewish trusts. The omission may have been intentional, or it may have been the result of an oversight on the part of the scribe.

A Karaite endowment exists as well, its assets appearing from time to time as a separate unit. All these endowments were under the administration of a member of this small community and leased to whoever so desired. At the end of the century, as part of the general decline in the status of the Jews, Karaite *waqf* property also suffered. Toward the end of 1584 a Karaite complained that a house that a generation before had been put in trust for the benefit of impoverished Karaites had ceased to serve this purpose. A number of the Jerusalem *subashi*'s associates had appropriated some of the rooms, and only after the previous kadi intervened had the rooms been returned to the rightful owner. He had even laid out a great deal of money for repairs, and now another

Karaite was demanding that the house be given to him, maintaining that he was a descendant of the endowment's founder. The latter showed the *waqfiyya* to the kadi and demanded the right to continue to benefit from the property, in accordance with his father's declaration at the time of the establishment of the trust. The house would go to the poor Karaites of Jerusalem eventually, but as long as a child of the owner remained, he was to live there. After examining the original writ and verifying the facts, the kadi ordered that the Karaite be reimbursed for repairs on the property and gave the other man permission to use the property as his father had stipulated.[50]

## *Economic Character of the Community*

The Jewish community in Ottoman-ruled Jerusalem, and in other towns in Palestine, has been depicted as pitiful and persecuted. This stereotype arose from the facts familiar to us from the late eighteenth and nineteenth centuries, when the heavy burden of debt led to the decline and partial disappearance of Jerusalem's Ashkenazi community. This image also arises out of the somber reports of the Rabbinical emissaries, whose descriptions of the state of affairs in Jerusalem were not confined exclusively to later periods but were applied equally to the early centuries of the Ottoman Empire. A factual examination casts doubt on this stereotype and the assumptions that support it. The situation that existed during the twilight of the Ottoman Empire did not exist in its early days, and this certainly includes its period of glory, the sixteenth century. As for the descriptions of the Rabbinical emissaries, our acquaintance with the modus operandi of their modern successors and the nature of their mission enables us to attribute considerable exaggeration to their statements. The situation of the Jews in Jerusalem must be examined on the basis of contemporary descriptions rather than subsequent developments; general conclusions are better arrived at by relying upon sources more objective than the emissaries and their reports.

In fact, such objective sources also seem to sketch a portrait of poverty and misery. The *jizya* collected from the Jews of Jerusalem during the sixteenth century was, without exception, calculated according to the lowest rate, that set for the poor. The volumes of the Jerusalem *sijill* occasionally record declarations made to the kadi by Jews who described themselves as "beggar[s] from among the Jewish beggars" and claimed to own nothing but the clothes on their backs.[1] In 1557 a Jew who occupied one of four shops in the community's religious trust described the shops as being in a state of imminent collapse, and depicted the poverty of their occupants, who had been obliged to vacate three of them. He himself, being the last to remain, was "unable [to pay for] the lighting of the lantern hung in the archway (*qanṭara*) of that quarter." The kadi acknowledged the poverty of the applicant and the other occupants of these shops, relieving them of this obligation.[2]

However, not all Jews were in the same straits. At least during the second half of the century a measure of economic differentiation was evident among the Jews, for in 1589 the kadi urged the shaykh of the Jews to treat all members of his community equally, and "think about the situation of the rich and of the poor, [each] according to his ability."[3]

As we have seen, many Jews were persons of means, and a few even owned considerable wealth. Among the persons of means we can number all those who appeared before the kadi to stand security for their brethren. Among the rich are owners of houses worth many scores of *sultani*, those who rented such houses, or dealers in gold and silver. Even outside these categories were men—principally the big merchants—who amassed great fortunes, evidence of which is found in the court records. The title *khawājā*, normally applied to wealthy Muslim merchants, was occasionally bestowed upon Jews (for example, *al-khawājā* Ma'īr ibn Ibrahīm, the cloth merchant who lived at the end of the century).[4] There are also more substantial clues. Ibrahīm ibn Ma'īr of Jerusalem lent 200 *sultani* to a Jew from Safed in 1550; four years previously the Karaite Ṣadaqa ibn Yūsuf owed the Rabbinical Jew Isḥāq ibn Ibrahīm ibn Natān Shullāl 200,000 *akçe* the equivalent of nearly 2000 *sultani*.[5] Loans between Jews, unlike the large sums of money owed by Jews to prominent Muslims cannot be dismissed as a form of extortion, although these payments too would have had to be made somehow.

Of course, debts declared by Jews in the law court might have been the product of some financial manipulation and do not necessarily express the true financial status of the lender. To provide better grounds for appraisal I examined proofs of the actual financial standing of Jerusalem Jews. On September 23, 1552, Isḥāq the Jew claimed in court that he had been attacked in his home by robbers, who wounded him and "robbed him of most of his goods."[6] They probably did so in the knowledge that his property was worth stealing. Jewish women also owned movable possessions in large amounts. In 1541, 75 *sultani* were deposited with two heads of the Jewish community as a Jerusalem Jewish woman's bequest to her sister. And in 1559, another Jewish woman deposited silver and gold jewelry, a blouse embroidered with silver threads, and other goods with the *muḥtasib* in bond for a loan she had received from one of the commanders of the city's garrison.[7]

Wealthy Jews found ways of holding on to their wealth. At the beginning of 1561, some months before his death, Isḥāq ibn Shentōv (or Yantōv) the Jew declared that he owed his wife 800 *sultani* in belated payment of her bride price.[8] This sum is many times larger than the average amount given by Jewish bridegrooms, and it seems probable that Isḥāq adopted this method of ensuring that most of his property would remain in the hands of his wife and eight children, instead of going to creditors or representatives of the government. Indeed, a study of the list of articles he bequeathed proves that he possessed very great wealth: cash was not listed at all, probably having been concealed from those drawing up the inventory, but there was an abundant amount of cloth of various kinds; large numbers of kitchen and household utensils of copper; 30 copper lamps; 12 chairs; two swords, one long and one short; three clocks made in Europe (*'ifranjī*); and 50 books and other objects. In all, the articles he left were valued at 221 *sultani.* An official valuation of the goods left by another wealthy Jew, Malīḥa bint Mas'ūd, in 1587 also totaled some 200 *sultani.*[9] The list of possessions left by the Jew Salamūn ibn Isḥāq at the beginning of May 1554 also included fabrics of various types, some being stored at his home and the rest at his shop in the cloth market; and their total value was estimated at over 150 *sultani.*[10] Inventories of other Jews' estates display a wealth of clothing, fabrics, and household articles.[11]

Available details about the estates of Jerusalem Jews allow us to draw two principal conclusions. First, the lists are intentionally incomplete, mainly with regard to coins and ready cash but also with regard to the value of the goods, not to mention those articles concealed from the eyes of the authorities.[12] Second, it is clear that, even throughout the second half of the century quite a number of Jerusalem Jews owned considerable wealth.

Another means of determining wealth emerges from descriptions that mention Jews who employed servants, whether for special occasions or on a permanent basis. In 1562 a Muslim hired himself out to Ya'qūb ibn Ibrahīm the Jew on the latter's journey from Jerusalem to Cairo, "in order to serve him in securing the load to the beast, and caring for it."[13] Notwithstanding the use of the term *khidma*, or "service," such a function denotes labor rather than personal service. In 1545–46 Yūdā the Jew was employed as servant (*khidmatkar*) to Ya'īsh the Jew, probably the famous commissioner Ya'īsh ibn Farḥān.[14] In this case the permanent nature of his employment is clearer, but both employer and servant were Jews. There were also non-Jews who served Jews on a permanent basis: Natān ibn *al-Mu'allim* Shamūyāl Cohen ibn Shams, who was the Jewish moneychanger in the diwan of the governor of Cairo, kept a Corsican Christian slave, whom he sold in 1576 to a Coptic Christian in Jerusalem.[15] The most interesting discovery is of the permanent presence of servant girls in the households of Jewish women. In 1557 the jewish maid Sārā bint Da'ūd declared before the kadi that Yūsuf ibn Ya'qūb ibn Yahūdā, known as Karpas, had redeemed her in Alexandria for 40 *sultani*, freeing her from bondage to Europeans, apparently pirates (*ṭā'ifat al-'ifranj*). In return, she had paid him one quarter of the sum, as well as hiring herself out to him for ten years as his wife's servant for whatever she should demand, "like those of her ilk."[16] Christian women were also employed by Jews as their servants: in the early 1550s Mordekhai ibn Mināḥīm, a Jew from Jerusalem on a visit to Edirne, hired Katarīnā the 'Ifranjiyya for 3 *sultani* a year to help his wife; he brought her back to Jerusalem, where she served him for many years.[17] Muslim women too were employed by Jews as servants. After a complaint by the assistant to the *subashi* of Jerusalem, who accused Marḥaba bint Yūsuf, the wife of an Egyptian Jew, of employing "a white Muslim woman slave" (*jāria bayḍā muslimat al-dīn*), the offender was brought to court on June 19, 1579. She claimed to have bought the slave, Fāṭima, two years previously for 60 *sultani* on the understanding that she was not a Muslim. But Fāṭima testified that she was Muslim, and that she had been bought six years previously from a Muslim. To verify her words she recited the *shahāda* and declared that she was neither Jewish nor Christian, whereupon she was taken away from the Jewish owner and entrusted to the commander of the Citadel.

At that same time there was a group of Jewish pilgrims from Cairo in Jerusalem, and Muslim dignitaries in the city exerted pressure upon the kadi to deport them. The Muslims leveled a number of charges against the Jews, including the accusation that they were keeping Muslim women as slaves.[18] The employment of Muslim women as slaves was perceived as a case of imprisonment or captivity.

The employment of women servants by Jewish women was an undoubted indication of luxury and prosperity.[19] This phenomenon is in principle interesting and significant, but in practice such cases were certainly rare. Far more widespread was the possession of silver and gold jewelry. This was certainly more than mere ostentation, serving principally as a method of investment and savings. From the woman's viewpoint it also promised a certain measure of financial security. In addition, that part of the bride price that the Jewish bridegroom undertook to pay was also set aside for the woman, while any landed property she inherited from her father or received from her husband was registered in her name.

Of course these examples of wealthy men and women were extraordinary cases. Wealth was not typical of the community as a whole. Nevertheless, these examples permit one to state with certainty that there were undoubtedly some Jews fortunate or capable enough to succeed at their craft or in business, even in sixteenth-century Ottoman Jerusalem.

The overall profile of Jerusalem's Jewish community shows them to have been an active element in the city's economy. The Jews engaged in a variety of occupations, embracing most spheres of the economy: trade, crafts, finance, farming, and civil service.

Although the more prestigious callings employed few Jews, others engaged a fairly large number. In all but a few exceptional cases, Jewish trades- and craftsmen were part of the general professional structure, even belonging to the guilds. Their integration into the city's economic structure was so far reaching that a Jew who acquired a high degree of proficiency in his craft or trade could even become head of his guild; this was not the case in the empire's other urban centers.[20] In addition, Jews and Muslims lent and borrowed money, set up mixed partnerships, and represented one another in monetary transactions.[21]

Some Jews engaged simultaneously in two or more trades. In 1572 Mas'ūd ibn Naftalī, a jeweler, joined with a Muslim to export a large consignment of soap from Jerusalem to Cairo. In 1573 the Jewish spice merchant Yūsuf ibn 'Abd-al-Karīm bought a large shipment of soap for a merchant from Damascus. The well-to-do cloth merchant Yāsif ibn Sha'bān accepted the post of moneychanger for the Khasseki Sultan *waqf*, and received a regular fee.[22] In general, the mode of payment—still largely payment in kind, discharged principally in agricultural produce as well as other merchandise, especially cloth—required the Jews, like the rest of their countrymen, to deal from time to time in commodities outside their usual sphere of activity.

In addition to trades and crafts, the Jews were also involved in real estate. Jews bought and sold property and leased and let houses and rooms, tracts of land, and public buildings. They engaged in this activity among themselves as well as with Christians and, primarily, Muslims. Some of these properties the Jews renovated, thus contributing to the development of the city. Moreover, in the construction and development of public buildings—mainly markets, but also a bathhouse—the Jews played a prominent role, particularly during the first two-thirds of the century.[23]

Their economic preeminence exceeded their proportion of the city's population. This held true, for example, in the heavily Jewish jewelers' guild as well as in trades employing few Jews. The number of Jewish moneychangers, for instance, was not large; but in the spring of 1535, when new coins were sent to Jerusalem to be put into circulation, the Jewish moneychangers received fewer than the Muslims but much more than the Christians, and on a scale that bore no relation to their numerical representation within the general population.[24]

Neither was the economic activity of the Jews confined to the city itself. Jewish merchants ranged into the rural hinterlands of the Jerusalem district and beyond, to all the economic centers in Palestine and the farther reaches of the empire. This trade created wealth for a significant number of Jews, who were then able to gain power and social status. Although their estates rarely included ready cash, savings were bequeathed in the form of textiles. The existence of savings and the accumulation of wealth in the form of investments in buildings and land are evidence of firm economic standing.

This does not imply a complete reversal of the stereotype. Without doubt there were Jews who lacked a livelihood; there were the old and the destitute, whose upkeep fell upon the community. In short, the concept of Jewish beggars (*ṣaʿālīq-al-yahūd*) was not unfounded. In the last quarter of the century this problem grew even more acute, when the community as a whole became encumbered by an ever-increasing burden of indebtedness. As we have seen, the heads of the community undertook various obligations in order to try to lighten the load, and some financial assistance came from other Jewish centers.[25]

In sum the picture shows poverty and increasing debt but also considerable prosperity, lively and diverse economic activity, and full participation in the city's business life. The Jews of Jerusalem were more than a religious minority; they constituted a vital and constructive element in the economy of the city and that of the country as a whole.

E I G H T

# *Conclusion: The Importance of Being Tolerated*

THE JEWS OF JERUSALEM enjoyed the status of a tolerated minority, that of a "protected people." This concept of protection by definition implied a degree of humiliation, but how far was this reflected in reality? On the one hand the Jews enjoyed social autonomy and religious freedom to an impressive extent. On the other hand there is a very different picture, such as that described by Francesco Suriano, head of the Franciscan order in Palestine and a resident of Jerusalem for many years, reporting on the situation of the Jews there at the end of the fifteenth century in the following words:

> Brother: I wish you to know how these dogs of Jews are trampled upon, beaten and ill-treated, as they deserve, by every infidel nation, and this is the just decree of God. They live in this country in such subjection that words cannot describe it. And it is a most extraordinary thing that there in Jerusalem, where they committed the sin for which they are now dispersed throughout the world, that they are by God more punished and afflicted than in any other part of the world. And over a long time I have witnessed that. Among themselves they are likewise divided, and one hates and persecutes the other in such a way that the Saracens worry them like dogs. No infidel would touch with his hand a Jew lest he be contaminated, but when they wish to beat them, they take off their shoes with which they strike them on their moustaches; the greatest wrong and insult to a man is to call him a Jew. And it is a right notable thing that the Moslems do not accept a Jew into their creed unless he first becomes a Christian. And in point of fact I saw two

> Jews in Jerusalem, men of reputation and among them not of the lowest condition, who wished to abandon their Mosaic law and become Saracens to be in a position to take revenge of other Jews their enemies, so first they had themselves baptised by the Greeks, seeing that otherwise the Saracens would not accept them. And if they were not subsidized by the Jews of Christendom, the Jews who live in Judea would die like dogs of hunger.[1]

True, Suriano is describing Jerusalem in the final years of Mamluk rule while this book has dealt with the century that followed; but through the period of Ottoman rule Christians continued to write similar accounts. To a certain extent, the appalling aspect of such descriptions lies in the conviction on the part of those representatives of Christendom that the Jews deserved their cruel fate. Granting the intense anti-Jewish bias of such accounts, we still must wonder whether the conditions they describe—the humiliation and wretchedness—indeed typified life in the Jewish community of Jerusalem.

To answer that question we must first recall the general conditions under which Ottoman subjects lived in those days. It was the norm throughout the empire for the ruler to mistreat his subjects, Jews and non-Jews alike. In Damascus, for example, in the spring of 1549 a lengthy deposition was recorded in the Shari'a court wherein the Muslim residents of Damascus gave detailed hair-raising testimony as to the suffering and humiliation caused by Sinan Pasha, who had been governor in 1545–46.[2] There had also been rulers and officials in Jerusalem who gravely oppressed the people. In the second half of the century, particularly in its final decades, the city's inhabitants complained more and more frequently to the sultan in Istanbul about the heavy hand of the local ruler and his henchmen, as well as about scoundrels among the local population. This study has been concerned with the lot of the Jews, but the *sijill* volumes offer abundant evidence of the sufferings of Christians and even Muslims at the hands of the Ottoman rulers.

To be sure, the word Jews, particularly on the lips of a Muslim, had derogatory connotations. There was also very real anti-Jewish discrimination in the enforcement of laws and regulations, and in the levying of special taxes on the *ahl al-dhimma.* Moreover, the Jews were perceived of as deviant, as people whose attachment to the city was somehow more tenuous than that of their Muslim neighbors. Although I have spoken of the Jews of Jerusalem or the Jewish community of Jerusalem these terms are virtually nonexistent in the kadi's records. There the Jews are called *al-mustawṭinīn bi'l-quds*—that is, those who had chosen Jerusalem as their place of residence. They were also occasionally referred to as *al-qāṭinīn* or *al-sākinīn*, "residents of" or "those who dwell in" Jerusalem. Although less frequently used, these terms implied, perhaps inadvertently, a degree of alienation.

Nevertheless, it is inadvisable to draw wholly negative conclusions from this evidence. The total picture of the lives of the Jews is more varied and complex than that. Despite internal differences and distinctions, the Jews were seen by the public as a single group, and as such as an important component of Jerusalem's population, while the Christians were fragmented into sects and fractions that never coalesced into a unified entity.

At the end of 1573 the kadi of Jerusalem sent a lengthy petition to Istanbul appealing to the central government in the name of the residents of Jerusalem to extend the tenure of Sulayman Bey, governor of the city and the province, for an additional term.[3] The petition, initiated and signed by representatives of the city's inhabitants, enumerated the many beneficial actions of the governor. Even though at this time there were fewer Jews than Christians in Jerusalem, the names of the heads of the Jewish community appear before the names of the various Christian priests, indicating the relative importance of the Jewish minority. More important for our purposes, however, is the insight this petition, as well as other documents, gives us into the relationships and attitudes that prevailed between Muslims and Jews. The appeal proclaimed the governor's fairness and decency to his people, his important contribution to their health, security, and prosperity and to the well-being of the city. The testimony of the Jews is significant not only in that it indicates that the governor treated the Jews with consideration but also because it reflects the relative important attributed to them by the central government, and therefore by the provincial authorities as well. The Jews were among the weaker classes of Jerusalem's diversified social structure—classes that almost inevitably evoked scorn and discrimination. A good ruler was expected to restrain such attitudes, enabling the people to benefit from the example of his tolerance.

Of course, there were also bad rulers who oppressed the Jews. But even then the Jews could register their protests in Istanbul. They could also take their grievances to the kadi in Jerusalem. As a local judge the kadi had independent authority, and he had no need to curry favor with the local ruler since his appointment came directly from Istanbul. There was wisdom in this separation of administrative and legal authority in the provinces, with the kadi responsible for maintaining the religious law. It was incumbent on the kadi to demand that the Jews behave in accordance with Islamic law and strictly observe the regulations circumscribing the *ahl-al-dhimma.* At the same time he had to safeguard their legal, economic, and social standing against unlawful incursions and ensure that they were treated fairly. The protocols leave no doubt at all that the law court was generally concerned with the welfare of the Jews and protected them against hostile rulers as well as against local malefactors.

As the court protected the rights of weak elements of society in accordance with the provisions of the Shari'a, so the Jews brought to the Muslim court all those matters over which their own religious court had no authority. But the kadi was more than a last resource for them. There were many disputes between Jew and Jew, criminal and civil cases, and even issues involving personal relations that the Jews brought to the kadi rather than the dayyān for adjudication. Men learned in the laws of Judaism tried to limit the kinds of issues Jews were permitted to bring before the Muslim judge. Rabbi David Ben Zimra, the Radbaz, for example, stated that bills of divorcement were not to be brought to the Gentiles, nor were Jews to take an oath before them.[4] But as we learn from the Responsa literature, even this limitation was breached during his own lifetime. Essentially an unlimited variety of issues was brought to the Muslim court by Jews, and neither their language nor their religion seems to have been a barrier between them and the judge.

The economic aspect of the picture also gives vital information about Jews in Jerusalem in the sixteenth century. It emerges from the *sijill* that fiscal restrictions imposed on the Jews by the Shari'a were not applied in accordance with the letter of the law.

Not all the Jews of Jerusalem who owed the *jizya* tax paid it; and even those who did were expected to pay only the lowest official rate. Had all the Jews been paupers, as they sometimes claimed, this could have been understandable; but there were some among them with substantial incomes and still others who had assets in property and capital. It may seem surprising that some of the Jews were able to accumulate wealth, but this was not an exceptional or passing phenomenon. The fact that scores of Jews owned houses in Jerusalem and ran profitable businesses attests to the presence of at least an affluent few. Of course there were also many impoverished Jews—some of them old and destitute, and others Yeshiva students too engrossed in their studies to earn a living. But the majority were engaged in productive activities within the local economy. The *sijill* records show that although the Jews were isolated socially, they were quite actively involved in the economic life of the city and the country. Jewish craftsmen belonged to the crafts guilds, and Jewish merchants traded with their Muslim counterparts, buying and selling real estate, food, and other commodities. Some Jews even held high public office.

It is evident that the "fiscal disabilities and social limitations"[5] so well described by Bernard Lewis were not too conscientiously imposed by the Muslim authorities, and the entire supervisory mechanism governing implementation of the religious law was often slanted in favor of the Jews, thereby counterbalancing pressures exerted by local society, the ruler, and his soldiers. In addition, the ruling authorities themselves created conditions for good living in Jerusalem, which spurred an influx of Jews and resulted in the development of the Jewish community. Finally, the Muslim population, despite the contempt it leveled at the Jews, considered them a vital component of society. For the most part they spoke the same language and lived in the same neighborhoods, sometimes even in the same houses; their dress was similar; and even the names of the Jews, after undergoing certain metamorphoses, sounded like those of the Muslims. The Jews were represented alongside their Muslim neighbors in all the trades and professions and even became heads of important guilds.

Jerusalem's spurt of development and subsequent decline were the result of processes that took place throughout Palestine and Syria as well as in other parts of the empire during the sixteenth century. These processes also had a profound influence on the Jewish community, an influence that lasted into the centuries that followed and steadily diminished the public stature of the Jews in the years to come. But that in no way changes the fundamental proposition of this book: an autonomous Jewish life was carried on in Ottoman Jerusalem under the protection of, and even encouraged by, the Muslim rulers from the time they rose to power. Closed within itself as Jewry may have been, it nevertheless intermingled with the various circles that made the Jerusalem of those days function: the legal network, the administrative system, the economic and even social configurations. It was not a mingling of equals; everyone knew that the Jews were a "protected people." But beyond this basic understanding—and perhaps thanks to it in that it removed the element of competition from Jewish-Muslim relations—life was so arranged in Jerusalem that the Jews could survive, develop, and sometimes even prosper within Muslim society and under the aegis of Muslim rule.

*Abbreviations*
*Notes*
*Index*

# *Abbreviations*

| | |
|---|---|
| *AJS Review* | *Association of Jewish Studies Review* |
| *BSOAS* | *Bulletin of the School of Oriental and African Studies* |
| *EI* | *Encyclopedia of Islam* |
| *IJMES* | *International Journal of Middle Eastern Studies* |
| *JESHO* | *Journal of Economic and Social History of the Orient* |

# *Notes*

## *1. Jews and the Authorities: Millet?*

1. Archives of the Muslim court of Jerusalem (*sijill*), vol. 39, p. 437. References throughout this book to volume and page pertain to this source. See also Cl. Cahen, *Dhimma, Encyclopedia of Islam* (new edition, Leiden, 1960–    , henceforth cited as *EI*$^2$); G. Vajda, *Ahl al-Kitāb, EI*$^2$; E. Tyan, *Histoire de l'organisation judiciaire en pays d'Islam* (Leiden, 1960), pp. 642–643.

2. Vol. 39, p. 423.

3. Vol. 69, p. 148.

4. See Chapter 2.

5. H. A. R. Gibb and H. Bowen, *Islamic Society and the West* (London, 1957), vol. 1, pt. 2, pp. 212–227.

6. Vol. 48, p. 25; vol. 80, p. 17 (*ṭā'ifat al-yahūd al-qāṭinīn bi'l Quds al-Sharīf*). For similar references with regard to the Christians see vol. 44, p. 249; vol. 48, p. 84.

7. A very similar conclusion was recently reached by two young scholars in Jerusalem and in Cambridge, Mass., who had explored this problem from the other perspective, that of the center: Istanbul. J. Hacker, "The Jewish Community in Salonica in the fifteenth and sixteenth centuries" (Ph.D. diss., Hebrew University, 1979), pp. 122–126; B. Braude, "The Ottoman State and Non-Muslim Communities, 1500–1700: The myth of the Jewish Millet," *AJS Review* (Sept., 1976), 11–12. For a more detailed discussion of his findings see Braude's "Foundation Myths of the *Millet* System," in B. Braude and B. Lewis, ed., *Christians and Jews in the Ottoman Empire* (New York, 1982), 1, 69–88.

8. Vol. 44, p. 462, and an earlier draft on page 448. On shops leased

to Jews in the marketplace of Istanbul in the sixteenth century see H. Inalcık, "The Hub of the City: the Bedestan of Istanbul," *International Journal of Turkish Studies*, 1, no. 1 (1979–1980), 7–8.

9. Vol. 76, p. 37.

10. I systematically transcribed all Jewish names as they occur in the *sijill* records. This entails certain inconsistencies but does help convey how they were pronounced by their contemporaries, perhaps even among themselves.

11. Vol. 25, p, 186. The person in question was Rabbi Ya'aqov Pollack.

12. Vol. 25, p. 653.

13. Vol. 13, p. 70.

14. Vol. 75, p. 223.

15. Vol. 53, p. 55.

16. Vol. 82, p. 368; vol. 35, p. 178, respectively.

## 2. *Population of the Jewish Community*

1. S. J. Shaw, "Ottoman Archival Materials for the Nineteenth and Twentieth Centuries: the Archives of Istanbul," *IJMES*, 6 (1975), 421–459; K. H. Karpat, "Ottoman Population Records and the Census of 1881/82–1893," *IJMES*, 9 (1978), 237–274.

2. N. Schur, "The Jewish Community of Jerusalem in the Sixteenth–Eighteenth Centuries according to Christian Chronicles and Travel Descriptions," in A. Cohen, ed., *Jerusalem in the Early Ottoman Period* (Jerusalem, 1979), pp. 343–434 (in Hebrew); Y. Ben Arieh, "The Population of the Large Towns in Palestine during the First Eighty Years of the Nineteenth Century," in M. Ma'oz, ed., *Studies on Palestine during the Ottoman Period* (Jerusalem, 1975), pp. 49–50.

3. B. Lewis, "Studies in the Ottoman Archives—I," *BSOAS*, 16 (1954), 469–501.

4. For a more detailed discussion of the *taḥrīr* series in general, and the population of Jerusalem in particular, see A. Cohen and B. Lewis, *Population and Revenue in the Towns of Palestine in the Sixteenth Century* (Princeton, 1978), pp. 1–41, 80–94.

5. Estimates of the actual size of the *khāne* vary between five and seven members, so I invariably used a coefficient of six for Muslims and non-Muslims.

6. The number of households refers to *khāne.* The number of family members equals the number of *khāne* times six. The category of individuals includes bachelors, invalids, and others living alone.

7. H. Inalcık, "Impact of the Annales School on Ottoman Studies and New Findings," *Review*, 1 (Spring 1978), 71–80.

8. See Chapter 6.

9. The widow Bella-Rosa, daughter of Yahūdā the 'Ifranjī, had eight children: Isra'īl, Mūsā, Salamūn, Ibrahīm, 'Azariya, Simḥa, Bellīnā, and the baby Yahūdiyya; vol. 43, p. 265. Yahūdā ibn 'Abd al-Karīm had five grown children: Shamīla, Shālūm, 'Abbūd, Davīd, and Le'a; vol. 77, p. 134. J. Finn, the British consul general in Jerusalem, described Jewish families in the mid-nineteenth century that comprised four, six, and even eight people; *Stirring Times*, (London, 1878), p. 443.

10. In Mardin, for example, the *taḥrīr* registers mention a "Jewish quarter" (*Yahudiyan mahallesi*); see N. Göyünç, *XVI Yüzyil Mardin sancağı* (Istanbul, 1969), pp. 101, 103–106.

11. A. Cohen, *Ottoman Documents on the Jewish Community of Jerusalem in the sixteenth Century* (Jerusalem, 1976), pp. 63–64, 96 (in Hebrew and Turkish). Mixed population, both Jewish and Muslim, from a Muslim point of view meant a possible erosion of the original character of the neighborhood. For specific *fatwā* rulings on these issues see M. Ertuğrul Düzdağ, *Şeyhülislâm Ebussuûd Efendi fetvaları ışığında 16 asır türk hayatı* (Istanbul, 1972), pp. 94–95.

12. See n5 above.

13. Vol. 74, p. 184.

14. For Safed see Cohen and Lewis, *Population*, pp. 156–161; for Salonica see Hacker, "Jewish Community," pp. 228–231.

15. See H. Inalcık, *Djizya*, *EI*$^2$; Düzdağ, *Ebussuûd*, pp. 97–98.

16. B. Lewis, *Notes and Documents from the Turkish Archives* (Jerusalem, 1952), p. 10. Information derived from the *sijill* confirms my contention, which seems to be more valid fiscally than Lewis's. A decree dated in late June 1587 (vol. 68, p. 11) refers to tax collection as an act to be carried out in accordance with "the number of their heads" (*'aded ru'usları*). Moreover, official documents dealing with *jizya* matters often tend to refer alternately to "household" (*khāne*) and "individual" (*nefer*); see, for example, vol. 73, p. 48, as compared to vol. 73, p. 69.

17. U. Heyd, "The Jews of Palestine at the End of the Seventeenth Century Based on Turkish Poll-Tax Registers," in *Yerushalayim—Meḥkerey Eretz-Israel* (Jerusalem, 1952), IV, 173–184 (in Hebrew).

18. Vol. 47, pp. 104–105.

19. Vol. 20, p. 167; vol. 21, p. 391.

20. The terms used are either *foreigners* (*aghrāb*) or *travelers* (*musāfirīn*).

21. Vol. 55, p. 207.

22. Vol. 68, pp. 4–5.
23. Vol. 63, p. 58.
24. Vol. 68, pp. 9–11, a decree dated 18 Sha'ban, 994 / August 4, 1586.
25. Vol. 68, pp. 13–14, a decree dated 20 Sha'ban 995 / July 25, 1587.
26. Vol. 68, p. 14.
27. Vol. 68, pp. 9–11.
28. C. Issawi, "Comment on Professor Barkan's Estimate of the Population of the Ottoman Empire in 1520–30," *JESHO,* 1 (1957–58), 329–331.
29. For example, Ibrahīm ibn Mūsā, recorded in the *taḥrīr* registers of 938 and 952, is not mentioned at all in that of 945; Ibrahīm ibn 'Abdallāh al-Najjār, although registered in the first census, disappeared from the lists of later years, but according to the court records he actually lived in Jerusalem during those years.
30. Yūsuf ibn Shmū'īl, for example, was a well-to-do merchant, very active during the years 945, 961, and 981, but his name never appeared in the population lists drawn up in those years.
31. Vol. 44, pp. 437–438 (*A'yān wa-akābir ṭā'ifat al-yahūd*).
32. One should point out that this by no means holds true for all of them. Ya'qūb ibn Fallāq, for example, whose career as shaykh al-yahūd was well recorded in the *sijill,* was not even mentioned in the *taḥrīr* of 1553–54 / 961 A.H. or in the preceding one, which coincided with the dates of his political career.
33. These names include first names that were not recorded at all in the combined list, such as Murdakhay and Samsūm (vol. 66, pp. 440, 480, respectively) and even full names, such as Shmū'īl ibn Khalīfa and Shmū'īl ibn Abi Jūkār (vol. 66, pp. 440, 494, respectively).
34. The latest survey listed in Jerusalem was that of 1596–97 / 1005 A.H., but unfortunately only the first part survived; the pages bearing the names of most of its Christian as well as all of its Jewish inhabitants are missing.
35. For example, the *sijill* records mention Yahūdā ibn Mūsā al-Ḥaddād both before and after the survey—in the years 967 and 974, and again in 983—but his name does not appear in 980.
36. Vol. 68, pp. 9–11.
37. Vol. 74, p. 153.
38. The breakdown in *para* (1/40 of the gold coin *sultani,* sometimes referred to as *qubrusi,* or the equivalent of two *akçe,* also called *'uthmani*) was as follows: for Christians, 46 under the old *jizya,* six on the accession of the sultan, and 30 for an additional *jizya* and a tithe on wine, for a total of 82; for Jews the figures are 52, 11, and 44, for a total of 107; vol. 73, p. 69.

39. This was the case when one of the officials tried to levy an additional sum of five gold coins on top of the regular *jizya* payments due (vol. 73, p. 69), or when attempts were made to collect unauthorized *jizya* from Jewish pilgrims, both according to the Shari'a and the Capitulations; vol. 108, p. 25.

40. The usual procedure for *jizya* collection was that a special collector referred to as *kharājjī,* or just *emīn,* was sent from Damascus, bringing along a copy of the *jizya* register to be used as his main reference. Deceased people were deleted from his list, while the names of those who had reached puberty or newcomers who had been living in town for three consecutive years were compiled in a new document: (*nev yafteh*). Once the tax was paid, an official receipt was issued and handed over by the *kharājjī;* vol. 32, p. 195; vol. 42, p. 39; vol. 60, p. 53; vol. 108, p. 25.

41. Vol. 68, p. 14. On this distinction see also U. Heyd, *Studies in Old Ottoman Criminal Law* (Oxford, 1973) p. 283.

42. Y. Rivkind, "Dapim Bodedim" (Scattered papers), in *Yerushalayim* (Jerusalem, 1928), p. 120 (in Hebrew).

## *3. The Leadership*

1. For the terms of reference of shaykh al-yahūd as described here see vol. 15, p. 465; vol. 36, p. 119; vol. 54, p. 436; vol. 79, pp. 235, 396; vol. 82, p. 163. On *bayt al-māl* see Cohen and Lewis, *Population,* pp. 73–74. On *bayt māl al-yahūd* see Chapter 4.

2. Vol. 82, p. 136.

3. Other names recorded in the *sijill* are: Minaḥīm (1529–1531), Mūsā (1535–36), Shamwīl ibn abi Jūkār (1555–1557, 1572–73, and 1588–89), Da'ūd ibn Yahūdā ibn 'Abd al-Karīm (1582), Shamīl ibn Yahūdā (1587–88), Sāsī ibn Faraj-Allāh (1592–1596), Ya'qūb ibn Barūkh al-Ḥāmī (1598–1600), Ibrahīm ibn Mūsā al-Barādi'ī (nominated in 1600 for five years).

4. Vol. 54, p. 436.

5. As late as 1579 Salamūn ibn Mūsā Shullāl was still regarded as one of the leaders of the community and was held responsible for part of its financial obligations, even though he did not bear any formal title; vol. 58, p. 415.

6. For examples of these individuals see, respectively, vol. 25, p. 616; vol. 4, p. 43; vol. 12, p. 502; vol. 39, pp. 429, 431–433; vol. 77, p. 521; vol. 78, p. 127; vol. 80, p. 336; vol. 78, p. 247.

7. Vol. 77, p. 86.

8. The predecessor was Kamāl ibn Mūsā, the Rabbinical physician, 1570–71 (vol. 54, p. 168); Tyan, *Histoire,* pp. 46–47.

9. S. A. Rosanes, *Qōrōt ha-Yehūdīm be-Turkiya ve-Artzōt ha-Qedem* (The History of the Jews of Turkey and the Countries of the Orient), (Sofia, 1937–38), II, 180.

10. See, for example, vol. 5, p. 115 (Rabbi Levī ben Ya'aqōv ben Ḥavīv, called in the register for 1535–36 Lāwī ibn Ya'qūb); vol. 15, p. 181 (Yūsuf ibn Ibrahīm in the year 1542–43).

11. "They chose him as a dayyān and a responsible spokesman for them"; vol. 54, p. 168.

12. Vol. 13, p. 70; vol. 15, p. 333; vol. 4, p. 188; vol. 40, p. 439; vol. 39, p. 429; vol. 27, p. 333; vol. 14, p. 335, respectively.

13. Vol. 36, pp. 153–154, 419.

14. Vol. 23, p. 105.

15. *Al-mu'allim* Ibrahīm Zardīn, the Rabbinical *dayyān*, 1559–1560 (vol. 39, p. 204); Isḥāq ibn Ya'qūb, the *dayyān* of the community of the Rabbinical Jews, 1547–48 (vol. 19, p. 395).

16. The dayyāns of Jerusalem whose names are cited in the court registers are: Lāwī ibn Ya'qūb (1533–1536), Yūsuf ibn Ibrahīm (1533–1536), Isḥāq ibn Ya'qūb ibn Ḥayyim (1533–1536), Bājī (1549), Sulaymān ibn Isḥāq al-Shāmī (1550), Ibrahīm ibn Yūsuf (1550), Nassīm ibn Faraj (1550), Salamūn ibn Yūsuf (1550), Abu Ya'qūb (1555–56), Ya'qūb (1557–58), Yūsuf ibn Ya'qūb (1557–1560), Da'ūd (1558–59), Ibrahīm Zardīn (1559–1560), Da'ūd ibn Zamīrū (1559–1564), Kamāl ibn Mūsā al-ṭabīb (1570–71), Yūsuf ibn Ibrahīm (1570–71).

17. Vol. 40, p. 376. Ibn Zamīrū was the name by which his community called him even earlier; see E. Strauss, *Tōledōt ha-Yehudīm be-Mitsrayyim ve-Sūriya taḥat shilṭōn ha-Mamlūkīm* (History of the Jews of Egypt and Syria under the Rule of the Mamluks) (Jerusalem, 1951), II, 458–459. I. M. Goldman, *The Life and Times of Rabbi David Ibn Abi Zimra* (New York, 1970), p. 199n17.

18. For further details based on Jewish sources, mostly Responsa literature, see M. Rozen, "The Jewish Community in Jerusalem for the End of the Sixteenth Century to the End of the Seventeenth Century" (Ph.D. diss., Tel-Aviv University, 1976), pp. 90, 132; Rosanes, *History*, pp. 180–181. There are many references in the *sijill* to various aspects of David ben Zimra's activity in Jerusalem; see vol. 40, pp. 376, 390, 439; vol. 40, p. 139; vol. 44, p. 574. Goldman, *Ibn Abi Zimra*, pp. 16, 90.

19. Vol. 31, p. 320; vol. 36, pp. 84, 158.

20. Vol. 33, p. 473.

21. Vol. 18, p. 304; vol. 19, p. 274; vol. 21, p. 475; vol. 40, p. 565.

22. For a more detailed discussion of this institution see Cohen and

Lewis, *Population*, pp. 38–40. For shaykh *al-ḥāra* in Ottoman Cairo see A. Raymond, "Al-qāhira al-'Uthmāniyya bi-waṣfihā madīna," in *Al-majalla al-ta'rīkhiyya al-Miṣriyya*, 20 (1973), 223–224. On *kafāla* as an institution in Istanbul see A. Refik, *On altıncı asırda Istanbul hayatı (1553–1591)* (Istanbul, 1935), pp. 145–146.

23. Vol. 44, pp. 437–438.

24. *'Uswat ahl al-maḥallāt.* For a similar example referring to the Greek-Orthodox community see vol. 31, pp. 173–174.

25. Vol. 10, p. 170; vol. 15, p. 401; vol. 37, p. 341.

26. Vol. 31, p. 450.

27. Some inhabitants of the Sharaf neighborhood complained in 1588 that the representative of the local governor was trying to have them elect a shaykh among them, although this position had been vacant for more than twenty years. The kadi endorsed their line and ruled that they did not have to nominate a neighborhood shaykh anymore (vol. 67, p. 248).

28. Vol. 25, p. 653; vol. 72, p. 367.

29. Vol. 77, p. 163; vol. 78, p. 415; vol. 80, p. 469.

30. Vol. 39, p. 429; vol. 44, p. 574. Both cases in the *sijill* deal with the cemetery on the Mount of Olives, a clear indication that Karaites also buried their dead there.

31. On the variety of Jewish congregations in Safed see Cohen and Lewis, *Population*, pp. 156–161. The Jew who walked around Jerusalem with phylacteries on his forehead was severely punished by order of the kadi; vol. 66, p. 296. On the al-Aman congregation see also vol. 39, p. 73; vol. 49, p. 484.

32. Rozen, "Jewish Community," pp. 97–98.

33. Alaman Jews, though not mentioned as such in the *taḥrīr* registers of Jerusalem, were specifically referred to in this form in contemporary Safed (Cohen and Lewis, *Population*, pp. 158, 160). Moreover, an Ashkenazi (*al-siknājī*) Jew brought before the kadi in 1560 argued that he had done no wrong in allegedly breaking into a room, for the room had belonged to the "al-Aman Jews" for many years. For him, and for the Shar'i court as well, Ashkenazi and al-Aman were identical in meaning; vol. 39, p. 73. See also M. Franco, *Essai sur l'histoire des Israélites de l'Empire Ottoman* (Paris, 1897), pp. 49–51.

34. Vol. 25, p. 27 for 1551; vol. 49, p. 484; vol. 58, p. 415 for 1579–1580; vol. 67, p. 222 for 1587–88.

35. Vol. 53, p. 371. See also vol. 58, p. 300, *Nātān al-mutakallim 'alā mūristān ṭā'ifat al-yahūd al-Aman.*

36. Vol. 92, p. 424.

37. Rozen, "Jewish community," p. 98.

38. The Jūkārs served in 1557–58; vol. 33, p. 486, vol. 36, p. 136. The Shullāls served in 1562–63; vol. 44, p. 354).

39. Vol. 31, pp. 304, 435, 533; vol. 39, p. 429; vol. 44, p. 574; vol. 54, p. 168; vol. 43, p. 140; vol. 55, p. 208; vol. 76, p. 201.

40. Vol. 82, p. 57.

41. The front page and sometimes also the back page of the *sijill* volumes often have several important dates or other information scribbled by the kadi. This was in no way an orderly list of references but rather some useful notes, such as the date of the arrival in town of a new governor, the date of his departure, and so on. The date on which the dayyān died is also noted in vol. 39, p. 643.

42. For a list of his belongings see vol. 39, p. 519.

43. Vol. 64, p. 515.

44. On his misfortunes see vol. 14, p. 336; vol. 7, p. 374. On his public career see vol. 8, p. 253; vol. 12, p. 502; vol. 18, p. 304; vol. 21, p. 391; vol. 23, p. 535. Ya'qūb Fallāq maintained close links with the Ottoman high officials; when he needed cash to pay the *jizya* of the community in 1551 he was lent the impressive sum of 33 *sultani* by the *subashi*, which he paid back much later, after he had collected the debt from the members of the community; vol. 25, p. 115.

45. Vol. 10, p. 607.

46. The same pattern held in the Christian communities. The Greek Orthodox shaykh was relieved from office "because he became an old man and could not conduct his duty anymore"; vol. 76, p. 390.

47. The fact that "someone . . . has openly been at enmity" with the injured party weighed heavily in the process of justice; Heyd, *Studies*, p. 106, article 43.

48. Vol. 25, pp. 186, 190, 191, 197–198.

49. Vol. 28, p. 317; vol. 31, pp. 188, 591, 599. On Ya'qūb Fallaq's family after his death see vol. 33, p. 466; vol. 35, pp. 128, 135.

50. For a case of an alleged beating by the dayyān see vol. 39, pp. 4–5. On the beating of the shaykh al-yahūd by a member of the community who had served in the same capacity on an earlier date see vol. 36, pp. 51, 119.

51. Vol. 15, pp. 181, 333.

52. For a clear distinction between the Ashkenazic shaykh al-yahūd Ya'qub ibn Isḥāq and the Sephardic Ya'qub ibn 'Ilyā the Damascene, both serving in Jerusalem in 1613, see vol. 94, p. 134; vol. 92, p. 424.

## 4. Legacies, Debts, and Financial Obligations

1. For information on reporting deaths in the Armenian community see vol. 4, p. 43.

2. Vol. 4, p. 109. See also "Bayt al-Māl" in *EI*[2]. See Cohen and Lewis, *Population*, pp. 73–74.

3. Vol. 5, p. 366.

4. Vol. 17, p. 590. An original Ottoman decree is reproduced in my *Ottoman Documents*, p. 74.

5. Vol. 25, p. 285; Düzdağ, *Ebussuud*, pp. 98–99, nos. 425, 426.

6. Vol. 27, p. 161.

7. Vol. 40, pp. 124–125.

8. Vol. 49, p. 14.

9. Shamīla ibn Yūsuf al-Sayrajānī, who served as shaykh al-yahūd, was the lessee in 1571–1581 (vol. 59, p. 558); three heads of the community leased it in 1596–97 (vol. 77, p. 501); Isḥāq ibn Murdakhāy, one of the most affluent Jews at the time, leased it in 1598–99 (vol. 79, p. 288).

10. In early 1561 a Jew declared that the real estate at his disposal belonged to the *waqf* of the Jewish community and that fifty jars (*jarra*) of his olive oil were actually the property of a certain Jewish woman. In addition he declared several debts owed to other Jews, and finally a debt of 50 *sultani* still owed to his wife as part of her dowry.

11. This was important not only for the Jewish community of Jerusalem but also for Jews in other parts of Palestine. See, for example, a case dated 1573, in which the person in charge of *bayt al-māl* ruled that although Rabbi Mināḥīm ibn Shamū'īl had died in Hebron, his property should be inherited by his wife and nephew, who still lived in Safed; vol. 55, p. 562.

12. Vol. 35, p. 178. For a somewhat different version of this ruling see vol. 32, p. 167, and the original Ottoman text reproduced in my *Ottoman Documents*, p. 87. The term *qisma* or *qismet* when used in Jewish sources also means a receipt given by the authorities. See J. W. Hirschberg, "Ottoman Rule in Jerusalem in the Light of *Firmans* and Shari'a Documents—Preliminary Note," in *Israel Exploration Journal*, 2 (1978), 243.

13. Vol. 3, p. 273.

14. Vol. 7, p. 166; vol. 17, p. 260.

15. Vol. 36, p. 242; vol. 37, pp. 286–287; vol. 55, pp. 58–65, 123, 131, 163; vol. 33, p. 422.

16. Vol. 35, p. 86; vol. 39, p. 562; vol. 43, p. 129; vol. 64, p. 349; vol. 55, p. 371.

17. Some doubtful loans are the 60 *sultani* owed to shaykh ʻAlī al-Mardīnī (vol. 21, p. 544) and the 25 *sultani* owed to another Muslim (vol. 30, p. 268).

18. Vol. 78, p. 247.

19. Vol. 77, pp. 345, 403; vol. 78, pp. 149, 485. On other debts to the *waqf* of Abu Sayfayn see vol. 76, p. 448; vol. 78, p. 66; vol. 79, p. 43.

20. Vol. 78, p. 127.

21. Vol. 79, p. 573.

22. Vol. 77, p. 521.

23. Vol. 80, p. 336.

24. Vol. 77, p. 387.

25. Vol. 82, p. 57.

26. Vol. 82, p. 51.

27. Vol. 77, p. 387.

28. The adjective that usually follows his name is undotted, which makes its reading unclear; it may read either *al-ʻArabī* (the one who speaks Arabic, the native) or *al-Gharbī* (the North-African); vol. 79, p. 396.

29. Vol. 79, pp. 438, 471, 532.

30. Vol. 79, p. 532.

31. Heyd, *Studies*, pp. 84, 122.

32. J. Schacht, "Ribā'," *EI*[1]; Th. W. Juynbol, *Handbuch des Islamischen Gesetzes* (Leiden, 1910), pp. 274–275.

33. Vol. 80, p. 17.

34. A 15 percent annual interest rate on loans was common in the Ottoman Empire during the sixteenth and seventeenth centuries. A higher rate was regarded as unlawful; Neş'et Çağatay, "Riba and Interest Concept and Banking in the Ottoman Empire," *Studia Islamica*, vol. 32 (Paris, 1970), pp. 62–65.

35. Vol. 67, p. 222. The same legal fiction may be found in later years also; see, for example, vol. 69, p. 214. On a 20 percent and even a 25 percent interest rate that the community had to pay in 1594, see vol. 76, p. 206. It appears that interest rates in the mid-nineties gradually increased over the levels of the eighties.

## *5. Religious Practice and Institutions*

### JEWS AND ISLAM

1. Vol. 1, p. 225. On the use of yellow for Jewish clothing in earlier centuries under Islam see Ibn Qayyim al-Jawziyya, *Aḥkām ahl al-dhimma* (Damascus, 1961), p. 740n2, 764n3.

2. Vol. 32, p. 7. For the original document see my *Ottoman Documents*, pp. 83–84. For further details on this custom, which predated Ottoman rule in Palestine, see Ibn Qayyim al-Jawziyya, *Aḥkām*, pp. 759, 763. In seventeenth-century Egypt Jews had to wear a necklace, either red or black, while in the bathhouse; G. H. El-Nahal, *The Judicial Administration of Ottoman Egypt in the Seventeenth Century* (Chicago, 1979), p. 56. On similar discriminatory regulations against Jews and Christians in sixteenth-century Istanbul see Refik, *On altıncı*, pp. 47–48, 51–52.

3. The Ottoman college was situated south of Bāb al-Maṭhara, a small gate south of the Gate of the Cotton Weavers (Bāb al-Qaṭṭānīn).

4. Vol. 24, p. 465.

5. For a more comprehensive version see vol. 49, p. 344; for a similar shorter version see vol. 18, p. 207. On wider aspects of conversion to Islam see Düzdağ, *Ebussuûd*, pp. 89–91.

6. Vol. 1, p. 225; vol. 48, p. 215.

7. Vol. 76, p. 184.

8. Vol. 76, p. 331. In other centers of the Ottoman Empire a similar phenomenon can be traced. In Salonica, for example, a Jewish convert to Islam and his Jewish partner jointly leased the right to collect certain taxes on salt in the late fifteenth century; M. A. Epstein, *The Ottoman Jewish Communities and Their Role in the Fifteenth and Sixteenth Centuries* (Freiburg, 1980), p. 35. See also Goldman, *Ibn Abi Zimra*, p. 130.

9. Vol. 1, p. 225.

10. Vol. 80, p. 507.

11. Vol. 27, pp. 161–163.

12. Vol. 49, p. 344. For an example of the economic gains attained by way of exemption from *jizya* taxes, and also from outstanding debts on *jizya* arrears, see Ibn Qayyim al-Jawziyya, *Aḥkām*, p. 57.

13. Vol. 79, p. 134; vol. 18, p. 207, respectively. The marriage of a Jew to a Muslim was of a most delicate nature; five kadis had to affix their seals to the official *sijill* document in order to attest to the validity of the facts described therein.

SYNAGOGUES

1. A. Ya'arī, *'Igrōt Eretz-Israel* (Letters from Palestine) (Ramat-Gan, 1971), p. 129. Rabbi 'Ovadia described the synagogue as "narrow and dark," while an Ottoman *firman* dated 1587 speaks of it as a "cellar"; vol. 71, p. 31, and see also my *Ottoman Documents*, p. 93. Another interesting comparison is the "water cistern" mentioned by Rabbi

'Ovadia, while an official decree in 1583 referred to a "ritual bath" or "toilet" that the Jews allegedly had built there; U. Heyd, *Ottoman Documents on Palestine, 1522–1615* (Oxford, 1960), p. 171n8.

2. On the disputes in earlier days see Strauss, *Toledoth*, II, 402–415. For the entire episode of the reconstruction of the synagogue after it had been pulled down see Mujīr al-Dīn, *Al-'uns al-jalīl bi-ta'rīkh al-Quds wa'l Khalīl* (Cairo, 1282), II, 300–314. On the prohibition against maintaining a church or even houses inhabited by Christians close to a mosque in Istanbul see Refik, *On altıncı*, pp. 14–15, 45–46.

3. Vol. 12. p. 509.

4. Vol. 12, p. 502. On Kastro's activity in Jerusalem see my article in *Zion* (1982), no. 4, 409–418 (in Hebrew, with an Arabic original document Xeroxed).

5. Vol. 22, p. 112.

6. Vol. 9, pp. 72–73. For the original decree see my *Ottoman Documents*, pp. 69–70.

7. Vol. 77, p. 149.

8. Vol. 64, p. 248.

9. Vol. 33, p. 197.

10. Vol. 23, p. 406; vol. 29, p. 79. The official document is reproduced in my *Ottoman Documents*, p. 80. On other aspects of this issue see Goldman, *Ibn Abi Zimra*, pp. 124–125.

11. Vol. 58, p. 268.

12. Vol. 57, p. 31.

13. Vol. 35, p. 66.

14. Vol. 40, p. 439.

15. Vol. 59, p. 44.

16. The person in charge of the synagogue reported the following items missing: three altar covers, 40 silk curtains, 70 covers for the Torah, and many other silver ornaments; vol. 59, p. 93.

17. Vol. 77, p. 149. See also Heyd, *Documents*, pp. 170–171. See also Düzdağ, *Ebussuûd*, p. 95, nos. 406, 407.

18. Vol. 64, pp. 248, 318. This was very likely the same "water house" (*ab khane*) mentioned in Heyd, *Ottoman Documents*, p. 171.

19. Vol. 66, p. 331.

20. Vol. 71, p. 31. See the original decree reproduced in my *Ottoman Documents*, p. 96.

21. Y. Ben Zvi, *She'ar Yishūv* (Jerusalem, 1966), pp. 195–196 (in Hebrew); A. Ya'ari, *Zichrōnōt Eretz-Israel* (Jerusalem, 1947), pp. 56–57, (in Hebrew). The latter are memoirs, written in Jerusalem in 1626, which refer to the synagogue as having been closed some forty years before. The *sijill* indicates, however, that in November 1586 the synagogue was still held by the Jews.

22. See my *Ottoman Documents*, p. 96.
23. Vol. 67, p. 159; vol. 77, p. 149.
24. Sixty copies of the scrolls were listed; see vol. 77, p. 512.
25. Heyd, *Ottoman Documents*, pp. 169–171. For further details on the amount of energy and resources that the Jews of Istanbul, as well as those of Jerusalem, invested in their attempts to mobilize support for their cause see Rozen, "Jewish Community," pp. 21, 29.
26. The introduction of pictures was regarded as an indication of the transformation of a private house into a synagogue as early as the Mamluk period; S. D. Goitein, "Ibn 'Ubayya's Book on the Destruction of the Jewish Synagogue in Jerusalem in 1474," *Zion* (1948–49), no. 13–14, 24 (in Hebrew). See also a *firman* on a similar topic dated 1604 in A. Galanté *Documents officiels* (Istanbul, 1931), p. 166.
27. The term used is *miḥrāb*—the niche in a mosque that indicates the direction of prayer toward the holy city of Mecca. This is the Muslim equivalent of the Jewish *mizraḥ*—the eastern wall indicating the symbolic direction of Jerusalem. The oblong form of the *mizraḥ* and the ornamentation surrounding it are reminiscent of a holy ark in the synagogue.
28. Vol. 73, p. 3. For the original decree see my *Ottoman Documents*, p. 98.
29. This is a correction of Y. Press's contention that after the closing of the Ramban synagogue in 1586, a new one, Talmud Torah, was inaugurated; "If I Forget Thee, Oh Jerusalem," in *Yerushalayim*, II, 4–5. Several additional synagogues are referred to in a decree dated 1587 that describes conditions in Jerusalem a few years before; vol. 71, p. 31. For the original decree see my *Ottoman Documents*, p. 96.
30. Vol. 11, p. 86. The original document is my *Ottoman Documents*, pp. 71–72. Vol. 76, p. 376.
31. Vol. 80, pp. 20, 28, 336.
32. Although there was no formal prohibition against maintaining a synagogue in close proximity to a mosque, this was undesirable. In the early nineties, therefore, when the Jews of Jerusalem approached the Sublime Porte in an attempt to regulate their prayers, they specified that they did not live or pray "near large or small mosques"; vol. 11, p. 86. In Damascus during the same years, and in Istanbul in the eighteenth century, Jews were told to move out of buildings located close to a mosque; Galanté, *Documents officiels*, pp. 170–172. See also Düzdağ, *Ebussuûd*, pp. 104–107.
33. Vol. 77, p. 512. The other "burglars" were Ya'qūb ibn Yāsif, Shamwīl ibn Mas'ūd, Yūsuf al-Baradi'i, and Shiḥāda. The rabbi claimed that the scrolls had been at his disposal in the past.

BURYING THE DEAD

1. An exceptionally long and detailed ruling was given in mid-1560; vol. 39, pp. 431–433. A sentence, usually to be found at the bottom of the document, was added to the name of each witness specifying that he had actually attended the court session. By affixing his signature, the witness attested to the accuracy of all details in the *sijill.*

2. Vol. 12, p. 433. The *waqfiyya* (document of establishment) of Ṣalāḥ al-Dīn, however, is dated three years earlier; vol. 95, pp. 424–428.

3. This spring was famous among Jews for its healing qualities. In October 1577, for example, Yahūdā, the dayyān of the community, sent his wife, Qamra, who had been suffering from an incurable illness, to ʿAyn Silwān. Having spent some time bathing there, she left the water and sat on a nearby bench, then suddenly passed out and died; vol. 57, p. 485.

4. This is located to the south of present-day ʿAyn Silwān, almost totally covered with rubble, but as late as the nineteenth century it was still full of water.

5. The description includes further details that must have been meaningful at the time but that can hardly carry any weight for the modern student: "the plot of land of so-and-so," "the plot of radish," and so on; vol. 2, p. 126.

6. Vol. 36, p. 419.

7. Vol. 39, p. 98. See also J. W. Hirschberg, "Ottoman Rule in Jerusalem," *Israel Exploration Journal,* 2, no. 4 (1952), 236, 240; W. Foster, ed., *The Travels of John Sanderson in the Levant, 1584–1602* (London, 1931), p. 105.

8. D. Possot, *Le Voyage de la Terre Sainte* (Paris, 1890), p. 184.

9. Jewish as well as Christian sources indicate that during the Mamluk period the Jewish cemetery stretched west of the bed of the Kedron stream, and it started climbing eastward only under the Ottomans; see Schur, "The Jewish Community," p. 355 and n60. In the nineteenth century, as a result of an ongoing process along these lines, most of the cemetery was situated east of the Kedron; see E. Pierotti, *Jerusalem Explored* (London, 1864), II, plate 2.

10. Vol. 23, p. 372.

11. Vol. 25, p. 349. The al-ʿAmri mosque is found in the very heart of the present-day village of Silwān. The villagers, who pronounce its name either al-ʿAmri or al-ʿImri, assert that in old times this was the site of the tomb of a saint (*willī*) by that name, to which pilgrims came and where Sufi darwishes would perform their *dhikr* ceremony. The present building is a modern one, built only four years ago by the local peo-

ple, but some remainders of the original niche of the old mosque, as well as a deep cistern, can still be seen.

12. E. Tyan, "Idjara," *EI*[2].

13. Vol. 2, p. 126, dated May 29, 1532. Later references in the *sijill* fail to mention the term *maliye.* On the *maliye* system see H. Sahillioğlu, "*Siviş* Year Crises in the Ottoman Empire," in M. A. Cook, *Studies in the Economic History of the Middle East* (London, 1970), p. 233.

14. J. Schacht, "Adjr," *EI*[2]; Tyan, *Histoire,* p. 269.

15. Vol. 24, p. 28. The Jewish case was that since one *dirham* actually weighed one quarter of a "legal" *dirham,* the annual rate of 2250 silver *dirhams* came up to 41⅔ gold coins.

16. Vol. 36, p. 419, is the source of the discussion that follows.

17. Vol. 39, p. 98.

18. Vol. 39, p. 253.

19. For further references to him see Heyd, *Ottoman Documents,* pp. 149, 178.

20. Vol. 39, p. 320.

21. Vol. 39, p. 429.

22. Vol. 39, pp. 431–433.

23. For the original text see my *Ottoman Documents,* pp. 90–91.

24. Vol. 39, p. 447.

25. Vol. 39, p. 487.

26. Vol. 39, p. 580. This new *taḥrīr* was apparently concluded in Jerusalem during those days. The official date recorded in the register now kept in Ankara is 1562–63 / 970 A.H., and the time it took to finalize the results may account for the lapse of time. For a copy of the original *firman* taken from this volume (no. 516) see my *Ottoman Documents,* p. 32.

27. Vol. 40, p. 348. Conspicuous among them were other sons of the Shullāl family (Salamūn ibn Mūsā, Ibrahim ibn Hilal), a representative of the Karaites ('Abd al-Karīm ibn 'Abd al-Laṭīf), and two *dayyāns*—the Radbaz, David ben Zimra, and Yūsuf ibn Ya'qūb, "the Egyptian."

28. Vol. 44, p. 574.

29. For more details see vol. 39, pp. 431–433. This ruling was diametrically opposed to the one passed by the earlier kadi and may well be an indication of his relatively low moral standard. He may have turned a blind eye to all these arguments as a result of Jewish bribes. On the gradual deterioration of the judiciary institution during the sixteenth century see Heyd, *Studies,* pp. 212–215.

30. This argument was raised by the Jews only once, in early 1554; vol. 29, p. 72. This may indeed indicate that the threat to stop them from burying their dead there was an empty one.

31. Vol. 53, p. 55. These gravediggers were of somewhat more productive occupation: one was a harness marker and the other a shoemaker.

32. Vol. 80, p. 31.

33. Vol. 43, p. 269.

34. Vol. 45, p. 161.

35. Vol. 82, p. 364.

36. For later years see A. Haim, "The Salvation of the Plots of the Mount of Olives according to Seventeenth-Century Shari'a Documents," in Cohen, *Jerusalem in the Early Ottoman Period*, pp. 233–270.

PILGRIMAGE

1. Vol. 29, p. 122; vol. 80, p. 344. For a comprehensive list of the villages in the district of Jerusalem see E. Toledano, "The Sanjaq of Jerusalem in the Sixteenth Century," in Cohen, *Jerusalem in the Early Ottoman Period*, pp. 72–73. For further details on the village of Rama see Ya'ari, *Letters*, pp. 139, 160, A. Ya'ari, *Travels in Eretz Israel*, (Jerusalem, 1946), p. 146 (in Hebrew).

2. Vol. 28, p. 251. On the *kafar* tax see Heyd, *Ottoman Documents*, pp. 182–183; Cohen and Lewis, *Population*, pp. 56–58; A. Combe, "A Note: Qafar-Khafara," *BSOAS* (1940–1942), 10, 790.

3. Vol. 28, p. 220.

4. Vol. 28, p. 251.

5. For further details on the special relationship the Karaites developed with this synagogue see Rabbi Cook, "Notes on the history of the Synagogue Located at the Burial Place of the Prophet Shmu'il," in *Yedīʻōt ha-Ḥevra ha-ʻIvrīt la-Ḥaqīrat Eretz Israel ve-ʻAtīqoteyha* (Jerusalem, 1939), VI, p. 143. See also Foster, *Sanderson*, p. 100.

6. Vol. 29, p. 122. See also my *Ottoman Documents*, p. 81.

7. Vol. 48, p. 16.

8. Vol. 10, p. 602.

9. Vol. 23, p. 460.

10. Vol. 28, p. 220.

11. Vol. 29, p. 167. See also my *Ottoman Documents*, p. 82.

12. This description is by Pantaleão de Aveiro, *Itinarario da Terra Sancta e suas Particularidades* (Coimbra, 1927), p. 424.

13. Vol. 80, p. 344.

14. Vol. 8, pp. 42, 46, 47; vol. 56, p. 123. Although the document gives the letter *ghayn* (*mustaghrib*) and not 'ayn (*musta'rib*) it appears to be an error (not unusual considering the sloppy manner in which these records were copied). A juxtaposition in the text of European

(*ifranj*) with Oriental (*musta'rib*) Jews makes much more sense than any other reading.

15. Vol. 19, p. 106.
16. Vol. 56, p. 123.
17. Vol. 29, p. 73. For the original text see my *Ottoman Documents*, p. 79.
18. Vol. 29, p. 29. For the original text see my *Ottoman Documents*, p. 76.
19. Vol. 42, p. 123. On the effects of plague on the population of Egypt and Syria see M. W. Dols, *The Black Death in the Middle East* (Princeton, 1977), pp. 172 ff.
20. Vol. 58, pp. 444, 533, 536.
21. See also Rozen, "Jewish Community," p. 53n1.

## *6. Social and Judicial Status*

### JEWS IN THE MUSLIM COURT

1. Vol. 80, p. 20.
2. Vol. 55, p. 172.
3. Vol. 76, p. 226; vol. 48, p. 465.
4. Vol. 26, p. 151.
5. Vol. 10, p. 328. On *ta'zīr* in Islam see Tyan, *Histoire*, pp. 569–570.
6. Vol. 51, p. 20.
7. Vol. 2, pp. 70, 125, 136.
8. Vol. 18, p. 491.
9. Vol. 26, p. 51.
10. Vol. 78, pp. 87, 88, 89, 97.
11. Vol. 56, p. 62.
12. Vol. 43, p. 129.
13. Vol. 33, p. 197.
14. Vol. 69, p. 143.
15. Vol. 53, p. 387.
16. Vol. 14, p. 436.
17. Vol. 19, p. 395.
18. Vol. 8, p. 72.
19. Vol. 62, p. 301.
20. In this case, concerning ownership of a saddle, Yahūdā could not produce conclusive evidence supporting his claim, and the shaykh, Ya'qūb Fallāq, was acquitted at the end of March 1538; vol. 7, p. 467.
21. On June 13, 1579, al-Mu'allim Da'ūd ibn Ya'qūb, a high-ranking

Jewish official from Egypt, sued Mūsā ibn abu Jūkār in Jerusalem over an order of soap that had not been delivered. The plaintiff brought witnesses on his behalf, and abu Jūkār was convicted; vol. 58, pp. 410, 415.

22. Vol. 78, p. 149; vol. 64, p. 449; vol. 48, p. 279; vol. 77, p. 174; vol. 78, p. 196.

23. Vol. 61, p. 148; vol. 62, p. 343; vol. 4, p. 410.

24. Vol. 24, p. 53.

25. Vol. 13, p. 500.

26. The man Sulaymān assaulted was also a Karaite, Barakāt ibn Ibrahīm; vol. 64, p. 277.

27. Vol. 37, pp. 527, 530.

28. Vol. 36, pp. 51, 68.

29. Vol. 16, p. 502; vol. 22, p. 211.

30. Vol. 39, p. 4. On some of the changes that this term underwent see Heyd, *Ottoman Documents*, p. 49n6; Heyd, *Studies*, pp. 152n8, 222n4.

31. Vol. 64, p. 85, dated mid-August 1584; vol. 51, p. 223, dated mid-May 1568, respectively.

32. Vol. 13, p. 70.

33. Vol. 75, p. 223.

34. Vol. 76, p. 184.

35. Vol. 18, p. 267. On the institution of *shāhid* or *'ādil* witnesses see Tyan, *Histoire*, pp. 236–242.

36. Vol. 40, pp. 432–433. For an earlier example see vol. 19, p. 274.

37. Vol. 56, p. 501.

38. Vol. 55, p. 562.

39. The witnesses were Sāsī ibn Faraḥ and his secretary Ya'qūb ibn Barūkh; vol. 77, p. 96.

40. The plaintiff, upon encountering his ex-wife, who had converted to Islam and married the accused, called her a whore (*yā qaḥba*). An argument ensued during which the convert hit the Jew and pulled out part of his beard; vol. 44, p. 58.

41. Vol. 79, p. 134.

42. Vol. 4, p. 555.

43. Vol. 12, p. 354. This serves to illustrate and to put into broader perspective Heyd's contention that "the testimony of a non-Muslim subject (*zimmī*) was, with certain exceptions, only accepted against another infidel"; *studies*, p. 245. See also Düzdağ, *Ebussuûd*, pp. 98–99.

44. Vol. 80, p. 507.

45. Vol. 66, p. 286. On the term *bayyina* and its meaning in Muslim law see E. Tyan, "Judicial Organization," in M. Khadduri and H. J. Liebesny, eds., *Law in the Middle East* (Washington, D.C., 1955), p. 253.

46. Vol. 1, p. 420. On the significance of the oath of the defendant in the Muslim court see Heyd, *Studies*, pp. 250–252.

47. Vol. 2, p. 229.

48. Vol. 22, p. 489.

49. Vol. 30, p. 390.

50. Vol. 33, p. 30; vol. 31, pp. 432, 436, respectively.

51. Vol. 49, p. 179.

52. Vol. 64, p. 277.

53. For two marital cases presented to the court in mid-1538 see vol. 8, p. 72, concerning Sa'īd ibn Tamām, who gave his daughter Mas'ūda in marriage to Hārūn ibn Nassīm ibn Shū'ā, and p. 81, concerning Nassīm ibn Mūsā ibn Sītūn al-Maghribī, who gave his daughter to Hārūn ibn Sa'īd.

54. Vol. 2, p. 112.

55. Vol. 6, p. 36; vol. 22, p. 444, respectively.

56. Vol. 43, p. 265. The term *'ifranjī* means "European," and it applies to both Christians—usually the Franciscan monks, most of whom were from Spain and Italy—and Jews. It is hard to tell when this term acquired the more modern connotation in its Jewish context, that of signifying "Ashkenazi." I did come across one example in which *'ifranjī* was used as an equivalent of "Ashkenazi": a reference to a Jew of Central European (German) origin; vol. 19, p. 139. See B. Lewis, "Ifrandj," *EI*$^2$.

57. The monks are referred to as *al-firanj al-jurjān*. This does not mean "the Georgian Catholics," which is a contradiction in terms. It applies to the town Jaraja, which is the Arabic form of Reggio, Italy; hence, "the Italian Catholics who came from Reggio"; vol. 18, p. 277.

58. Vol. 64, pp. 505, 515. For similar cases surprisingly early in Ottoman history, when they were rare and atypical, see U. Heyd, "Ritual Murder Accusations in Fifteenth and Sixteenth Century Turkey," *Sefūnōt* (1961), 5, 135–144.

STATUS OF THE JEWISH WOMAN

1. Vol. 24, p. 384; vol. 20, p. 236.

2. Vol. 79, p. 532.

3. Vol. 5, p. 9.

4. Vol. 51, p. 650.

5. On the flogging of one Manūḥa bint Mūsā see vol. 62, p. 343. On the lifting of the veil see vol. 49, pp. 501–502. Here my findings tally with those of R. C. Jennings on Kayseri. There were no specific days on which Jewish women appeared in court; R. C. Jennings, "Women in

Early 17th century Ottoman Judicial Records—the Sharia Court of Anatolian Kayseri," *JESHO*, 18 (1975), 58.

6. Vol. 28, p. 316. Their names were Raḥil bint Isḥāq, [’I]stir bint Ya‘qūb, Sanina bint Ibrahīm, Simḥa bint Ishmū’īl, Sanīna bint Mūsā, Raḥma bint Ya‘qūb, Qamar bint Shmū’īl.

7. Vol. 8, p. 328.

8. Vol. 64, p. 340. For a similar case in seventeenth-century Cairo see El-Nahal, *Ottoman Egypt*, p. 30.

9. Vol. 49, p. 613.

10. Vol. 54, p. 168.

11. Vol. 31, p. 534.

12. Vol. 33, p. 350.

13. See for example vol. 18, p. 207. Shortly after having converted to Islam the woman married a wealthy Muslim who gave her an impressive dowry.

14. Vol. 39, pp. 250, 289–290.

15. Vol. 31, p. 463.

16. Vol. 5, p. 115. On a specific ruling of the shaykh al-Islam of the time concerning support see Düzdağ, *Ebussuûd*, p. 93.

17. Vol. 24, p. 199.

18. Vol. 58, pp. 122, 253.

19. Vol. 31, p. 435.

20. Vol. 76, p. 115.

21. Vol. 58, p. 235. See also vol. 15, p. 312; vol. 7, p. 394; vol. 36, p. 148.

22. Vol. 36, p. 84.

23. Vol. 61, p. 227. On this criminal offense and its punishment (flogging and fine, not divorce) see Heyd, *Studies*, p. 103.

24. Vol. 55, p. 448.

25. Vol. 8, pp. 72, 81.

26. Vol. 49, p. 251.

27. Vol. 62, p. 438; vol. 76, p. 103.

28. Vol. 19, p. 156.

29. Vol. 28, p. 318. Since the widow was expecting a child at the time of her husband's death, a sum identical to that inherited by the son was set aside for the baby.

30. Vol. 25, p. 194.

31. Vol. 2, p. 48.

32. Vol. 58, pp. 122, 157.

33. Vol. 44, p. 200.

34. Among those listed are Ḥannā and ‘Azīza, wives of Yahūdā ibn Mūsā al-Ḥaddād, 1594 (vol. 76, p. 87); Sāra and Simḥa, daughter of the rabbi, wives of Mūsā al-Buṭaynī, 1569 (vol. 53, p. 193); Sulṭāna and

Braylā, wives of the dayyān Yūsuf of Karkūz, 1561 (vol. 40, p. 472); Istīr and Sulṭāna, wives of Nassīm ibn Faraj, 1552 (vol. 25, p. 415); and Sāra and Simḥa, wives of Salamūn ibn Yahūdā ibn Mūsā Shullāl, 1582 (vol. 61, p. 119). On more general aspects of this issue see Goldman, *Ibn Abi Zimra*, pp. 132–133.

35. Vol. 40, p. 442; vol. 37, p. 163.
36. Vol. 37, p. 431; vol. 61, p. 22.
37. Jennings, "Women in Kayseri," pp. 53–114.
38. Jennings, "Women in Kayseri," p. 112.

### SOCIAL STATUS: THE EXTENT OF INEQUALITY

1. Vol. 23, p. 599. Compare the description given by William Biddulph, an Englishman who visited Jerusalem in 1600, in M. Ish-Shalom, *Christian Travels in the Holy Land* (Tel-Aviv, 1965), p. 309.
2. Vol. 32, p. 169. For the original text see my *Ottoman Documents*, pp. 88–89.
3. Vol. 29, p. 78.
4. Vol. 32, p. 167.
5. For further examples from Christian European sources see Ish-Shalom, *Christian Travels*, pp. 280, 301, citing Johan Helfrich and Voldrich Pefát. On the widespread concepts of discriminating against *ahl al-dhimma* see Düzdağ, *Ebussuûd*, p. 94, no. 402.
6. Vol. 32, p. 7.
7. Vol. 18, p. 510.
8. Vol. 21, p. 464; vol. 25, p. 1.

## *Economic Activity*

### JEWS IN THE BUREAUCRACY

1. Vol. 39, p. 384; vol. 55, p. 631. In the latter case the Jew paid 25 *sultani*, which entitled him to a salary (*waẓīfa*) of 6 *'uthmani* per day. For Jewish *multazims* (tax farmers) in seventeenth-century Egypt see El-Nahal, *Ottoman Egypt*, p. 56.
2. *Al-'āmil 'alā al-amwāl al-sulṭāniyya wa-khārij al-daftar* (commissioner of the sultan's taxes and of the taxes that are outside of the book [the original *taḥrīr* ]); *al mutakallim 'alā jihāt al-khāṣṣ* (the one responsible for the *khāṣṣ* income); *al-multazim bimā yataḥaṣṣal min jihāt al-khāṣṣ al-sharīf* (lessor of everything that will be collected from the exalted *khāṣṣ* revenue); vol. 10, p. 453; vol. 12 p. 128; vol. 14, p. 458, respectively. See also B. Lewis, *Emīn*, $EI^2$.
3. Vol. 10, pp. 248, 464.

4. On this term see Cohen and Lewis, *Population*, p. 162n24.
5. On this term see ibid., p. 74 and n91.
6. Vol. 10, p. 458.
7. Vol. 14, pp. 135, 421, 428, 460; vol. 17, pp. 285, 300; vol. 21, p. 29; vol. 22, pp. 6, 542; vol. 23, p. 609; vol. 27, p. 65.
8. Vol. 12, p. 149.
9. Vol. 16, p. 542.
10. Vol. 17, p. 369; vol. 18, p. 102; vol. 33, p. 528; vol. 18, pp. 8, 17. On bitumen in the Dead Sea see Cohen and Lewis, *Population*, pp. 59, 100.
11. Vol. 24, p. 120; vol. 31, p. 604.
12. Vol. 18, p. 36, a reference to Yūsuf ibn Shū'ā.
13. Vol. 23, p. 609.
14. Vol. 1, pp. 263, 383; vol. 8, p. 341; vol. 10, p. 191: vol. 14, p. 98; vol. 48, p. 372; vol. 18, p. 348; vol. 21, p. 516.
15. Vol. 17, p. 477.
16. Vol. 1, p. 380, dated early 1530s; vol. 19, p. 273, dated midcentury; vol. 76, p. 67, dated mid-1590s.
17. Vol. 76, p. 67, dated March 20, 1594.
18. Vol. 18, p. 267; vol. 14, p. 421; vol. 7, p. 9; vol. 24, p. 55. The Jewish moneychanger of the sixteenth century was a link in a long chain that dated back to the 'Abbassid Empire; see W. J. Fischel, *Jews in the Economic and Political Life of Mediaeval Islam* (London, 1937).
19. Vol. 2, p. 92.

JEWISH SLAUGHTERERS AND BUTCHERS

1. Lewis, *Notes and Documents*, pp. 7–8.
2. Cohen and Lewis, *Population*, p. 84n23.
3. Ibn Qayyim al-Jawziyya, *Aḥkām*, pp. 244–245; Düzdağ, *Ebussuûd*, p. 91. Meat slaughtered by Jews in Istanbul was officially fixed at a higher price than the average in 1576; Refik, *On altıncı*, p. 93.
4. Vol. 1, p. 15.
5. Vol. 8, p. 120.
6. Vol. 8, p. 378.
7. Vol. 24, p. 182, dated 1550.
8. Vol. 25, pp. 273, 276.
9. Vol. 44, p. 401.
10. Vol. 25, p. 276.
11. The guild of butchers had to supply the inhabitants of Jerusalem daily, both summer and winter; vol. 66, p. 527, dated April 1587.
12. Vol. 25, p. 403.
13. Vol. 28, p. 491, dated 1554. See also vol. 23, p. 144; vol. 25, p. 431.

14. For an example from the early 1560s see vol. 40, p. 144. The situation was the same in the other cities; on Damascus and Safed see Heyd, *Ottoman Documents*, p. 134.

15. For various aspects pertaining to the activity of the head (*rayyis*) of the guild of slaughterers, or to the members of the guild themselves, see vol. 13, pp. 190, 249–251; vol. 17, p. 297; vol. 27, p. 370; vol. 33, p. 18.

16. Vol. 31, pp. 304, 452, dated October 1556. On the involvement of the heads of the guild in the performance of the Jewish slaughterers see vol. 12, p. 263. In seventeenth-century Egypt the Jewish slaughterers constituted a guild of their own headed by three Jewish *naqībs;* El-Nahal, *Ottoman Egypt*, pp. 58, 60.

17. Vol. 25, p. 431.

18. "He [the governor] issued an exalted decree imposing the *siyāsa* on him and branding him by ringing bells so that others be deterred" ("Fabaraza amruhu al-sharīf bi-mu'āmalatihi bi'l-siyāsa wa-ishhārihi bi'l-tajrīs 'alayhi li-yurda'a ghayruhu"); vol. 31, p. 507. *Siyasa* may imply not only severe punishment but also execution of the culprit. On this term see Tyan, *Histoire*, pp. 446–451; Heyd, *Studies*, pp. 259–270. On *tashhīr* or *tajrīs* see Tyan, *Histoire*, p. 650.

19. Vol. 31, p. 251. See also vol. 5, p. 337.

20. Vol. 36, p. 316.

21. Vol. 44, p. 401.

22. Vol. 66, p. 466.

23. Vol. 72, p. 263; vol. 75, p. 74.

24. Vol. 75, p. 387.

25. Vol. 82, p. 339.

26. Vol. 76, p. 21.

27. Vol. 8, p. 59. It was specifically stated that this price was fixed with the full consent of the Jewish community. For a similar case in seventeenth-century Egypt see El-Nahal, *Ottoman Egypt*, p. 61.

28. Vol. 43, p. 359.

29. Vol. 16, p. 263.

30. This act of branding the meat was called *tasmiya;* vol. 8, p. 120. For further complaints dated February 1552 and May 1571 see vol. 25, p. 273; vol. 54, p. 168. The mark branded on various parts of the animal was termed a seal (*khatm, damga*); vol. 31, p. 250; vol. 49, p. 60.

31. Vol. 51, p. 485. This was not just a hypothetical possibility. For a case in which a Jew admitted that he had slaughtered without assistance and outside the *maslakh* see vol. 15, p. 394.

32. Vol. 12, p. 263; vol. 14, p. 335. On nonkosher meat and the various orthodox approaches to it in Islam see Ibn Qayyim al-Jawziyya, *Aḥkām*, pp. 267–269. On the original Hebrew term in an Arabic poem

dating from the eleventh century see B. Lewis "An Ode against the Jews," in *Islam in History* (London, 1973), p. 161. On the Ashkenazic pronunciation of some vowels in Hebrew words see P. Kraus, "Hebraische und Syrische Zitate in ismailitischen Schriften," in *Der Islam*, vol. 19 (Berlin, 1930), pp. 243–263. My thanks to Professor B. Lewis, who drew my attention to these two sources.

33. Vol. 58, p. 571; vol. 59, p. 87.
34. Vol. 75, p. 199.
35. Vol. 14, p. 335.
36. Vol. 28, p. 258.
37. Vol. 36, p. 316.
38. Vol. 24, p. 182.
39. Vol. 54, pp. 168, 181.
40. Vol. 75, p. 318.
41. Vol. 75, pp. 74, 318.
42. Vol. 80, p. 507.
43. Vol. 75, pp. 387, 318; vol. 76, p. 215.
44. For further details see S. D. Goitein, "Banū Isrā'īl," *EI*[2].
45. The term refers to Jews and Christians and also designated *ahl al-dhimma;* vol. 59, p. 87.
46. Vol. 40, p. 510.
47. Vol. 31, p. 250; vol. 36, p. 136.
48. Vol. 55, p. 351.
49. Vol. 61, p. 506.
50. Vol. 76, p. 215; vol. 80, p. 507.
51. Vol. 16, p. 236.
52. For two separate lists of butchers and venders, each of them including one Jews, see vol. 58, p. 404. See also vol. 5, p. 249.
53. Vol. 27, p. 314; vol. 31, p. 187.
54. Vol. 33, p. 486.
55. Vol. 25, p. 403; vol. 82, p. 339.

## SHOEMAKERS AND PROCESSORS OF HIDES

1. In the year 1533–34 five Jewish *adamī* were mentioned: Mūsā ibn Yaḥyā, Shū'ā, Da'ūd, Ṣafaniā, and Sham'ūn; vol. 4, pp. 114, 198. On Jewish *ḍabbāgh*s see vol. 27, p. 188; vol. 51, p. 114.
2. Vol. 23, p. 599.
3. Vol. 66, p. 176.
4. Vol. 19, p. 105.
5. Vol. 21, p. 158; vol. 36, p. 231; vol. 57, p. 344; vol. 61, p. 284; vol. 79, p. 119.

6. Vol. 64, p. 266; vol. 66, p. 299; vol. 69, pp. 143, 214; vol. 82, p. 274.

DEALERS AND WORKERS IN PRECIOUS METALS

1. Vol. 75, p. 49.
2. Vol. 37, p. 477. He is referred to elsewhere (vol. 37, p. 382) as Mūsā ibn Ibrahīm, who was nominated as shaykh and *mutakallim* of the jewelers upon a request submitted by their notables (*a'yān*) to the kadi.
3. Vol. 49, p. 125. Whether or not these practices constituted an exception to the rule followed by other guilds in Jerusalem is unclear. These powers substantially exceed those defined by G. Baer in "Ottoman Guilds: a Reassessment," in O. Okyar and H. Inalcık, eds, *Social and Economic History of Turkey (1071–1920)* (Ankara, 1980), p. 100.
4. Vol. 75, p. 49.
5. Vol. 37, p. 477. Musa, the Jewish jeweler, was nominated there.
6. Vol. 75, p. 242. For similar conditions stipulated in 1585 by the kadi at the request of the head of the jewelers' guild see vol. 64, p. 266. On other occasions more general formulations were used, such as "adhina lahu an ya'murahum bi'l 'iffa wa'l amāna wayanhāhum 'an 'isti'māl al-ghishsh wa'l waghl wa'l khiyāna"; vol. 61, p. 11.
7. *Sūq al-ṣāgha* or *al-ṣiyāgha.*
8. Vol. 1, p. 22; vol. 14, p. 264; vol. 22, p. 223.
9. Vol. 31, pp. 550, 560; vol. 33, pp. 140, 144, 145.
10. Vol. 33, p. 145.
11. "They will practice jewelry in silver of one type"; vol. 33, p. 144.
12. Vol. 75, pp. 164, 242. For a detailed description of many of these pieces see E. W. Lane, *Manners and Customs of the Modern Egyptians* (London, 1908), pp. 566–577. See also G. C. Miles, *Dirham, EI*$^{2}$.
13. Vol. 66, p. 563.
14. Vol. 31, p. 432; vol. 27, p. 3; vol. 23, p. 60, respectively.
15. Vol. 18, p. 57; vol. 22, p. 570; vol. 23, p. 61; vol. 30, p. 390.
16. Vol. 75, p. 107.
17. Vol. 6, p. 424.
18. Vol. 8, p. 171.
19. Vol. 13, p. 382.
20. Vol. 30, p. 248.
21. Fallāq ibn Ḥayyim, for example, purchased various items of gold jewelry from a Muslim goldsmith; vol. 25, p. 191.
22. Heyd, *Documents,* p. 68n20.
23. G. Baer, "The Organization of labour," in G. Spuler, ed., *Handbuch der Orientalistik* (Leiden, 1977), VI, 42. Jewish sources give fur-

ther evidence of the prevalence of Karaites among the jewelers of Jerusalem several years later; Rozen, "Jewish Community," p. 85.

24. His wealth may be gauged from references to various trade transactions, some very impressive in size (vol. 33, pp. 127, 128; vol. 25, p. 699); his acquisition of an orchard in the *waqf* of Aḥmad al-Thawrī outside Jerusalem (vol. 45, p. 136); his administration of various estates that belonged to the Karaites of Damascus (vol. 46, p. 152); and his nomination as moneychanger to the lessor of the *jizya* from Christians as well as Jews (vol. 48, p. 372).

25. Vol. 43, p. 140.

26. Vol. 54, pp. 570–574. For an indication of the affluence of Ibrahīm ibn Mas'ūd, the Jewish jeweler, see vol. 66, p. 378.

## SPICE MERCHANTS

1. H. Inalcık "The Heyday and Decline of the Ottoman Empire," in *The Cambridge History of Islam* (Cambridge, 1970), I, 332.

2. Vol. 47, p. 36.

3. Vol. 46, p. 143. For further details on this and related matters see my "Local Trade, International Trade, and Government Involvement in Jerusalem during the Early Ottoman Period," *Asian and African Studies*, 12, no. 1 (1978), 5–12. On international trade in spices reaching Palestine during the sixteenth century see Cohen and Lewis, *Population*, pp. 55–56, 129. On similar, almost identical developments in other towns of Syria and Egypt, see A. Raymond "The Ottoman Conquest and Development of the Great Arab Towns," *International Journal of Turkish Studies*, 1, no. 1 (1979–1980), 86–90, 93–97.

4. Vol. 66, p. 440. On the *sūq al-qaṭṭānīn* and developments therein see my "On the Realities of the Millet System," in Braude and Lewis, eds., *Christians and Jews in the Ottoman Empire*, II, 7–18.

5. Vol. 48, p. 325; vol. 58, p. 289; vol. 67, p. 449.

6. Vol. 66, p. 440; vol. 72, p. 263; vol. 35, p. 38.

7. Vol. 58, p. 157; vol. 66, p. 7.

8. Vol. 37, p. 406; vol. 45, p. 221; vol. 72, p. 263.

9. Vol. 6, p. 661; vol. 17, p. 107; vol. 2, p. 144, respectively.

10. Vol. 6, p. 38; vol. 35, p. 38; vol. 3, p. 324; vol. 66, p. 7, respectively.

11. Vol. 12, p. 354: vol. 72, p. 263.

12. Vol. 75, p. 29.

13. Vol. 46, p. 146.

14. Vol. 10, p. 68.

15. Vol. 25, p. 464.

16. Vol. 44, p. 354; vol. 45, p. 221. On special privileges granted to

merchants in the *suq al-'aṭṭārīn* see Ö. L. Barkan, *XV ve XVIinci asırlarda Osmanlı Imparatorluğunda Zirai ekonominin Hukuki ve Mali Esasları* (Istanbul, 1943), I, *Kanunlar*, p. 218; R. Mantran and J. Sauvaget, *Règlements fiscaux Ottomans, les provinces Syriennes* (Beirut, 1951), p. 38.

JEWISH PHYSICIANS

1. M. Franco, *Essai*, pp. 39, 68, 86. See also my article in E. Kedourie, ed., *The Jewish World* (London, 1979), pp. 186–191. Less famous examples are "Yusuf the Jew," who served as a physician bearing the title *Jarrāḥ* in 1557–58, "Kamal the Jew," who, in the very same year, was referred to as one of the *Cerrahin-i Hassa*, and so on. For these and other examples see R. M. Meric, "Osmanlı tababeti tarihine ait vesikalar: I. Cerrahlar-Kehaller," *Tarih Vesikaları*, 1, no. 16 (1955), 42, 43, 49.

2. Vol. 57, p. 265 ("annahu lā yataṣarraf fī faṣl wa-lā fī takḥīl ḥattā yata'allam 'umūr al-jirāḥa"). See also M. Meyerhof-T. Sarnelli, *Djarrah*, *EI*$^2$.

3. For the use of the term *kahhal* to indicate a physician see the long lists in Meric, "Osmanlı tababeti." On this term see also M. Z. Pakalın, *Osmanlı Tarih Deyimleri ve Terimleri* (Istanbul, 1951), II, 237.

4. Vol. 14, p. 436.

5. Vol. 19, p. 177.

6. Vol. 54, p. 261.

7. Vol. 47, p. 11; for the original decree see my *Ottoman Documents*, p. 94; vol. 48, p. 465; vol. 49, pp. 5, 78.

8. Vol. 2, p. 44; vol. 25, pp. 715, 730; vol. 56, p. 496; vol. 58, p. 188.

9. Vol. 40, p. 376; vol. 44, p. 574; vol. 54, p. 168.

10. Vol. 54, p. 92; vol. 23, p. 3.

11. Vol. 46, p. 123.

LOCKSMITHS

1. Vol. 31, p. 450; vol. 48, p. 196.

2. For further details see my article "Local Trade," *Asian and African Studies*, 12 (1978), 7–10.

3. Vol. 16, P. 354.

4. For a case of a natural death, of Da'ūd ibn Makhlūf, the Jewish locksmith, in 1531 near the village of Dayr Ghassāna see vol. 1, p. 218. For the two locksmiths mentioned above who received approval in 1549 see vol. 6, p. 55; vol. 22, p. 559.

5. Vol. 39, p. 408.

6. Vol. 72, p. 263; vol. 22, p. 559; vol. 6, p. 55.

7. Vol. 10, p. 170; vol. 58, p. 571: vol. 59, p. 44; vol. 64, p. 125; vol. 67, p. 222.

8. Vol. 64, p. 266.

9. On a partnership between a well-to-do Jew, Mas'ūd the spice merchant, and the Jewish locksmith Mūsā see vol. 44, p. 57.

10. Vol. 82, p. 274.

### CLOTH MERCHANTS

1. Cohen and Lewis, *Population*, pp. 54, 59–62.

2. Vol. 79, p. 445. On the term and its meaning see Cohen and Lewis, *Population*, p. 150n14.

3. Vol. 36, p. 398.

4. Vol. 7, p. 19; vol. 12, pp. 313, 869; vol. 24, p. 445; vol. 37, p. 27; vol. 48, p. 340; vol. 69, p. 424.

5. Vol. 61, p. 169.

6. Vol. 62, p. 403; vol. 31, p. 303; vol. 58, p. 541; vol. 48, p. 467; vol. 57, p. 386; vol. 76, p. 294.

7. Vol. 76, p. 131.

8. Vol. 24, p. 325.

9. Vol. 5, p. 7.

10. Vol. 19, p. 108; vol. 48, p. 467; vol. 76, p. 206; vol. 18, p. 52; vol. 77, p. 86.

11. Vol. 76, pp. 201, 540. The shaykh *al-tujjār*, the head of the merchants of Jerusalem, added his name, Muḥammad al-Dahīna, as a witness to this transaction.

12. For another example of Jewish interpreters see Foster, *Sanderson*, p. 103.

### DEALERS IN GRAPES AND WINE

1. For example see vol. 20, p. 38; vol. 39, p. 253.

2. Vol. 53, p. 479; vol. 56, p. 243.

3. Vol. 35, p. 85.

4. Vol. 56, p. 535.

### CHEESE MAKERS

1. Vol. 23, p. 554; vol. 5, p. 9.

2. Vol. 33, p. 235.

3. Vol. 53, p. 387.

4. Vol. 31, pp. 304, 250, 435.
5. Vol. 23, p. 273; vol. 20, p. 317.
6. Vol. 4, p. 128.

MILLERS AND BAKERS

1. Vol. 1, p. 369.
2. Vol. 6, p. 591.
3. It should be pointed out that in several registers, in the untidy handwriting of the scribe this word could also be read as *ḥaddād*, or "locksmith." There is no doubt, however, that the reference is to peasants who provided the town with grains (*al-ḥaddārīn al-fallāḥīn al-jallāba*); vol. 5, p. 125. The term is currently used in the local Arabic dialect of Jerusalem to indicate peasants harvesting wheat and barley. Jewish sources also mention Jewish merchants who supplied Jerusalem with grain purchased in nearby villages; Rozen, "Jewish Community," p. 228.
4. Vol. 5, p. 125.
5. Vol. 33, p. 159.
6. Vol. 4, p. 305; vol. 5, p. 125; vol. 23, p. 621; vol. 25, p. 285; vol. 58, p. 353.
7. Vol. 10, p. 393; vol. 17, p. 336; vol. 37, p. 335; vol. 49, p. 306.
8. Vol. 1, p. 131; vol. 6, p. 506; vol. 25, p. 398; vol. 37, p. 127.
9. Vol. 19, p. 139; vol. 22, p. 332; vol. 23, p. 284; vol. 17, p. 319; vol. 37, pp. 335, 343.

DEALERS IN OLIVE OIL AND SOAP

1. Vol. 1, pp. 10–11; vol. 66, p. 9.
2. Vol. 19, p. 356; vol. 21, p. 383; vol. 22, p. 495.
3. Vol. 21, p. 383; vol. 24, p. 39; vol. 31, p. 591.
4. Vol. 56, p. 61; vol. 58, p. 415.
5. Vol. 58, p. 410.
6. Vol. 62, p. 53; vol. 75, p. 229.
7. Vol. 55, p. 535.
8. Vol. 27, p. 307; vol. 59, p. 558; vol. 56, p. 535. For more examples of Jewish merchants referred to as *sayrajānī* see vol. 18, p. 267; vol. 22, p. 211; vol. 28, p. 383.

JEWS IN TRADE

1. Vol. 4, pp. 15, 36; vol. 19, pp. 109, 170; vol. 8, p. 354.
2. Vol. 57, p. 488; vol. 31, p. 432; vol. 69, p. 288.

3. Vol. 38, p. 133. This volume is exceptional in that it deals only with matters pertaining to villages and their inhabitants.

4. Vol. 36, p. 233; vol. 77, pp. 162, 163.

5. Vol. 77, pp. 565–569.

6. Vol. 64, p. 184.

7. Vol. 72, p. 305. On the depreciation of the Ottoman coins see Cohen and Lewis, *Population*, pp. 43–44.

## JEWS AND REAL ESTATE

1. Vol. 22, p. 447; vol. 23, pp. 372, 374; vol. 25, p. 469; vol. 37, p. 467; vol. 46, p. 184; vol. 46, p. 124.

2. Vol. 44, p. 31.

3. A Karaite physician let his house in 1547 (vol. 20, p. 115); the Hanafi kadi rented a room from the Karaite *waqf* in 1558 (vol. 36, p. 6); another *'ālim* rented a house from the Karaite *waqf* in 1565 (vol. 46, p. 152).

4. For example see vol. 13, p. 398; vol. 24, pp. 55–56: vol. 7, p. 411.

5. Dūna bint Ya'qūb in 1537 (vol. 6, p. 497); Naṣriyya bint Rūbīn in 1547 (vol. 19, p. 65); Sāra bint Sīmūn in 1548 (vol. 20, p. 319); Sulṭāna bint Yūsuf in 1558 (vol. 36, p. 100); Simḥa bint Isḥāq in 1573 (vol. 56, p. 418).

6. Vol. 13, p. 398; vol. 7, pp. 411, 436.

7. Vol. 13, p. 398; vol. 20, p. 404; vol. 24, pp. 55–56; vol. 72, p. 305.

8. These transactions were recorded whether the owners were residents of Jerusalem or not. For a detailed description of how a Jew from Cairo purchased a large building in Jerusalem from a local Jew in 1554 see vol. 28, p. 222.

9. One of these cases dates from 1506–07—that is, before the Ottoman conquest; vol. 7, p. 360.

10. Cohen and Lewis, *Population*, p. 92.

11. For example, a house bought by a Jew in May 1529 near Zion Gate was sold by his son on November 1, 1566, to a Muslim.

12. In some instances the woman inherited the house from her father (vol. 24, p. 384); sometimes she bought it (vol. 28, p. 447); and sometimes it was given as her dowry at the time of her marriage (vol. 28, pp. 310–311).

13. Vol. 56, pp. 199, 211.

14. See, for example, vol. 66, p. 299.

15. Vol. 23, p. 105; vol. 56, pp. 199, 211.

16. Vol. 58, p. 299.

17. "I'ādat al-binā' al-munhadim ... al-tarmīm wa'l-ta'mīr wa'l-

takḥīl ẓāhiran wa-bāṭinan wa-ḍarb al-qasrmal 'alā asṭiḥatihā" ("reconstruction of the dilapidated building . . . repair, refurbishing and painting inside and outside, and insulating its roof"); vol. 59, p. 167.

18. Vol. 75, p. 42.

19. Vol. 23, p. 369; vol. 36, p. 280; vol. 59, p. 260. In one case a building with a large plot of land attached to it was sold for the impressive sum of 250 *sultani;* vol. 64, p. 185.

20. Vol. 25, p. 127.

21. Ibrahīm ibn Hilāl, in 1553 (vol. 27, p. 336).

22. Vol. 36, p. 280.

23. See my article "Local Trade," pp. 5–7.

24. Vol. 28, p. 445.

25. Vol. 39, p. 537.

26. Cohen and Lewis, *Population*, p. 104.

27. Vol. 28, pp. 139, 169, for al-Rīsha; vol. 25, pp. 198, 521, for al-Sharaf. See also vol. 51, p. 173; Heyd, *Ottoman Documents*, pp. 149–150 and n8.

28. Vol. 19, p. 337. The area was also called ḥārat Ṣahyūn al-Juwwāniyya; vol. 43, p. 151.

29. Vol. 23, p. 369.

30. Vol. 58, p. 83.

31. Vol. 26, p. 139.

32. On the last three institutions see vol. 62, p. 260; vol. 69, p. 259.

33. Vol. 53, p. 193; vol. 80, p. 74.

34. Vol. 58, p. 353. This may not necessarily have been a separate gate of the Jewish quarter but rather a reference to Zion Gate, located nearby ("bāb madīnat al-Quds al-Sharīf al-kā'in bi-maḥallat al yahūd," vol. 66, p. 13). As for the "new gate" close to the 'Umari mosque, see vol. 19, p. 311.

35. The first shaykh mentioned was 'Alī ibn Rajab from Funduqūmiyya; vol. 51, p. 187. The second was Muḥammad ibn Takrūr; vol. 72, p. 367.

36. Vol. 69, p. 475.

37. Vol. 43, p. 140.

38. Vol. 31, p. 560; vol. 55, p. 511; vol. 54, p. 102; vol. 33, p. 530; vol. 56, p. 278.

39. Vol. 31, p. 450.

40. Cohen and Lewis, *Population*, p. 40.

41. Vol. 67, p. 248.

42. Vol. 4, p. 305, dated the mid-1530s; vol. 17, p. 162, dated 1545.

43. Vol. 4, p. 365; vol. 20, p. 547; vol. 21, pp. 107, 146; vol. 45, p. 136. Jewish agricultural activity is mentioned in the following villages

around Jerusalem: Ṣūr Bāhir, Bayt Ṣafāfā, 'Azariyya, Bayt Mazmīl, Mālḥa, Walaja, Qalūnia, Kafr Samwīl, Bayt Ḥanīna, Shaykh Jarrāḥ.

44. Vol. 4, p. 277; vol. 5, pp. 82, 98.

45. Vol. 2, p. 48. In medieval Egypt "many charitable foundations were established by women"; S. D. Goitein, *Mediterranean Society* (Berkeley, 1967), II, 113. For the traditional positive approach of Islam to the establishment of an endowment meant for "the Jewish poor" see Ibn Qayyim al-Jawziyya, *Aḥkām*, p. 300.

46. Vol. 27, p. 292.

47. Vol. 14, p. 461.

48. Vol. 53, p. 339.

49. Vol. 28, p. 333. See also Jennings, "Women in Kayseri," pp. 105–106.

50. Vol. 64, p. 131.

## ECONOMIC CHARACTER OF THE COMMUNITY

1. Vol. 4, p. 109; vol. 6, p. 299; vol. 37, p. 516.

2. Vol. 33, p. 294.

3. Vol. 69, p. 82. On the legal differentiation between a "rich" person, who owned property exceeding 40,000 *akçe*, and a "poor" one, who owned less than 5000 *akçe* in property, see Heyd, *Studies*, p. 284. Of course, if the kadi considered some Jews to be rich, that still leaves the question as to why he applied the same *jizya* tax to all. Doubtless he had his reasons.

4. Vol. 62, p. 30.

5. Vol. 23, p. 471; vol. 18, pp. 297–298; vol. 33, p. 466.

6. Vol. 25, p. 653.

7. See vol. 20, p. 236; vol. 36, p. 434; vol. 37, p. 423; vol. 2, p. 70; vol. 48, p. 225; vol. 59, p. 351 for these and other examples.

8. Vol. 40, p. 441.

9. Vol. 40, p. 440; vol. 66, p. 378.

10. Vol. 28, p. 318.

11. For examples see vol. 39, p. 519; vol. 51, p. 402; vol. 61, p. 119; vol. 40, p. 142; vol. 66, p. 7; vol. 80, p. 55.

12. See n9 above.

13. Vol. 43, p. 370.

14. Vol. 17, p. 310.

15. Vol. 56, p. 585.

16. Vol. 33, p. 71. Sārā is described as "medium built, slim, of fair complexion, dark eyed, eyebrows asunder, a scarred eyelid."

17. Vol. 37, p. 520. On the wider issue of Jews and Christians em-

ploying Muslim servants see Düzdag, *Ebussuûd*, p. 94, no. 400; Refik, *On Altıncı*, p. 43.

18. Vol. 58, p. 444. For another example see vol. 28, p. 323.

19. Employment of Muslim maids by Jewish families is widely described in Jewish sources; Rozen, "Jewish Community," pp. 241–242n7.

20. It seems, therefore, that my findings call for the addition of a third dimension to the two put forward by G. Baer in "Ottoman Guilds," pp. 96–97. Gerber found in Bursa separate guilds for the various religious groups, while Rafeq and Raymond suggested that although they were open to all, the head was always a Muslim. In Jerusalem Jews reached the top position, even over non-Jewish members.

21. On Jewish real estate interests protected by a Muslim see vol. 2, p. 114; on a Christian who was a go-between for Jewish merchants in Jerusalem and Damascus see vol. 33, p. 406; on Jewish-Muslim partnerships see vol. 21, p. 138; vol. 22, p. 251. For similar instances in seventeenth-century Egypt see El-Nahal, *Ottoman Egypt*, p. 56.

22. Vol. 55, p. 343; vol. 56, p. 61; vol. 76, p. 131.

23. For example, the Jews were among those instrumental in the rebuilding of the vegetable market in 1563–64. The people notified the kadi of their willingness to pay for the repairs, the sums later to be credited to their rent payments. The forty renovated shops were divided equally among the three communities, but the Jews were clearly the majority of those who were first to take out leases and begin trading; vol. 44, pp. 382, 448.

24. The Jews received 2900 *akçe*, the Christians 2000, and the Muslims 4000; vol. 4, p. 612.

25. For example, the great sum of 20,000 *akçe* was sent from Istanbul for distribution among the poor Jews of Jerusalem; vol. 76, p. 540.

## *8. Conclusion*

1. Francesco Suriano, *Itinerario de Hierusalem: Treatise on the Holy Land*, tr. E. Hoad and T. Bellorini, preface B. Bagatti (Jerusalem, 1949), pp. 101–102.

2. Heyd, *Studies*, pp. 211–212.

3. Vol. 55, p. 738.

4. Goldman, *Ibn Abi Zimra*, pp. 154–155.

5. Lewis, "Ode against the Jews," p. 164.

# *Index*